EXPLORERS *of the* INFINITE

EXPLORERS *of the* INFINITE

The Secret Spiritual Lives of
Extreme Athletes—And What They Reveal
About Near-Death Experiences, Psychic Communication,
and Touching the Beyond

MARIA COFFEY

JEREMY P. TARCHER/PENGUIN
a member of Penguin Group (USA) Inc.
New York

JEREMY P. TARCHER/PENGUIN
Published by the Penguin Group
Penguin Group (USA) Inc., 375 Hudson Street, New York, New York 10014, USA • Penguin Group
(Canada), 90 Eglinton Avenue East, Suite 700, Toronto, Ontario M4P 2Y3, Canada (a division of Penguin
Canada Inc.) • Penguin Books Ltd, 80 Strand, London WC2R 0RL, England • Penguin Ireland,
25 St Stephen's Green, Dublin 2, Ireland (a division of Penguin Books Ltd) • Penguin Group (Australia),
250 Camberwell Road, Camberwell, Victoria 3124, Australia (a division of Pearson Australia Group
Pty Ltd) • Penguin Books India Pvt Ltd, 11 Community Centre, Panchsheel Park, New Delhi–110 017,
India • Penguin Group (NZ), 67 Apollo Drive, Rosedale, North Shore 0632, New Zealand
(a division of Pearson New Zealand Ltd) • Penguin Books (South Africa) (Pty) Ltd, 24 Sturdee Avenue,
Rosebank, Johannesburg 2196, South Africa

Penguin Books Ltd, Registered Offices: 80 Strand, London WC2R 0RL, England

From LETTERS TO A YOUNG POET by Rainer Maria Rilke, translated by Stephen Mitchell,
copyright © 1984 by Stephen Mitchell. Used by permission of Random House, Inc.

Grateful acknowledgment is made for permission to reprint from the following:
Margaret Avison, *Always Now: The Collected Poems* (in three volumes). Permission granted by
the Porcupine's Quill. Copyright © 2003 by Margaret Avison.
T. S. Eliot, *The Waste Land.* Permission granted by Faber and Faber Ltd/The T. S. Eliot Estate.

Most Tarcher/Penguin books are available at special quantity discounts for bulk purchase for sales promo-
tions, premiums, fund-raising, and educational needs. Special books or book excerpts also can be created
to fit specific needs. For details, write Penguin Group (USA) Inc. Special Markets, 375 Hudson Street,
New York, NY 10014.

ISBN: 978-1-58542-651-5

Printed in the United States of America
3   5   7   9   10   8   6   4

BOOK DESIGN BY NICOLE LAROCHE

For my mother, Bee

CONTENTS

PART FOUR

EXPLORERS *of the* INFINITE

INTRODUCTION

2003.

*Opening night at the Banff Mountain Film Festival. We sit
in a large, packed auditorium, watching fast-paced clips of people
throwing themselves off high cliffs, kayaking over huge waterfalls, and skiing down precipitous mountain slopes. Crazy, seemingly impossible feats that bring cheers, whoops, and whistles
from the crowd. My own pulse races, my palms sweat. What
intrigues me is not just that these adventurers willingly go to the
edge, but how at ease they seem there.*

*After the showing I seek out the Norwegian explorer Børge
Ousland, a man who has made epic treks to the South and North
poles, across Antarctica and the Patagonian Ice Cap. Completely
unsupported. A man who has refused to stop at research stations,
eschewing any warmth and company on his missions. Why does
he undertake such journeys?*

*"Because they strip me away," he says simply. "I become like
an animal. I find out who I really am."*

*Later that night, in my warm hotel room, I gaze through
double-glazed windows at a snowy mountain face looming up
from the Bow Valley. Somewhere on its slopes a man climbs in
the dark. Alone. Earlier in the evening I'd met him, a local in the*

area, dressed in his climbing gear, backpack at his feet, having a quick drink in the bar before setting off. He had a simple happiness about him; he was relishing the prospect of a night on the icy slopes. At this very moment, he is moving upward, like an animal, vulnerable to the elements. I think about all the layers surrounding me, insulating me from everything he is experiencing. I know I couldn't do what he is doing, or what Børge Ousland does. Nor do I want to. But I envy them for being so at home in the wild world, wide open to its beauty, plugged into its power. For whatever it is they find there that proves so irresistible.

I was at the Banff festival to receive a prize for a book I'd written about the personal costs of climbing. All of the climbers I had interviewed for that book described an overwhelming sense of aliveness they felt in the mountains, and at moments of great danger. To my surprise, many of them referred to this as a spiritual sensation, something I interpreted as entering a "transcendence zone." I'd been even more surprised when some of the climbers shared stories of the further reaches of this zone: encounters with ghosts and spirits, telepathic communications, precognitive dreams, astral travel, bouts of superhuman strength.

Extreme adventurers, of any ilk, must do more than just master the skills of their sport. Their survival depends on their maintaining a constant focus and paying close attention to all the forces of nature, becoming hyperaware of the slightest breeze, a change in temperature, the way snow feels under their boots or rock on their fingers. And when disaster hits—the avalanche breaks loose, the parachute collapses, the boat overturns—in a split second they must throw together past experience with what is happening in the present, and react. Their lives depend upon this process—what some psychologists call "thin slicing"—of finding patterns in situations and behavior based on very narrow segments of experience. It's what most of us call intuition, a "knowing without knowing."

Knowing without knowing. Was it possible, I now wondered, that as these adventurers tune into the natural world, they unwittingly open channels to hidden powers and realms of experience that we call mystical and paranormal? That these channels lie dormant in us all, shut down beneath layers of insulation? And that the process of risk-taking strips away that insulation, opening the way to spiritual transcendence?

These questions were the genesis of this book. My work on it began with another question: Is reaching a state of spiritual transcendence the fundamental lure of extreme adventure? Needless to say, the more I looked for answers, the more questions accumulated, but as the work progressed I became increasingly convinced that extreme adventurers break the boundaries of what is deemed physically possible by pushing beyond human consciousness into another realm. Their experiences give a glimpse of those unimagined levels of existence, signing the way for others to follow.

Before I set out to write this book, I was a fence-sitter about all things spiritual, mystical, and paranormal. What stopped me from settling firmly on the side of rationalism were memories of puzzling incidents in my life—a mystical "awakening" after I nearly drowned off the coast of Morocco; a premonition of my lover's death on Everest and the "visitations" I received from him after the news was confirmed; the spirit of a river that protected me from illness and banditry while I kayaked hundreds of miles down its course. At the time, I'd rationalized each of these sensations as being the result of fear, worry, grief, or exhaustion. But listening to the stories of adventurers made me wonder if, perhaps, they were more than just products of my imagination.

I gathered accounts of spiritual, mystical, and paranormal experiences from an array of extreme adventurers: BASE jumpers, highliners, astronauts, solo sailors, freedivers, kayakers, surfers, big-mountain skiers and snowboarders, as well as mountaineers. I cross-checked their accounts against the research and opinions of scientists, psychologists, and spiritual teachers. This journey back and forth from wonder to science, mystery to explanation, is documented in these pages. It begins with my premise that reaching a spiritual state of being is the principal lure of extreme adventure, but that until there is a common language for this experience there will be no common acceptance of it. The next section of the book examines fear, suffering, and focus as components that enable adventurers to release hidden powers and access other realms of experiences; it also explores the possibility that a close connection to the natural world is a vital part of how adventurers access these realms. There follows a wealth of stories from adventurers about precognition, intuition, telepathy, and encounters with spirits, "paranormal" powers that I view through the lens of scientific opinion. The final chapters suggest that extreme adventure is not only a spiritual search, but also a spiritual tool. And that it is the same for all of us, adventurers or not. The hardest, most challenging experiences of our lives can enrich our existence, revealing our true identity, awakening us to a greater awareness of our own potential, and opening us to the infinite beauty of the universe.

PART ONE

The fairest thing we can experience is the mysterious. It is the fundamental emotion which stands at the cradle of true art and true science. He who knows it not and can no longer wonder, no longer feel amazement, is as good as dead, a snuffed-out candle.

ALBERT EINSTEIN, "The World As I See It"

Chapter 1

SPIRITUAL ADDICTION

Across the table from me sits a woman whose idea of a pleasant Sunday afternoon outing is spidering up a frozen waterfall, attached only by the tips of her crampons and ice picks.

"The scariest thing for climbers," she says, "is having to look at why they climb."

"So, why do they climb?" I ask.

"For emotion," she says. "For ego. For attention. Sometimes for excitement and money and fame. But mostly it's about attaining spiritual heights."

Like a tiny bug, its wings glinting in the sunlight and its drone cutting through the post-storm stillness, the search plane makes turn after turn across the vast South Face of Mount Foraker. Rock spires, avalanche chutes, hanging glaciers, cornices, crevasses. And the climbers' route: a sharp arête, rising nine thousand feet to the top of the mountain. The Infinite Spur.

Peering down through binoculars, the rangers strain their eyes for a tent, a length of rope, footprints in the snow. Any sign, a shred of hope to cling to. They know it's impossible. The two women have been on the mountain for twenty-six days. Their food would have run out a week ago.

They cancel the search. They are sure the climbers were blown off the mountain. At the height of the storm, winds were gusting at a hundred miles an hour. It would have been fast. Unconscious in seconds. Dead on impact. The best thing to believe.

She knows it didn't happen that way. She knows that they dug into a crevasse during the storm. She knows she can find them. Without maps. Or GPS. She'll follow the information that came to her in visions, during deep meditation. From her friend, lying dead in a snow cave on the Infinite Spur.

Throughout her teens and much of her twenties she'd been a wild child, defined by drugs, drink, and reckless living. Then she moved to Canmore, Alberta, where a boyfriend introduced her to ice climbing. The dizzying exposure as she scaled frozen waterfalls on the tips of crampons, swinging her axes hard into the ice—it was a new kind of risk-taking that appealed to her drive and sucked up her restless energy. It also brought her far more satisfaction than the drugs and drink ever had—though, at the time, she didn't understand why.

There were few other women in the ice-climbing scene and none Margo Talbot felt close to. Until Karen McNeill flew in from New Zealand, carrying her picks, helmet, and crampons. The friendship developed fast and stayed strong. Talbot became one of North America's top female ice climbers. McNeill gravitated to serious mountaineering. An expedition a year, in India, Alaska, Peru, with her climbing partner, Sue Nott. In between trips, she was making a home in Canmore with her boyfriend, and taking advantage of all the ice climbing the area had to offer. She and Talbot grew ever closer. They recognized each other—determined, driven women, chasing the demons of unhappy childhoods. Searching for the same thing, and finding it in climbing.

"When you leave to go into the mountains, at first all you're concerned about are your daily routines back home," says Talbot. "Your head is full of chatter. Within hours, you're in this rhythm where you're thinking only about food and fuel and camps. Then, when the climb gets technical, and especially when there is a level of danger, you become utterly present. There's no stress, sometimes even no fear. You literally become simple consciousness."

Margo Talbot insists that climbers are addicts—not to the activity itself, but to the mental state it enables them to reach.

"Something larger than you takes over. It's mysterious and inexplicable. You need to go out there again and again to find it. It's what Karen was looking for when she died."

Over the last few years, Talbot has been taking meditation courses. She practices "energy work"—reading her own and other people's energy, seeing how it moves through the body, and helping to change it when it's blocked or negative. This, she believes, is a continuation of her climbing career, a natural part of its growth. Her climbing and her spiritual work feed each other.

She was in deep meditation, in her apartment in downtown Vancouver, when the first messages came through from Mount Foraker. She'd heard that McNeill and Nott were missing, and that a search was on for them. Now, she knew they were already dead. McNeill was sending her visions of what had happened before she died.

"I saw her making herself as relaxed and warm as possible in an ice cave. I saw her running out of food and fuel. I picked up on her fear and anxiety, what she was thinking. I heard her listening to the initial search planes flying overhead."

Talbot was confused, and afraid of the knowledge coming through about her friend's struggle. She went to talk to some of her spiritual teachers, people she believed had psychic powers. She told them she was getting messages, but gave them no details. She asked them to try to tune into her friend. They all picked up exactly the same information. One of the women told her that McNeill had been desperately trying to telepathically communicate with people at home in her last hours, because she knew it was the only way she could be saved.

Talbot has no idea why she didn't pick up those first messages. But she maintains that her channels of communication to Karen McNeill are now open, and strong. She knows McNeill wants her body recovered. And Talbot wants to be the one to do that. She's hoping to find a partner who will climb Mount Foraker with her, via the Sultana Ridge. So far, the climbers she's approached have backed away from the plan. Not because it's dangerous—apart from altitude, crevasses, and the possibility of storms, for an experienced mountaineer the physical risk on this route is relatively low. But the emotional risk will be high. Encountering her friend's frozen body. Extricating it from the cave. Moving it to a place where the park service can winch it off by helicopter. An even bigger factor, says Talbot, is that most climbers are skeptical of her claims. But she has no doubt that, on this big wild mountain, she will find her friend's remains.

"I have a good idea of where I'll look. Karen's shown me."

During my first conversation with Margo Talbot, she confided that it was a relief to be able to tell her story, "without people thinking I'm crazy." She was surprised to learn that a number of her peers had said the same thing. That they too had stories they rarely shared with others. Because, as the mountaineer Carlos Carsolio informed me, in their world, talk of ghosts and spirits is "forbidden territory."

M ystical and paranormal experience runs counter to the rational and scientific parameters of our time. But this doesn't necessarily reflect people's beliefs. In the United States, a 2005 Gallup poll showed that out of a thousand people interviewed, 47 percent believed in ESP (extrasensory perception), 32 percent in the existence of ghosts, 26 percent in clairvoyance, and 21 percent in the possibility of contact with the dead. In a similar survey done in the United Kingdom, 43 percent of interviewees believed they had been in contact with the dead, 71 percent believed in the existence of the soul, and 53 percent believed in some form of afterlife. In general, older people were more skeptical and women were more prone to such beliefs than men.

The inexorable yearning for something beyond the mundane or the explainable runs deep in the human psyche. It arises from an urge to find meaning in existence, for something bigger than ourselves. It also comes from a need to belong, to experience life in terms of a harmonious interaction—with others, with nature, with God, with the universe. An interaction that was once part of the human condition.

In hunter-gatherer societies, religious belief was always linked to nature. Facing constant danger, people sought ways to live in harmony with the unpredictable environment by worshipping the earth, its elements, its wild animals. Life was shot through with spirituality. And the powers of ESP, or psi—contact with the dead, premonition, telepathy, astral travel—were accepted as an essential part of man's interconnection with nature.

The Neolithic revolution, ten thousand years ago, changed all that. Along with a shift to agriculture, it brought the beginnings of institutionalized spirituality. With the growth of the Judeo-Christian tradition, psi powers were viewed as divine or demonic. But pockets of the old order remained, and still exist to this day in Eastern religions and among cultures generally regarded in the West as hindered by superstition, like the Aboriginal songline walkers, the shamans of Mongolia and the Amazon, the shark callers of the South Pacific, the witch doctors of Africa. And among people in our society who refuse to accept the dogmas of organized religion, and remain open to mystery.

Many of the adventurers I spoke to were raised by religious parents, and in teenage years had turned away from their church. Such apostasy often leaves what Jean-Paul Sartre called a "God-shaped hole." Spiritual hunger is rampant in our society, evidenced by the burgeoning of the New Age movement, the interest in Eastern religions, and, perhaps, by the growing number of people who chose for their "re-creation" to go out into nature and open themselves up to its power.

"The God of my childhood is not the God I'm talking about now," says extreme skier and mountaineer Stephen Koch, who was brought up a Catholic. "That's not the God that I feel. My God is nature's beauty. It's the earth in its most natural state, untainted by man. You can still find that in the mountains, the oceans, the desert. Those are the places where I find the most profound sense of peace."

Like Koch, most extreme adventurers are fiercely independent individuals who are making unusual tracks in life. It's not surprising, then, that their spirituality is often deeply personal, homegrown, and inextricably tied to nature and their experiences within it.

"Being on the high peaks brings me a sense of intimacy with the infinite," says Everest mountaineer Pete Athans. "I'm more in touch with nature there. More alive. I don't think climbers are just an eclectic bunch of misfits. In some ways, I believe we are torchbearers of having a relationship with the natural world. A lot of us are disaffected with contemporary Western religion and we've substituted it with our own brand of faith."

In 1978, Michael Murphy and Rhea A. White wrote that many athletes had problems accepting the "sublime" aspects of their sport, because they had no words to frame the experiences, no philosophy to support them. The problems remain: if we cannot find a name for something, it's difficult for us to accept that it really exists, and adventurers still have no commonality of ritual or language to adequately define and express their more esoteric experiences.

"What we are doing, without really meaning to, in our wild play, is making a kind of religion," writes adventurer and author Rob Schultheis. "An incoherent catch-as-catch-can kind of religion, but a religion nonetheless. . . . the connections we make out there are hallowed, through and through, religious in the deepest sense of the word."

Reverend Neil Elliot, an Anglican vicar and chaplain to the University of Central England, is trying to help adventurers find a language for this new brand of faith. He believes that once they accept the idea that their experiences can be spiritual, they will begin to experience them as spiritual. Then they can start to take them further and, in time, find a way to express them.

In 1997, the year of his ordination, Elliot discovered the delights of snowboarding powder—deep, light, freshly fallen snow—on ungroomed slopes, a variation of the sport known as "soul riding." Instantly, he was hooked on the activity, and intrigued by the term— to what did "soul" refer? No one could tell him, so he began his own research, which led to his Ph.D. on the spirituality of snowboarding.

One of Elliot's early powder runs was on a beautiful sunny day in the French Alps, just after a big snowfall. With a guide and some friends he took the lifts up to a high point of a resort. From there they started climbing, until they crested a ridge. Around them, mountain peaks gleamed in the morning sun. At their feet lay powder fields, perfect clean canvases awaiting their touch. One by one, Elliot's friends pushed off down the slope. Then it was his turn. At first, like the others, he was whooping and laughing in exhilaration as the feathery snow sprayed up around him, filled with sparkling light. Then calm descended on him. The sensation of constant turning, and the effort it required, disappeared. Completely focused on his riding, aware of every nuance of the snow and his board, he became detached, as if the board were guiding itself and taking him along as a passenger.

"Suddenly, everything was flowing," he recalls. "I was both in and out of time. There and not there. It was just pure being. . . . I was very close to God at that point. Such moments are the heart of the soul-riding experience, and they come as a gift from God."

He calls these moments "raw spiritual experiences."

In the past, he says, most people would have needed to interpret such experiences in some kind of religious framework. Elliot still does. He believes in a personal God who "wants to give and reveal himself/herself to all of humanity, in various ways." Soul-riding is one of them. But he acknowledges a growing interest in what he calls "noninstitutional spirituality," free from the aegis of a church, where people are putting together their ideas and beliefs from a variety of traditions, and where spirituality is linked to action and risk in the outdoors.

So how is Elliot doing with his quest to find a language for this new spirituality—particularly for those "out of the moment" moments he feels when snowboarding? When asked this, he laughs ruefully. "Part of me wants to say that this is such holy ground that we should not try to name it."

Of all extreme adventurers, surfers come closest to having a common language for the spiritual aspect of their sport, and an ease in using it. Many of them refer to the sea as "Mother Ocean." They talk unselfconsciously about "soul surfing." William Finnegan writes about feeling "the heightened sense of a vast, unknowable design" in big waves, and refers to the places he has surfed as "stations on some looping ragged pilgrimage...a long search through a fallen world for shards of a lost bliss."

Mark Fawcett, a professional kite surfer, feels that some greater power must have deliberately created the perfect venue of waves and breaks that he plays in, worldwide.

"It's just too much of a coincidence to have happened accidentally. Every time I come out of the water, I feel immensely grateful to that power, whatever it is. You'll find a lot of surfers saying the same—that to go out every morning and jump in the water and become part of it, flowing with it, that's their church. It's a beautiful, beautiful thing."

It's not surprising that expressing sublime experiences comes more easily to surfers, for whether they are conscious of it or not, each one of them is part of a long and deeply imbued spiritual tradition.

What we now know as surfing was brought to Hawaii in the fourth century A.D. by the Polynesians, who had journeyed by canoe across the Pacific Ocean from Tahiti and the Marquesas. One of their customs was playing in the surf on *paipo* (belly) boards. The Hawaiians took it from there, perfecting the art of standing up on boards that varied in length from twelve to twenty-four feet. Surfing became much more than a pleasurable pastime: it was an integral part of the

Hawaiian culture, social hierarchy, and spiritual lore, and subject to the code of *kapu* (taboo) that governed all of life. When a craftsman cut down a sacred *koa* or *wiliwili* tree to make a surfboard, he dug a hole at its roots and placed a fish there as an offering to the gods in return for the tree. The *kahuna*—local priests and sorcerers—intoned chants to bless new surfboards, to call up big waves, and to give courage to the men and women who rode them. Hawaiian society was stratified into royal and common classes, with *ali'i* (chiefs) having their own private reefs and beaches for surfing, which were strictly out of bounds to commoners.

In the 1700s, the arrival of Christian missionaries almost brought an end to surfing in Hawaii. They taught that it was highly immodest to disport in the waves with few clothes on, especially with members of the opposite sex. Hiram Bingham, the chief American missionary, wrote with obvious satisfaction that "the decline and discontinuance of the use of the surf board as civilization advances may be accounted for by the increase in modesty, industry and religion."

But the tradition ran too deep to entirely disappear, and by the early 1900s, when the American writer and adventurer Jack London sailed into Waikiki, surfing was flourishing again. London was entranced; he proclaimed it to be "a royal sport, for the natural kings of the earth." He was keen to learn it himself, and was introduced by the journalist Alexander Home Ford to a twenty-three-year-old Irish-Hawaiian named George Freeth, a consummate surfer. "There's something spiritual about Freeth that makes him stand out from the rest, like a bright light," Ford told him. "Water is his God, and it's all around and inside of him. When he rides the waves he's almost—dare I say it?—a Christ-like figure."

Big-wave surfers face some of nature's greatest powers unencumbered, unprotected—practically naked. To survive waves that the writer

Daniel Duane likens to "a three-story building going at twenty-five knots," they must hone their bodies and minds until their physical fitness and skill are matched by highly tuned powers of focus and intuition. The ultimate moment comes when the surfer rides the hollow inside the curling lip of a big wave, a place known in surfer-speak as "the green room" or "the barrel." Being inside it, crouching slightly, one hand on the hard wall of wave to slow the speed of the board, is "getting locked in," "shacked," or "tubed." It's the epitome of experience for surfers. It's where they all want to be.

"It's *wild*," says Rabbi Nachum Shifren. "All that speed and power and energy—you're engulfed in water but breathing air, going at forty miles an hour—it's like rapture."

Every day, close to his home in Venice Beach, California, Shifren exchanges the traditional Hasidic attire of a *bakishe* and *gartel* for a wetsuit, tucks his long Hasidic sideburns under a hood, and paddles his board into the ocean with the fervor of a pilgrim. Now in his early fifties, Shifren was brought up an agnostic in the San Fernando Valley. He discovered surfing in his teens, on a visit to Malibu Point, and for the next fifteen years sought out good breaks all along the coasts of California, Hawaii, and Mexico. When he was twenty-seven, he went to Israel as a combat fitness instructor for the defense forces. At the age of thirty-five he immersed himself in *pnimiut,* a Hasidic word meaning "to delve into the true inner self." Four years later he was ordained as a rabbi. Although he studied the laws of the universe as taught by the Torah, it was in the ocean that he found a manifestation of his spiritual beliefs. Surfing big waves, he believes, allows him "to see God in a very different way than most human beings could imagine."

For Shifren, the spiritual experience of surfing can be explained through Judaism, in its purest form.

"In the Kabbalah we're taught that prayer has four different forms starting with four different worlds. These culminate in a world where you are nullified in the Infinite Light which is a manifestation of God's power in the world.... All religions have this one commonality, of the soul trying to rise above the material world and toward the infinite light."

This, he believes, is the essence of "soul surfing."

"There's no surfer worth his grain of salt who does not want to just fly off the wave, to use that wave with every ounce of its power to go faster and faster. Surfers especially want to have the feeling of moving, of constant dynamic, or overcoming their physicality. This happens in big, fast, steep waves, where there is so much energy, force, and speed that at some point the body goes on autopilot and it's all the spiritual makeup of the person. This is what the soul is trying to do. To escape the body and gain spiritual release. When you're surfing...if you're fast enough, that transcendence automatically happens. It's the ultimate, sensual, spiritual high."

There might be another explanation for the addiction to those spiritual highs. Surfing a big wave, climbing a high mountain, kayaking a waterfall, snowboarding an avalanche-prone slope—in all these activities the adventurer takes away the safety nets and becomes vulnerable to natural forces, with every sense on high alert. Stripped down and tuned into the surrounding environment, as our ancient ancestors were, in a life that was all about survival.

At the end of 2004, news broke of a devastating tsunami in Southeast Asia. Among all the compelling stories of human survival was an account of a tribe of hunter-gatherers on Sentinel Island, part of the Andamans in the Indian Ocean. Frozen in time, their culture is

Stone Age, and they shy away from contact with the outside world. The tsunami engulfed Sentinel at a time of year when the tribe would have come down from the forest and onto the coastline, to fish. They were all feared dead. Two days later, however, officials in a coast guard helicopter spotted a tribesman standing naked on the beach. How had he—and others of his tribe who later appeared—survived the devastating waves? The officials couldn't land to find out; according to reports, the tribesman shot a warning arrow at the helicopter. But Ashish Roy, an environmentalist lawyer who lobbies to protect the tribes, believes he has the answer. They sensed the approach of the waves, and fled back to higher ground. They used skills that have been crucial to their survival throughout the ages.

"They can smell the wind," says Roy. "They can gauge the depth of the sea with the sound of their oars. They have a sixth sense that we don't possess."

But maybe we *do* possess it; maybe it lies dormant in us until we need it. All the extreme adventurers in this book spoke of a "sixth sense" that comes from being keenly attuned to the environment they are moving through. Mountaineers feeling uneasy on a route, just before a serac shears off above them. Surfers predicting exactly where the next wave will break. Sailors sensing a brewing storm. Is this different in essence from whatever allows Margo Talbot to pick up messages from her dead friend? Or what enabled Clay Hunting to save his friend's life, after a climbing trip that went horribly wrong?

Hunting, an experienced ice climber, was doing a winter ascent in the Canadian Rockies with his friend Sean Smeardon. The beginning of the route was a frozen waterfall. Hunting led the first pitch, but the ice was so poor that he moved onto rock, set up an anchor, and started belaying Smeardon. Neither man can remember why, at the moment the waterfall collapsed, Smeardon was not tied onto the rope.

"All I remember is an earsplitting sound, and turning to see Sean falling amid tons of ice, for a hundred and fifty feet," says Hunting. "When I got to him he was very badly broken up. A big mess. He had smashed his hips, legs, ribs, and one arm. His face was caved in, he'd lost a bunch of teeth, he had a massive hematoma on his head, and one eyeball had popped out. I had to leave him to hike many miles through a canyon, to get help. It took me most of the night. I was in a terrible state. I had climbed with Sean for a very long time, he was my best friend and I thought I had lost him. The strangest thing was that when I was hiking out I had a small light in front of me the whole time. It wasn't my headlamp. It was a blue light. It led me out. I don't know what it was but there was no way I could have got out as fast as I did without its help. Every so often I would stop, and turn off my headlight and look for that blue light. It might be a bit higher up or lower, or to the left or right and I would follow it."

Eventually he reached a place from where he could call for help. A helicopter rescue was mounted.

"By the time they got Sean to the hospital, he was so hypothermic his heartbeat was almost gone," says Hunting. "It was close. Without the blue light showing me the way, I'm sure he would have died."

What was that blue light? A reflection from his own headlamp? Or was it a "sixth sense" accessed through a portal opened by the extremes of his situation? A portal to that transcendent state which helps keep adventurers alive.

Carlos Carsolio, a Mexican climber, told me how he was guided through a terrible storm down K2, the world's second-highest peak, with the help of the spirits of the mountains and the ghost of a climber who had perished on its slopes. Accessing such "moments of extended reality" was the main motivation for his audacious ascents of the world's fourteen highest mountains, without oxygen.

"One thing I know for sure," he said. "Once you have these experiences it gets easier to reach them again. You open the channel. I looked for such moments in every expedition. It's why I wanted to climb alone and to do such hard routes. It's a kind of spiritual addiction."

Part Two

But to gain a perfect view, one must go yet farther, over a curving brow to a slight shelf on the extreme brink.

John Muir, *The Yosemite*

Chapter 2

FEAR

Pressing us up against the limits of physical exertion and mental acuity, leading us up to the edge of the precipice separating life from death, sports may open the door to infinite realms of perception and being. Having no tradition of mystical experience, no adequate mode of discourse on the subject, no preparatory rites, the athlete might refuse to enter. But the athletic experience is a powerful one and it may thrust [him], in spite of fear and resistance, past the point of no return into a place of awe and terror.

GEORGE LEONARD, *The Ultimate Athlete*

Against the huge rock wall, his long, gangly body casts a bizarre shadow. A shadow walking in space. When the line sways in the wind, he balances on one bare foot, moving from the hips, his arms outstretched, his hands loose and relaxed. He's halfway between the wall of Yosemite Valley and Lost Arrow Spire, a towering rock outcrop. A walk of seventy feet. Half a mile off the ground. Without a safety tether.

At six feet five inches, American alpinist Dean Potter should be too tall for the finely tuned balance necessary for walking "highlines," lengths of narrow nylon webbing strung between points far off the ground. Philippe Petit, who walked a high wire between the tops of the World Trade Center's Twin Towers eight times on one day in 1974, is almost a foot shorter. Unlike Petit, Potter never uses a counterbalance pole. Perfect physical control is not enough; such activity calls for a mindset capable of dealing with extreme exposure.

"Essentially, it's like walking on air," says Potter. Almost as an afterthought, he adds, "If you fall and you don't grab the line, you'll go to the ground."

Why does he do it? For the same reason he climbed impossibly difficult faces on Patagonia's arrow-straight mountains, solo and without any form of protection. For the same reason he free-climbed Yosemite's Half Dome and El Capitan in a day, the first person to do so. For the same reason he took up BASE jumping in his thirties, throwing himself off bridges, buildings, and cliffs, opening his parachute at the last possible second. Not, he claims, just for sport, or adventure. He does these things for enlightenment. To search for the dharma, the higher truths of life. The activities are his spiritual path. His own form of Zen.

"When I'm jumping, climbing, or highlining, it's as truthful as I can be," he says. "What I'm seeking when I do these things is to break free from all my attachments."

Some of his peers scoff at this. Potter is a controversial figure, especially since he free-soloed Delicate Arch, a world-famous sandstone structure in Utah's Arches National Park. After news of the ascent broke, and word spread about how it was filmed and photographed, a firestorm of criticism grew. Potter was accused of doing the climb for purely commercial motives and, worse, of permanently scarring the fragile rock with his practice rope. He denies both charges. Visible groove marks in the sandstone were, he claims, caused by a couple of other climbers who had scaled the arch some years before on two separate occasions. And he's adamant that his motives were pure.

"I've lived a few miles away from the Arch for a decade, and I visualized climbing it on countless occasions," he says. "In the end, simply, I was uncontrollably compelled to climb it. I did no harm to Delicate Arch, other than blowing a little dust off the footholds and handholds. All rocks are sacred to me. Climbing it, in essence, was no different to climbing El Capitan, or Cerro Torre, or Trango Tower. My motives, as always, were to mesh with nature, using the art of climbing."

His motives, too, are to take risks which leave him wide-open to the possibility of death—his deepest fear, but a fear, he claims, which is the only thing that brings him to his full potential.

Sociobiologists, who in the 1970s applied evolutionary theories to social behavior, attribute the allure of risk to our biological inheritance from prehistoric times. Originally, so the theory goes, there were two types of humans, those who stayed at home in the cave guarding the young and those who ventured out into the wild world to hunt for food and find new territory. The most successful of those "adventurers" were the ones who developed the best survival skills, and thus could withstand the greatest risks. They lived long enough to have many children, successfully passing on their genes until risk-taking became part of human nature. In modern society, people have different levels of need to give our primitive brain a "workout" through facing up to fear. For some, a fast run down a groomed ski slope satisfies this need. At the other end of the spectrum are those

who are impelled to re-create the level of danger their distant ancestors faced.

Like Caitlin Perryman. She didn't just walk on tightropes, she
danced on them, she leaped into the air, executed pirouettes, and
landed again on what she called "the fine line." A move underpinned
with the challenge of overcoming fear. The sort of fear which was
"a concentrated stream of energy," electrifying her body from head
to toe.

"My body is calm but my mind races," she wrote in 2003. "As much
as I try to control it, fear sends sparks through my body, shaking my
knees and ankles. I am fighting. It is a simple jump, I know what to
do: push, stretch, tuck my knees up, shoot them back out, land and
absorb the shock. I force the rampant images of a missed footing out
of my head, and I jump!"

For her, fear was the eternal "what if" of falling from the rope.

"Once safe on the other platform," she wrote, "there is elation and
triumph. In the middle runs the cable of risk. A place of freedom
which can only be found between the two extremes…In this space,
risk is beautiful."

In a cruel stroke of fate, Caitlin Perryman was killed by a car that
mounted the sidewalk she was walking along in Montreal, on her way
to a tightrope practice. To honor his sister's memory, Benjamin Perryman now faces down fear in the mountains.

"My legs are wobbling, half in anticipation and half in fear of the
task ahead," he writes, about preparing to ski off a cliff in the British
Columbia Coast Mountain Range. "My heart is beating fast, knowing that a mistake will mean injury, possibly even death. I look out,
over and down the cornice. It seems as high as one of the skyscrapers
downtown. My brain sends out one last message of sanity, warning
me of my actions. But its message is in vain, an emotion deep down

inside of me has taken over. I am both fixed in my stance and compelled to proceed further by the same emotion. Finally the force over-
powers the restriction and I shoot off the cornice, pushed and guided
by fear."

In the early 1970s, Dr. Sol Roy Rosenthal, a medical researcher at the
University of Illinois, coined the term "risk exercise response" for the
exhilaration and euphoria that people report during high-risk sports.
Subsequent research revealed the biochemistry that triggers such
euphoria—the cascade of natural chemicals in the brain, including
dopamine, endorphins, and serotonin.

By the 1990s, several studies had indicated that individual differences in people's relationships to risk were associated with genetic
differences related to the neurotransmitter dopamine and its receptors. Dopamine has long been associated with the pleasure systems of
the brain; its release brings feelings of well-being and enjoyment, and
reinforces activities that provide those feelings, such as eating and
sex. But, as researchers at the University of Southern California discovered, it is also released in response to negative, stressful, and even
painful stimuli—the sort that extreme adventurers and athletes face
on a regular basis. The studies linked the "thrill-seeking" personality
to a specific gene, D4DR, which encodes the dopamine receptors in
the brain, and suggested that the length of the D4DR protein affects
how strongly cells react to dopamine. People with a long version of
the gene, it is claimed, are more sensitive to fluctuations in dopamine
levels, thus they begin to feel depressed at levels that would stabilize
the moods of people with an average length of D4DR. Conversely,
when the dopamine levels are increased, such people sense thrills
more intensely and thus crave more "hits" of the chemical.

The theory that there is a genetic basis to all human behaviors is a controversial one. Some scientists say a person's environment and circumstances have as much impact on behavior as genetics, or more; that Benjamin Perryman, for example, would not be skiing off cornices if his sister were still alive. It's also clear that not all risk-taking activities produce bursts of dopamine. Mountaineering involves frequent periods of drudgery, and Dalya Rosner, a British scientist, suggests that "the magnificence of the mountains ... the adventure of exploring the grandeur of nature, the thrill of experiencing the elements that carve out our world" bring rewards that are as valued and longed for as chemical changes in the brain.

While all this may help explain why extreme adventurers so willingly go to the edge, it doesn't shed light on how at ease they seem there. Are they immune to fear, or do they have a way of controlling and harnessing it? And does making friends with fear help bring spiritual and mystical rewards?

According to Celtic tradition, the earth has "thin places," where spirit and matter meet, where humans can touch the divine, and where the presence of the holy is strongly felt. When Christianity replaced paganism in Ireland and Scotland, these places continued to be revered, and to this day they are sacred pilgrimage sites. Many of them are high and rocky, windswept and storm-battered: mountaintops, like Croagh Patrick, or islets rising sheer from the open ocean, like Skellig Michael. Places that are hard to reach, exposed to the full forces of nature. Places where even unbelievers attest to feeling an energy they can't explain.

A long tradition of nature writers subscribe to the "immanent" view of the mystical—that God is in everything, and that spending time in nature, and paying attention to its details and its numinous qualities, enables one to touch the divine. Henry David Thoreau and Annie Dillard both found the mystical through a close observation of flora and fauna.

"Our life is a faint trace on the surface of mystery," writes Dillard, describing her moments of illumination in nature as "some enormous power brushes me with its clean wing, and I resound like a beaten bell."

Stephen Graham, in *The Gentle Art of Tramping,* also tries to describe this experience. "As you sit on the hillside, or lie prone under the trees of the forest, or sprawl wet-legged on the shingly beach of a mountain stream, the great door, that does not look like a door, opens."

For some people, finding that door takes more than gentle tramping. They need to go to the world's "thin places." They need to push themselves, to open up to the fear of annihilation. Then, with luck, they find their reward: "thin moments," when they break through to a different reality.

"Climbing, like any exacting activity, draws one deeper and deeper into its own territory," writes the mountaineer Maureen O'Neill, "a territory often as narrow as the ice blue thread of a couloir. In return for this extraordinary sacrifice of energy, the climber receives visions of the earth. In the moment before a difficult move she may turn her head away from what is directly before her, and the beauty—or is it the fear—lays her open. Her eyes are the eyes of God, the land flows in and through and from her like a river."

Dr. Joseph LeDoux, a neuroscientist at New York University and the Center for Neural Science Experiments, has spent years studying how the brain reacts to fear. To understand how our fear system works, he maintains, it is important to understand the neural systems that evolved as "behavioral solutions to problems of survival." The hub of these systems is the amygdala, an almond-shaped structure in the limbic system, an ancient part of the brain. Learning of and reacting to the stimuli that warn of danger involve neural pathways that bypass the thinking part of the brain, sending information straight to the amygdala. This triggers changes in the workings of the body's organs and glands, which produce the fight-or-flight responses: increased heart rate, blood pressure and sweating; muscles primed with nutrients; salivation and tear production inhibited. Using functional magnetic resonance imaging (fMRI), a method of scanning the brain to record localized changes in cerebral blood flows related to neural activity, LeDoux has studied the amygdala's response to dangerous situations. In humans, when the fear systems begin responding, the rational brain tries to assess what is going on and what to do about it. But the pathways connecting the cortex to the amygdala are much weaker than those from the amygdala to the cortex. According to LeDoux, this might explain why, once an emotion is aroused, it is hard to control. Why old fears often stay with us, as if imprinted on our neural pathways.

But if Elizabeth Phelps, a professor of psychology and neuroscience at New York University, is right, the response to fear can be unlearned. Phelps tested this theory by scanning volunteers' brains while showing them images and giving them mild electric shocks to create fear connected to those images. Their fear response—indicated by sweating and heart and blood pressure rate—was measured by a galvanic skin conductor. The volunteers were then told that something in the experiment was about to change. They saw the same pictures several times without the shock. As they realized there were no more shocks pending, their galvanic skin response went back to normal levels. Meanwhile, their brain scans showed both the amygdala and the prefrontal cortex lighting up during the process of their getting over their fears.

"As humans we actively try to control our emotions," Phelps told the BBC. "We know not to be anxious in certain circumstances but to be anxious in others. When we see a tiger in the zoo we know we should not be afraid. The question to answer now is, how do we regulate that?"

Is it possible that regular and intense "fear workouts"—in response to real and significant levels of threat—could alter our neural pathways? That fear, once faced and controlled, could be harnessed to bring a spiritual feeling of immense well-being?

One of Dean Potter's earliest childhood memories is of a powerful, recurring dream, in which some friends had told him how to fly. He was trying it out by jumping off a cliff. The fall went on and on, until he found himself plummeting toward a dead tree at the bottom. Just before impact, he woke up. The dream recurred regularly, right through his teens, and he became convinced that it was a premonition of his death. In 1998, when he was already an established rock climber, he was in Yosemite Valley, preparing to do some ascents of its big walls. Suddenly he caught sight of the cliff, and the tree, of his dream.

"It was a wall called the Rostrum, an incredibly hard climb. The tree was there at the bottom. The minute I saw the place I made the connection."

He started to have the dream again. It was the source of his deepest fear—the fear of death. He decided to confront it. That same year, he free-soloed the Rostrum. He climbed his dream—eight hundred feet and eight pitches of sheer unforgiving rock—several times without any form of protection.

"I did it to conquer the fear," he says. "But it doesn't seem to be the end of it for me. I haven't had the dream for a while but I think about it on a regular basis and ponder the meaning of it. Part of the reason for what I do is sensing what we have locked inside us, wanting to find that and have some control over it and be able to use it at will. Maybe it is possible to fly. Maybe through consistent exposure to these really powerful events that I'm forcing myself into, something will click inside of me and I'll get closer to this idea of being able to do anything. But I've read that a lot of Indian swamis make fun of the amazing tricks people can do, like walking on fire and so on. They say it's a waste of time on their path toward enlightenment, another stumbling block. I think a lot about that."

Kristen Ulmer, a former world champion extreme skier, also believes that fear is necessary for spiritual growth, although her relationship with the emotion has been a complicated one. A pioneer of the free-skier style—jumping off cliffs, doing huge midair flips, and descending mountains via near-vertical slopes and gullies—she claims to have had at least twenty near-death experiences. For ten years she took extreme risks for a living, and, with her blond good looks and daredevil nature, she became a poster girl of extreme skiing, appearing in numerous ski movies and magazines. She dealt with fear—the kind she describes as "vibrating in my body like a tuning fork"—by "breathing in good energy and breathing out the fear." Overcoming her fear, becoming fearless, was for a long time her route to a level of spiritual fulfillment.

"Skiing some sick ski descent or climbing the hardest routes," she says, "people like me really seem to seek this stuff out. It's only a century ago that people were discovering new territory on wagon trains going across the country. Now we're working in cubicles and having mundane lives. Things get pretty boring pretty fast. Humans want to feel alive and to feel deep emotion. They want drama in their lives. Maybe extreme adventurers have to experience something more intense to find that. And anything intense is going to be ultimately spiritual for us humans."

Fear always drew her. Facing up to it was the way she worked out childhood insecurities, how she came to define herself. If she hadn't been a skier, she thinks she would have ended up as a stripper, or doing drugs, or both.

"I have this real aggressive, manic edge to me that needed some sort of focus. I chose sports, and it was crucial for someone with a personality like mine to find something especially extreme. You're out there ripping big chunks of raw meat off life, with blood dripping down your face. I needed some sort of crazy way to express myself and there's part of me that just loved the near-death experiences. I wouldn't go home and be traumatized, I'd be invigorated."

Many extreme athletes jokingly describe themselves as having attention deficit disorder, and admit to needing constant stimulation. Ulmer admits to having been an extreme among extremes. Some years ago she was in Alaska, to do some heli-skiing film and photo work. For nine days the weather was bad, forcing her to sit in her motel room, bored and understimulated. Finally she decided to go home. She needed to get to the airport to sort out her ticket. It was thirty-five miles from her motel, and she didn't have a car. She went out onto the highway and stuck out her thumb.

"A guy in a pickup truck stopped for me and drove me out there. He seemed really nice. When we got there, he said he didn't have any-thing else going on, and offered to wait for me and drive me back to my motel. So we set off again and we'd only gone a few miles when he announced that he had just got out of jail. I said, 'Oh wow, what was that like?' He just snapped. He started screaming at me at the top of his lungs. About how he saw me hitchhiking on the side of the road and realized I was nothing but a piece of ass with money. That we were out in the middle of nowhere, and there was nothing to stop him from fucking me in the ass and slitting my throat, and throwing my dead body in the bush and that no one would ever find it. He went on and on like this, vulgar and violent and threatening."

And her reaction to this violation?

"I thought, *Thank God something interesting is happening.* I loved it. It was such an intriguing experience."

Proof of a dopamine junkie? A misfiring of the connections between the amygdala and the cortex? Ulmer doesn't know, but she's certain that her reaction saved her life.

"He screamed at me for almost thirty-five miles. I thought about jumping out of the truck, but there was no place to go. I just kept small-talking, saying things like, 'You're right, no one would find my body, and it really sucks that you had such bad experiences in jail.' So he never got the feeling of power over a victim, which is what he was looking for. Just outside of town he finally calmed down. He drove me up to my motel and let me out."

Ulmer was beginning to realize that her need for fear had become dangerously unbalanced, threatening to wipe out her life instead of enriching it. In the spring of 2001, *Skiing* magazine sent her to Chamonix, to research a feature about extreme skiing, and specifically about descending vertical couloirs—narrow chutes of snow between cliffs. The French Alps, and the Chamonix area in particular, offer skiers a huge and potentially dangerous playground; in 2006, fifty-three people died there while skiing and snowboarding, mostly off-piste. Ulmer and her two companions nearly became a statistic. Their plan was to ski down one of the most exposed extreme descents in the area, on the North Face of the Aiguille du Midi, part of the Mont Blanc Massif. They took ski lifts up the mountain, then traversed across to the start of their route. Ulmer, not easily fazed, stared at it in horror. Its top face sloped down at fifty degrees before ending abruptly at a one-thousand-foot sheer ice cliff. They would have to ski off to the right above the edge of the cliff, then rappel for three hundred feet to reach a couloir, which was, writes Ulmer, "so skinny it barely existed . . . and about a hundred and twenty vertical feet long."

For two hours she and her companions discussed whether they should go ahead with the descent. Finally they put on their packs and tightened their bindings—to lose a ski on this descent would mean certain death. The start of their route was "a sudden fifty-degree drop onto a bowl of powder that had no bottom." They reached the ice cliff. They weaved between a maze of deep crevasses. They rappelled into the couloir, which was sixty degrees steep and barely a ski length across. A perfect avalanche chute. By then the sun had come out and was shining on the snow-laden slopes above.

The first avalanche passed a few feet to their right. They clung to the fixed rope, standing one above the other in the gully, head to feet, pressing their bodies and faces into the snow. The avalanches came at five-minute intervals, increasing in size each time, throwing off wind blasts that coated the skiers in clumps of snow. Within an hour, they were getting direct hits. Five-story walls of snow traveling at a hundred and fifty miles an hour. What saved the skiers from being plucked off the mountain was a small rock buttress directly above them, which deflected the avalanches to pummel on their backs instead of their heads. Between hits, Ulmer's companions yelled at each other in panicked French. She took no part in the conversation. The experience had taken her to another place, where the avalanches were like beautiful white angels of death, roaring by in tidal waves that crashed against the rocks in great plumes of spray. Finally, the big one came. Seven stories high. Deafening. A violent beating that went on for twenty seconds. Ulmer's fear was so intense it closed her throat, constricting her breathing. She knew she was going to die. So why was she smiling?

"When the helicopter came and rescued us, my friends were really traumatized, but I wasn't," she says. "I had enjoyed the experience. As we flew away I thought, *This is really fucked up. I've got to stop doing this, before I get killed.*"

She gave it all up. She established a company that combines ski coaching with spiritual practice. During her four-day clinics, participants extend their skiing skills in challenging backcountry conditions, do yoga, and receive teachings from Genpo Roshi, a Zen master. On her Web site, she claims that the clinics give people the chance of "an unfiltered interaction with nature…and…poignant glimpses of transcendental states of being."

Ulmer says she started the clinics because she wanted to figure out what she had learned from being an extreme athlete. Most of all she wanted to work out her own relationship with fear.

"Before I was doing these clinics, I'd push back the fear, and it would show up in injuries. I got so burned out fighting fear that I would blow my knee, just so I could take a break."

These days, she sees the value of fear. She wants to have it in her life. She wants others to have it. When she's out on the slopes with workshop participants, she teaches them to breathe in their fear and breathe out the possibility of ever getting rid of it.

"As humans we have these disowned voices. For years I completely disowned fear; it was not going to help me accomplish being the best woman skier in the world. No fear, no fear—it was like having this screaming child in the basement desperate to get out. At some point it's going to start tearing you apart. Only when you embrace your fear can your fear relax. It's like a child that needs to be listened to. Once it's listened to, it calms down."

She calls her workshops Ski to Live. Her spiritual path is now about living life rather than courting death. But sometimes she slips back.

"The other day I was kite-boarding and I got going really fast. I didn't hold my edge and it looked like I was going to crash. I went to that place of intense focus, where I knew if I screwed up I could get really badly hurt—a place I hadn't gone to in a long time. It was a real rush. I still crave those moments."

She's finding new ways to get them. She went to the Burning Man Festival and worked as a "cooler," helping to calm and rebalance people who had taken too many drugs or were overstimulated in some other way.

"It was as much a rush as sports," she says, "because you have to be really, really focused. It's the aliveness of having a purpose."

Ask mountaineers why they climb and almost certainly they will tell you it's because it makes them "feel alive." Some take it no further than this; others, like Stephen Koch, who has climbed up and skied down some of the world's highest mountains, interpret the feeling in spiritual terms.

"If God's anywhere, he/she is in the mountains. A place that scares the shit out of you—that's where God is, I think. That's why we go and push it. I got into harder alpinism and went to Alaska with Marco Prezelj, a strong Slovenian climber. We opened a single push route on Denali together, nonstop. It was so beautiful to do that, to share that connection with him and the world and the mountain."

Few climbers have developed the idea of fear and spirituality as

thoroughly as Willi Unsoeld. In 1960, he led the first ascent of Mash-
erbrun, a 25,600-foot peak in the Himalayas. Three years later, he was
elevated to the status of a climbing legend when, with Tom Hornbein,
he made the first ascent of Everest's West Ridge. They also completed
the only traverse of the mountain, descending by the South East
Ridge. In doing so, they broke another record, bivouacking at 28,000
feet, with their oxygen all but depleted.

"You've climbed to the highest mountain in the world," said
Unsoeld, on his return to North America. "What's left? You've got to
set your sights on something higher than Everest."

He spent the rest of his life preaching to anyone who would listen
that it is essential to open oneself to the forces of nature, and to recognize its sacredness. Losing nine toes to frostbite on Everest didn't
dint his enthusiasm for high mountains, or the rapturous certainty
they gave him of being an integral part of nature's "seamless robe."
He advocated going into nature, "for an experience of the sacred...to
reestablish your contact with the core of things, where it's really at, in
order to enable you to come back to the world of people and operate
more effectively. Seek ye first the kingdom of nature, that the kingdom of people might be realized."

Unsoeld spoke a lot about the necessity for feeling "at home"—not
just in the mountains but in the universe. Our distant ancestors, he
claimed, were so deeply connected to their environment that this
"at homeness" came naturally to them. In the modern world, however, we have become alienated, from ourselves, from our emotions,
and, most important, from nature. The sum of these alienations, said
Unsoeld, is a loss of meaning in life. The way back to that meaning
is to go out into the wilderness with an open heart, "to feel it as a
mystery...something totally outside your ordinary thought patterns.
The Holy Other."

In 1951, Unsoeld graduated from Oregon State College with a B.A. in physics. Later he received a B.D. in theology from the Pacific School of Religion in Berkeley and a Ph.D. in philosophy from the University of Washington.

"I came to where I am by way of science," he said in 1974. "Then I went into philosophy and religion. And talk about cold turkey. I haven't had an answer since."

But he never stopped searching, and the place he looked hardest was in the mountains—from the time he started climbing, at age twelve, through the years he spent in Nepal as a Peace Corps director, on his Himalayan expeditions, and in the mountains close to where he lived in Washington State.

While at divinity school, Unsoeld became entranced by the teachings of Rudolph Otto, best known for his analysis of the experience that, in his view, underlies all religious and spiritual belief. Otto calls this experience "numinous," and says it has three components: *mysterium tremendum et fascinans*—a fearful and fascinating mystery. As *mysterium,* the numinous is "wholly other"—experienced with blank wonder, stupor, entirely different from anything we experience in ordinary life. As *tremendum,* it provokes terror because it presents itself as an overwhelming power, evoking a sense of one's own nothingness. Finally, the numinous is *fascinans:* in spite of the fear and terror, it is irresistible, full of potent charm.

For Unsoeld, this rang true with all his mountaineering experiences.

"Angst, existential fear, fear of radical dissolution...to be nullified by sheer overpoweringness. How many people ever feel this today?...You don't measure yourself against the sacred. You don't because there are just no calibrations small enough to notice you...against it we're completely insignificant. And I found this quality only in the mountains...keyed to the presence of physical risk."

I was sixteen years old, and in a pub on the West Coast of Ireland, when astronauts took their first momentous steps on the moon; the place was packed, we were standing shoulder to shoulder, straining to see the television set on the wall above the bar. During the lead up to the transmission there was an excited atmosphere, with waves of Guinness flowing across the counter, cigarette smoke hanging at ear level, and people shouting over the hubbub. But as the ghostly image of Neil Armstrong paused on the bottom rung of the ladder, and then planted a boot on the lunar dust, a reverent hush fell over the crowd.

"Jesus, Mary and Joseph," someone at my shoulder murmured. "That man is close to God."

Astronauts, like mountaineers, push out the boundaries of what is humanly possible, and for some this also pushes the boundaries of their consciousness. The author Frank White conducted interviews with a range of astronauts. Based on his findings, he coined the term "overview effect" to describe the paradigm shift in consciousness that many of them reported when they viewed the Earth from space. The most dramatic was that of Edgar Mitchell, the sixth man to walk on the moon. In 1971, two days into his homeward flight, he was lying in the console of *Apollo 14,* monitoring the spacecraft's systems and peacefully contemplating the scene through the small capsule window. Because there is no atmosphere in space, almost ten times more stars are visible to the naked eye than on Earth. As the craft rotated, multitudes of stars and planets, including Earth, tumbled in and out of his view. He had a wondrous sense of "being swaddled in the cosmos." He felt tranquil and relaxed, safe after his foray on the unforgiving surface of the moon. Then, without warning, something happened that would change the course of his life.

"Somehow I felt tuned into something much larger than myself," he writes, "something much larger than the planet in the window. Something incomprehensibly big. Even today, the perceptions still baffle me...looking beyond the Earth itself to the magnificence of the larger scene, there was a startling recognition that the nature of the universe was not as I had been taught. My understanding of the separate distinctiveness and the relative independence of movement of those cosmic bodies was shattered. There was an upwelling of fresh insight coupled with a feeling of ubiquitous harmony—a sense of interconnectedness with the celestial bodies surrounding our spacecraft....I was part of a larger natural process than I'd previously understood, one that was all around me in this command module as it sped towards Earth through 240,000 miles of empty black space."

Mitchell, with a doctorate in aeronautics and astronautics, was initially embarrassed to share this experience with his colleagues. To try to make sense of what had happened he turned to the mystical literature of Eastern and Western religions. Soon he became convinced that he had had a classic *savikalpa samadhi*—a moment when he reached a higher state of consciousness, perceiving time, space, and the universe in a new way.

"I vividly recall knowing I was separate from the stars and planetary bodies, but simultaneously knowing I was an intimate part of the same process....Not only was there a sense of unity and wholeness with the cosmos, but a duality. A schism between my early religious upbringing and my later scientific training was suddenly and quietly reconciled to a meaningful degree."

Such an epiphany, he believes, is a natural phenomenon, accessible to every human being. It is a sudden organization of information, a synthesis of ideas, producing a new insight.

Like Unsoeld, Mitchell felt compelled to share and further explore his experiences. He founded the Institute of Noetics Science, based in California, which has become an influential forum for New Age scientists and quantum physicists, with the mission of studying the nature of human consciousness.

Is it necessary for risk-takers to go to extremes for their metaphysical fixes? Not according to Royal Robbins. In the 1960s, his drive and fearlessness on the big walls of Yosemite Valley, in California, helped redefine what was possible in rock climbing. He was the first American to climb a 5.9 route, the first to make a big wall Grade VI ascent, the first to find and establish new routes up El Capitan. And he did it with rudimentary hardware—wires slung through machine nuts, pitons made from pieces of old Ford axles. Later, he took up whitewater kayaking and nearly died when he was trapped in a keeper hole while running a river in Chile.

When Robbins was a small child, his father deserted the family. He claims that climbing took the place of his father, teaching him what he needed to know about how to be a man. An agnostic for most of his life, in 1984 Robbins suddenly found God. Not, as one might have expected, high on a massive rock wall, or while fighting his way down a raging river. It happened one sunny June day, while he was paddling down a quiet stretch of the Little Fork of the Salmon River, which he had run many times before.

"I was just floating along, relaxed," he recounts. "It's typical Idaho country with sloping hillsides forested with pines and spruce. Nothing spectacular, except that it has a certain aura that has kept me going back. I had been through rapids the day before—not super-serious. But there was no connection between that and what happened. All of a sudden I felt this presence of God. It was unmistakable. It was there, just over my left shoulder. It was a very strong and powerful experience."

When I asked him to try to define the experience more clearly, his voice caught.

"It was like you've grown up without your father and you've only heard about him, and suddenly he came around again and you realized how much he loved you. That's what I felt."

Nothing in all his climbing or kayaking had ever given him the same spiritual high as his epiphany on the Salmon River.

"I thought, that was fantastic, I want to experience it again, to feel that close to God, because it's so powerful."

He hoped he would feel it again in the wilds. Not long afterward, however, he received a message in a dream, a voice clearly telling him that he would find God in Jesus Christ. So that's where he's been looking ever since. He became a Lutheran; now he's considering converting to Roman Catholicism. He still climbs and kayaks, but God, for Royal Robbins, is in church. And in nature's quieter reaches.

Where does man's sense of "God" come from? David Wulff, professor of psychology at Wheaton College, Massachusetts, has said that because spiritual experiences are so consistent across cultures, time, and faiths, there is the possibility of "a common core that is likely a reflection of structures and processes in the human brain."

Religion and science are usually at odds with each other, but during recent years there has been a burgeoning of studies looking for that common core by charting the changes in the brain during spiritual experiences, a nascent field known as neurotheology.

One of the pioneers of neurotheology is Dr. Andrew Newberg, a radiologist at the University of Pennsylvania. In the 1990s he began using brain-imaging techniques to study the neurological patterns of Franciscan nuns during prayer and Tibetan Buddhist monks during meditation, scanning them before and at the peak of their transcendent feelings. During that peak, the imaging showed that the prefrontal cortex—the part of the brain dealing with positive emotions—was seething with activity. At the same time, and more important, there was a substantial decline in neural activity in the parietal lobes. These lobes are associated with two functions: the orientation of the body in space and the perception of space. The left superior parietal lobe creates the perception of the body's physical boundaries, and the right superior parietal lobe creates the perception of physical space outside of the body. Newburg calls this the "orientation association area" and believes that a decrease in its activity is highly significant in the search for the root of spiritual experience. Without sensory stimulus to delineate the border between the self and the world, he concludes, the brain has no choice but to perceive the self as "endless and intimately interwoven with everyone and everything the mind senses."

During meditation, or intense concentration, this dulling of spatial perception could explain what Newberg calls a "state of hyper-lucid unitary being that is often experienced as mystical." He cautions, however, that "there is no way to determine whether the neurological changes associated with spiritual experience mean that the brain is actually causing those experiences, or is in fact perceiving a spiritual reality."

Recording which part of our brain lights up during spiritual rapture, however, doesn't explain why it happens, why the experience has such a profound impact, or why the aftermath of such an experience is a craving for more. Nor does it clarify why being in nature—particularly in its "thin places"—so often induces this rapture.

In the early history of the Western world, wilderness areas, and particularly their highest reaches, were feared. Ancient Greeks, passing through forests or mountains, dreaded an encounter with the god Pan; the word "panic" originated from their terror on hearing strange cries in the wilderness and believing them to signify Pan's approach. In the 1600s, a Swiss scientist, Jacob Scheuchzer, drew up a compendium of the species of dragons living in the Alps. In the 1700s, climbers arriving in Chamonix were warned by locals about the witches on the glaciers. Gradually, this fear of wild places began to lessen as a new doctrine spread, that the world in all aspects was an image given to man by God, what Sir Thomas Browne had, a century earlier, called a "universal and public manuscript," in which God's grandeur could be deciphered. To contemplate nature was to be elevated spiritually. The movement helped change the notion of the wild landscape as a malevolent force.

"Mountains," writes Simon Schama, "were at last admitted to the universe of blessed nature.... The informed contemplation of nature became not merely compatible with awe of the Creator but a way to affirm his omniscience...to offer a glimpse of his ingenuity."

The Romantic Movement, which began in Germany and England in the 1770s, viewed nature as a manifestation of spirit in the universe. In "Tintern Abbey," Wordsworth summed this up as:

A sense sublime
Of something far more deeply interfused
Whose dwelling is the light of setting suns,
And the round ocean and the living air,
And the blue sky, and in the mind of man:
A motion and a spirit that impels
All thinking things, all objects of thought,
And rolls through all things.

The Romantics, and the Transcendentalists who followed them, believed that in the contemplation of nature the mind can reach heightened moments of spirituality and enlightenment. That God can be sensed and communed with through nature. Such ideas affected the adventurers of the time, such as the German climber Leonard Meiser, who on reaching an Alpine pass in 1782 was overwhelmed by the new sense of space.

"Inspired, I raised my face to the sun; my eyes drank in the infinite space; I was shaken by a divine shudder; and in deep reverence I sank down."

By the mid-1800s, the wild world was no longer a place to be feared. But remnants of the old panic remain. Every climber who has scaled Ben MacDhui, Scotland's second-highest mountain on the Isle of Skye, has heard stories of its yeti-like ghost, the Big Grey Man. People who claim to have encountered the ghost describe seeing a giant, hulking figure, hearing loud footsteps, and feeling consumed with panic. The most famous accounts have been by mountaineers, such as Alexander Tewnion, who in 1943 wrote about pulling out a gun and shooting at the apparition.

According to British climber and author Andy Roberts, most of the ghost sightings don't stand up to scrutiny, but what is commonly reported by most witnesses is a sudden and inexplicable feeling of panic. Sifting through mountaineering literature, Roberts discovered that the core experience of "mountain panic" was relatively widespread in wild or mountainous areas.

"The solitude, exertion and oft overpowering awe of the surroundings," he writes, "together with the realization, consciously or otherwise, of being a fragile entity in an awesome and ultimately unknowable landscape could be said to overpower the heroic or rational ego. Effectively, people who experience [such] terrors suddenly perceive the grandeur and might of nature in a way which is terrifying."

He argues that mountain panic is the opposite of the benign experience of being at one with nature, expressed by the Romantic writers. He also points out that our ancestors, with their nature-based cosmologies, would have had no problem in explaining such experiences. Everything in the landscape had a spirit presence, which gave each place a particular atmosphere.

"Is this what these witnesses have experienced, the *genus loci* of particular locations, angry at human intrusion?" asks Roberts. "Or is it just all in the mind?"

To traditional Inuit hunters in the far north of Canada, the supernatural—spirits, premonitions, trances, transcendence—was in fact natural, part of the normal world. A world of wind, ice, cold, wild animals, and constant danger. When the 1920s Arctic explorer Knut Rasmussen asked his guide what Inuit believed, the man said, "We don't believe. We fear."

Beneath the beauty in nature, terror is ever present. William Finnegan understands this. He describes the experience of surfing big waves as dreamlike, yet a dream in which it is essential to be awake. "Terror and ecstasy ebb and flow ceaselessly around the edges of things," he writes, "...an unearthly beauty fills the world, scenes that seem mythic even as they unfold.... Truly big surf is a force field that dwarfs you, and you survive your time there only by reading those forces carefully and well. But the ecstasy of actually riding big waves requires placing yourself right beside the terror of being buried by them: the filament separating the two states becomes whisker-thin."

Beneath the beauty, terror.

On one of his early trips to the Himalayas, Willi Unsoeld was so entranced by his first sight of the beautiful mountain, Nanda Devi, the Shining Goddess of Bliss, that he named a daughter after it. Nanda Devi Unsoeld grew up to become a climber herself, and in 1977, she traveled to her namesake mountain with her father, to climb it with him. At Camp 4, however, she became seriously ill, and died in Willi's arms. He chose to leave his daughter on the mountain. With his teammates, he carried her body to the edge of a huge drop on the Northeast Face. He said a prayer of thanksgiving, "for the sheer beauty of the mountains...and for the constant element of danger without which the mountain experience would not exercise such a grip on our sensibilities." Then he pushed his daughter's body off the edge, watching it fall through swirling snow into the abyss, toward "the breast of the Bliss-Giving Goddess Nanda."

Willi and Nanda Devi Unsoeld had known about the legends of the goddess that resides on the mountain's summit. That her benevolence can quickly switch to a powerful wrath; that local people appease her with sacrifices of goats and buffalos. But the villagers and porters whom Nanda Devi had met during the expedition later insisted that the mountain hadn't claimed her out of anger. When Willi had named his daughter, they said, the Goddess of Bliss had entered the child's being and become incarnate in her. She wasn't really dead; the goddess had brought her home, and she would live there forever.

Willi Unsoeld kept returning to his "thin places" in the mountains. More than ever, they were places of solace for him. Two years after his daughter's death, he was on Mount Rainier, guiding a group of students from the Evergreen State College. They had been there a week, reached Camp Muir at 11,800 feet, and tried, unsuccessfully, to summit. Late on the Saturday night, a storm hit. By Sunday, the day they were due home, it was still raging. Unsoeld made a judgment call, leading the party down through high winds and heavy snowfall. At the unfortunately named Cadaver Pass, he chose a route that was slightly more dangerous than the alternative, but a quicker way to the mountain hut, which was only a few hundred yards away. Perhaps he was just unlucky. Perhaps he let his attention slip for a moment. Perhaps fear got the better of his decision-making. As he set off, with three students behind him on his rope, he triggered a slab avalanche. It swept the rope team down the slope and buried them under several feet of snow. Two of the team survived. It was forty-five minutes before they found Unsoeld and a young woman called Janie Dienpenbrock. By then, both had suffocated. In the mortuary, when Unsoeld's family gathered around him, they were amazed by how intact his body was. Not a bone was broken. His face was relaxed, and at peace.

Beneath the terror, beauty.

Chapter 3

FOCUS

Being ecstatic means being flung out of your usual self. When you're enraptured, your senses are upright and saluting. But there is also a state when perception doesn't work, consciousness vanishes like the gorgeous fever that it is, and you feel free of all mind-body constraints, suddenly so free of them you don't perceive yourself as being free, but vigilant, a seeing eye, without judgment, history or emotion. It's that shudder out of time, the central moment in so many sports, that one often feels, and perhaps becomes addicted to, while doing something dangerous.

DIANE ACKERMAN, *On Extended Wings*

Ed Lucero really loves running waterfalls. In layman's language, this means paddling a tiny kayak down massive walls of water cascading over high cliffs. To date, the highest waterfall that he has run—setting a world record at the time—is 105.6 feet. The equivalent of a ten-story building.

In the summer of 2003, a friend invited Lucero on a road trip to the Slave River, in Canada's Northwest Territories, to surf its huge standing waves. About four hours before they got to the Slave, they stopped to look at the Alexander Falls, on the Hay River.

"It's a big big big BIG waterfall," Lucero recounts. "I look at it. I think, I could run this and survive and it would be the largest waterfall ever run. It's like an offering. It's like it's saying, *Ed, this is the time in your life when you're supposed to run me.*"

He and his friend scouted the waterfall from all angles. Then they drove on, and played in the waves of the Slave River for a week. But Lucero couldn't get the Alexander Falls out of his mind. "I kept thinking, this is where the rivers have brought me. I'm supposed to run this waterfall. I have to run it."

Quickly, he assembled a team—a safety crew and a camera crew—from other kayakers who were up at Slave River. They went back to the falls, where Lucero spent a week studying the "perfect curling line" that flows over its left side, and visualizing the run. On July 31 he was ready. He strapped on the armor-like life jacket that he designed himself for white water. He climbed into his kayak, snapped his spray skirt over the cockpit of his small boat, and pushed off.

The camera follows him paddling along the river. Around waves called "holes" that drop over a rock or a ledge, creating a recirculating backflow akin to the rinse cycle of a washing machine. Through standing waves converging at angles, a haystack effect of chaotic unstable water. Toward the lip of the fall.

The river thunders over it, thousands of tons of water in free fall. An aerial view shows Lucero approaching the drop. His boat looks like a twig that's sure to be snapped in half. His arms windmill as he tries to keep on course. Suddenly, he's over. He disappears. Seconds tick by. Massive columns of spray rise up from where the falls hit the river. It's impossible. No one could survive this. Then a voice, the man behind the video camera shouting, "He's out! He's up! He's all right!"

Down below, a tiny bright dot. Lucero, bobbing to the surface, followed by his kayak.

What was it like going over that drop? Lucero tries to recapture the moment.

"Okay, I'm moving horizontally with the flow of the river. Now I'm approaching the lip and speeding up speeding up speeding up. The sound is deafening, but if you listen carefully, it's an oscillation. You can actually hear individual drops of water. I'm getting close now, I just focus on where I'm going, I don't see the people along the banks anymore, I'm just thinking about my line. I'm almost there now, everything is really simplified, I'm not thinking about anything but where my stroke is, I'm looking at the five feet in front of me, that's all there is. Then ZWEEEE, I'm over, I hit hyperspace, I flash into a different plane. I'm still in the river but now the water is free-falling vertically."

He pauses for breath.

"That's when it becomes really calm. And wavelike. And *silent*. Everything loosens up. I feel light and serene. The fall goes on and on—later, when they told me it was only three seconds, I couldn't believe it. Then BOOM, I hit the surface tension of the water, shock waves go right through my body and there's this ringing tone in my head like *Buuuuuhhyooooingeeeeee*. The water holds me under for several seconds. The impact has pulled me almost all the way out of my boat. My first thought is, *Am I hurt?* If I'd leaned over just a little on impact, I would have snapped my spine. But I'm up now, floating and moving slowly to make sure everything is still working."

In 2007, another kayaker ran the Alexander Falls. On impact with the surface of the river he stayed in his boat, thus, according to the rule book, claiming the world record. But for Lucero, going over the falls wasn't just about records. It was one of the most profound experiences of his life. An experience he'd been moving toward for years. During his childhood his family lived for a while in the Marshall Islands, where he spent hours on the beach, watching how each time a wave came in, it slowly sifted the sand according to weight, creating perfect patterns.

"I came to believe that human beings must be in that process as well," he says. "It's like everything and everyone is constantly interacting with nature, sifting into place. The more freedom I have to move around the world, the more I sift into place, my special niche."

Rivers are his niche. On them, he feels as if he's in a blood vessel of the earth, riding its great pulse. And going over waterfalls sends him into "hyper-attention," a state that brings him deep satisfaction.

"Everything else leaves, you're not thinking about the past, you're thinking about now, right now. And that seems to initiate the joy. To me that's very spiritual, the way that gravity focuses you to the present moment."

Psychologists call this state of mind by various names: "peak experience," "in the zone," and "flow." It happens when a set of finely tuned skills matches the absolute focus of attention on one action, screening out the usual chatter of the mind and producing a state of exultation that, according to authors White and Murphy, "approaches the richness of experience evoked by religious practice."

Paying attention to what is happening in the present moment is a central tenet of most spiritual traditions. For Hui-neng, one of the founders of Zen, "absolute tranquility is the present moment." For Sufism, the mystical branch of Islam, "a Sufi is the son of time present." For Meister Eckhart, the thirteenth-century mystic, "there exists only the present instant...a Now which always and without end is itself new." For the modern-day spiritual teacher Eckhart Tolle, experiencing "the Now" is the only way to go beyond the limited confines of the mind.

However framed, it is a state extreme adventurers must achieve in order to survive what they do. A state many of them end up craving in ordinary life.

For Dolores LaChapelle, a pioneer of powder skiing in the 1940s and one of the early voices in the deep-ecology movement, her sport was "life, fully lived in a blaze of reality.... Once experienced, this kind of living is recognized as the only way to live."

LaChapelle began skiing in the fourteen-thousand-foot mountains around her home in Denver, climbing up them with a pair of army surplus, seven-foot-long wooden skis strapped to her back, then skiing down via fifty-degree avalanche chutes. Staying alive in the sort of terrain she frequented—back-country snow bowls vulnerable to avalanches—was achieved only by maintaining a constant state of focus.

"I moved cautiously out along the windblown edge of the ridge I'd been standing on," she writes, about a ski tour in the San Juan Mountains, "very conscious that it could fracture into a hard slab slide at any moment.... I peeled off down the ridge in perfect snow. No effort at all, just moving with gravity and sun and snow—bliss—it always is. But at the same time there's total attention, watching to see if there are any telltale sudden little cracks in the snow beginning to form.... Total attention was mandatory."

"Si tu tombes, tu meurs"—if you fall, you die—was the mantra of the late Patrick Vallencant, one of the French pioneers of extreme skiing. In the 1970s he tackled mountain faces in the Alps and South America that were deemed impossible to ski. He did so in "pure" style, only descending on skis what he could first climb up on crampons. His margin of error was zero, and his level of control was, according to one journalist, "verging on the supernatural."

"At the beginning of any speed descent," writes Vallencant, "concentration of incredible intensity fills me...the world disappears....

To ski a very steep slope is completely beautiful; it is pure, hard, vertical, luminous in a dimension that, by its nature, is foreign to us, yet
I become a part of this cosmic dimension....I have the impression,
after a descent, of dropping all restraints—my heart is open and
free, my head is clear...all the beauty of the world is within the mad
rhythm of my blood."

Dharma practice," writes the spiritual teacher Tenzin Palmo,
"is not a matter of learning more and more and studying more and
more....It's a matter of emptying out, peeling off layer after layer.
We're already so full of junk, so stuffed to the top, that first we need
to empty out....We need to start peeling off all our opinions, all
our ideas, and all our cleverness and just remain very naked, in the
moment, just seeing things as they are, like a small child."

Explorer Peter Matthiessen recalls observing his three-year-old
son Alex in such a state.

"Forsaking all his toys, [he] would stand rapt for near an hour in
his sandbox in the orchard, as doves and redwings came and went on
the warm wind, the leaves dancing, the clouds flying, birdsong and
sweet smell of privet and rose. The child was not observing, he was
at rest in the very center of the universe, a part of things, unaware of
endings and beginnings, still in unison with the primordial nature of
creation, letting all light and phenomena pour through...there was
no 'self' to separate him from bird or branch."

It is this childlike state that extreme athletes such as Ed Lucero
revert to during their moments of extreme focus. The state before the
accumulation of experiences and memory, which, according to Susan
Greenfield, a leading British neuroscientist, makes us "self"-conscious,
aware of ourselves as separate from others, and from the world.

At birth, a child's brain has approximately 100 billion neurons. As the child grows, the number of neurons remains the same, but the connections between them, the synapses, along which neurotransmitters travel, develop as each new experience is cross-checked against previous ones. Gradually, a unique configuration of neuronal connections personalizes the brain, allowing the child to interpret the world in the light of previous experience. It is these thought processes and associations, built on accumulated experience and memory, that Greenfield claims constitute the "self."

Becoming self-conscious takes time. If an eighteen-month-old baby looks in the mirror and sees a dirty mark on her cheek, she will most likely try to wipe it off her reflection. By the time she is two years old, she will recognize herself in the mirror, but it will be another year before she understands that the self she sees in the mirror is enduring through time. Researchers at the University of Louisiana videotaped a group of young children playing, and at one point surreptitiously placed large stickers on the backs of the children's heads. When the children were shown the video later that day, those who were over three years of age reached up to their own heads to check if the stickers were still there, recognizing the "self" in the video as their present self. Younger children didn't make that connection.

But this self-consciousness is not fixed; it ebbs and flows from one moment to the next, as emotions shift and change. In fear, in rage, in ecstasy or during intense focus, self-consciousness, the Self, is forgotten. It can happen at parties, in church, while skiing or dancing or having sex—or while climbing a sheer cliff or running a wild river. At such times, writes Greenfield, "our brains can transiently reconfigure in some way, to revert back to the state where our carefully controlled life, our personal reality, increasingly fades in favor of the moment, the context-free, meaningless sensation where we have quite literally let ourselves go."

Since small children have accumulated relatively few experiences, it is easier for them to go into the state in which they experience the world on a sensory level, without interpretation. As we age, however, this sense of wonder and the power of imagination become stunted. Krishnamurti, studying the workings of the human mind over half a century ago, wrote, "A complex mind cannot find out the truth of anything, it cannot find out what is real—and that is our difficulty. From childhood we are trained to conform, and we do not know how to reduce complexity to simplicity. It is only the very simple and direct mind that can find the real, the true." As we age, the truth is replaced by analysis and understanding—until strong emotions sweep them away.

By eight years of age, Matthiessen's son was already "shutting out the wildness of the world," just as he had done in his own childhood. But certain situations bring back memory traces of that state. In 1954, Peter Matthiessen was on bow watch on a navy ship in the Pacific during a big storm. The sailor who was due to take over from him got badly seasick, so Matthiessen spent a nerve-wracking night at the helm.

"Again and again waves crashed across the deck, until water, air and iron became one," he writes. "Overwhelmed, exhausted, I lost my sense of self, the heartbeat I heard was the heart of the world, I breathed with the mighty risings and declines of earth and this evanescence seemed less frightening than exalting."

Greenfield says it's not surprising that a "loss of self" during moments of focus is so often equated with the spiritual. As well as an escape from the mundane concerns of everyday life, there's also a sense of removal from the physical world. And the sense of well-being that all those chemicals in the brain produce? "Pleasure is, literally, a sensational moment of life," she writes. "A higher plane of pleasure can often be identified with joy and in turn with religious experiences."

And such experiences, as Sam Drevo knows, are highly addictive. A professional kayaker from Oregon, he and a group of extreme paddlers had just done the first-ever run of a ten-mile section of the Rio Jimenoa, in the Dominican Republic. It was what he calls "real gnarly"—rapids and waterfalls, lateral waves, a maze of boulders with massive "keeper" holes behind them, big drops into troughs, eddy lines racing up, the sides of the canyon flashing by. Finally, they reached a steep, deep, narrow canyon where the water was serene. From behind, Drevo could hear the roaring of the river, like a loud pulse, but the canyon was still and quiet. He just floated, staring up at the rock walls, intensely aware of the millions of years and the immense powers it had taken to carve out this place. Suddenly a feeling overwhelmed him, a mixture of euphoria and profound peace.

"It was like I reached a place where clarity and intuition and effort and focus all came together to bring me to a higher level of consciousness," he says. "A level where I was no longer me; I was part of the river. It was an amazing experience; it definitely draws me back."

A sense of oneness, boundlessness, a connection to the whole world—"oceanic" in the words of Romain Rolland, a colleague of Freud. Infantile narcissism, Freud called it, a stage of pure ego, when the child is unable to distinguish between the subjective self and the objective outside world. A state which has parallels to Greenfield's "loss of self."

Men are afraid to forget their own minds, fearing to fall through the void with nothing on which they can cling," wrote the eighth-century Cha'an master Huang-Po. "They do not know that the void is not really the void but the real realm of the Dharma.... It cannot be looked for or sought, comprehended by wisdom or knowledge, explained in words."

When the Self disappears, so does doubt, and with it the fears and anxieties that inhibit human potential, both physical and mental. Letting go of the mind can open the way to the seemingly impossible, like the superhuman strength Alan Burgess found on the slopes of Lhotse Shar in the Himalayas. Burgess, a British mountaineer who now lives in Utah, was on the mountain with his twin brother, Adrian, and another climber, Dick Jackson. The three men were roped together, with Alan in the lead, at about 23,000 feet. They had just got above some 150-foot-high seracs, and Alan had started to traverse a thirty-degree snow slope. The sun was warming the snow, and he knew it was time to be turning back, but he was anxious to get to a place from where he could see the upper slopes of the mountain, and the rest of their planned route. When he had climbed about a third of the way, he heard a loud crack. Beneath his feet, the whole slope began to slide. A massive slab avalanche, about two hundred feet wide and five feet thick, had broken off above him.

"Suddenly I was engulfed," he recalls. "Something went over my head, blocking out the bright light of the day—it must have been a wave of snow. I was spun to the left and I thought, *This is what it's like to die.* Then the light reappeared and I was looking straight down the slope toward my brother and Dick. I was up to my waist in snow, being pulled down by this avalanche."

That's when he did the impossible. He freed his hips and hurled himself upward. Like a Hollywood martial artist, he did a backflip, out of thousands of tons of avalanching snow. And then he held the two other climbers.

"I landed on my upper back on the slope, which was now just hard ice. Below me, Adrian and Dick were engulfed by the snow, heading for the edge of the seracs. I was tied to them. I had to hold them. It was a massive amount of weight. I was on perfect *neve,* wearing crampons, my feet were hip-width apart, and the rope was running straight down below. I remember sitting down on the ice, totally focused on holding them while the avalanche drained through them. The front of my quads felt like steel, burning."

Adrian Burgess and Dick Jackson came to a halt at the edge of cliffs. They struggled to their feet, shaking snow out of their hair and eyes, astonished by what Alan had achieved: "a perfect standing belay" holding the weight of two men and masses of snow.

"All I did was react," he says, "and do what my training had given me."

Training. With enough training, would it be possible to tap into that sort of control at will? Hans Lindemann, a German physician, believed so. In 1955, after crossing the Atlantic alone in a dugout canoe, he landed on the shores of Haiti. During the two months he spent on the island, he became fascinated by voodoo and its belief that the practice of deep concentration can dispel fears and doubts. When he decided to cross the Atlantic again, this time by kayak, his only physical training was to swim one and three-quarter miles a day. But his psychological training was rigorous. He forced himself to go without sleep, and for one week managed on only five minutes a night. He studied autogenic training, a method developed by the German psychiatrist and neurologist Dr. Johannes Schultz to teach the mind to calm and focus itself. It involves going into a state of meditation or "passive concentration" while repeating "autosuggestions" and focusing attention on different parts of the body. In this way, Schultz claimed, the subject can have control over the state of the autonomic nervous system, warmth in the solar plexus, the rate of the heartbeat, and emotions, such as fear.

Knowing that fear, doubt, and hesitation would be his worst enemies during the ocean crossing, for months Lindemann regularly repeated a series of autosuggestions: "I shall succeed," "I shall make it," "Never give up, keep going west," "Don't take any assistance." Gradually, his confidence grew, along with a deep-found conviction that he would reach his goal. "I had a feeling of cosmic security and protection," he writes, "and the certainty that my voyage would succeed."

On October 20, 1956, he set off from Las Palmas in the Canary Islands. His craft was a Klepper folding kayak, seventeen feet long and thirty-six inches wide, with a plywood frame, a canvas-and-rubber hull, built-in air tubes, an outrigger for buoyancy, and a sailing rig. He couldn't lie flat in the boat, and, unless he was becalmed, he had to steer constantly with the foot pedals.

After the first twenty-four hours he wrote in his diary, "The torture has started." To endure it, he began his autosuggestions, and meditated to keep his pulse rate slow. To ease the cramp in his legs and buttocks, he spent fifteen minutes each day focusing his thoughts on those parts of his body and visualizing warm blood flowing through them.

Thirty-six days passed. He was catching fish and eating them raw—the flesh for food, the blood for liquid. A freighter appeared, and came alongside him. A young officer called down from the bridge, asking Lindemann if he wanted food, and inviting him aboard for a rest. *Don't take any assistance.* He turned down both offers.

Forty days into the trip, a series of big storms moved in. After hours of struggling against strong winds and walls of water hitting him broadside, his hallucinations began. Waves talked to him. A black servant pulled him along a road in a rickshaw. His outrigger was an African with whom he had long conversations. Horses galloped by. He had the sensation of his boat going backward. During this period he survived by "concentration on nothing—becoming one with nature, being able to neither see nor hear, not even knowing my name, though knowing that I must have one.... I felt enormously happy and content as though I were in another world in which I had no discomfort sitting, where I no longer heard the incessant howling of the wind and knew nothing of my desperate situation."

On the fifty-sixth day of his crossing, the worst storm hit. Winds gusting to force 9 kicked up huge seas that capsized his kayak. For hours he clung to the upturned hull, with twenty-foot waves breaking over him. Cold and exhaustion ebbed at his strength until he was drifting in and out of consciousness. Yet he never lost his grip on the boat, or his paddle.

"I marveled at the intensity of my grasping reflex," he writes. "My spirit grew weak and seemed to want to leave my body, but in all these critical situations, *I'll make it* and *Never give up* broke through time and time again to help me to persist."

Dawn broke, and the storm abated. He righted the kayak, baled it out, and retrieved what he could of his damaged gear. He was sure he had survived the worst. Unfortunately, he was wrong. Within hours another storm blew up. It raged for days, repeatedly capsizing him. Throughout the ordeal he focused only on keeping himself alive. All his pre-trip training, to embed the autosuggestions so securely in his subconscious that they would automatically help him in difficult situations, had paid off.

"I was empty," he writes. "A shell, unthinking, kept going only by a complete concentration on the words, *Keep going west, never give up, I'll make it.*"

Seventy-two days after setting out from the Canary Islands, he surfed his kayak onto a beach on the Caribbean island of Saint Martin. He stepped ashore, fifty pounds lighter than when he'd set out, shaky as a very old man, but able to walk without support. The whole trip, he wrote later, could be viewed as meditation. A lesson in focus.

How did Lindemann do it? Scientists at the Weizmann Institute of Science in Israel believe they have observed the brain in the act of losing its "self." To explore sensory processing and introspection, they asked volunteers to look at pictures and listen to music while performing different tasks. Meanwhile, their brains were scanned. The researchers found that sensory processing activated the sensory cortex and introspective tasks activated the prefrontal cortex. It is important to note that activity in the latter was silenced during intense sensory processing.

"The picture that emerges from the present results," Ilan Goldberg, one of the researchers, concludes, "is that during intense perceptual engagement, all neuronal resources are focused on the sensory cortex, and the distracting self-relating cortex is inactive. Thus, the term 'losing yourself' receives here a clear neuronal correlate."

His colleague at the institute, Rafael Malach, led a similar study, in which volunteers watched a highly engaging popular movie while having their brains scanned. In almost all cases, there was a "robust and widespread activation of most of the posterior part of the brain." Malach muses that this is "intriguingly reminiscent of recurrent Eastern philosophical themes which emphasize the 'silencing' of the self during intense engagement."

So when the brain needs to carry out a demanding task, it has the ability to switch off the "self." This, says Goldberg, might be a protective mechanism. When the slope under Alan Burgess's feet began to avalanche, he didn't stand there pondering how he felt about the situation—his subconscious snapped into an extreme state of focus, and took action.

"The reason why some people love to engage in dangerous activities such as mountain climbing," writes Eckhart Tolle, "is that it forces them into the Now—that intensely alive state that is free of time, free of problems, free of thinking, free of the burden of the personality. Slipping away from the present moment for even a second may mean death."

During extreme focus, however, the "present moment" takes on a whole different meaning. Time perception shifts in remarkable ways. Jim Buckley vividly remembers a fall he had while ice climbing in Wales, almost thirty years ago. He was on Cwm Glas in the Snowdon area. There had been a long, hard freeze, and the ice was solid. Using crampons and a borrowed ice axe, he started ascending a frozen stream bed, angled between fifty and seventy degrees. He quickly got into a rhythm, swinging his axe so that it bit into the ice. On one swing, however, the axe just bounced off the frozen sheet of water. Buckley lost his balance and fell backward. In the split second before he fell, he remembers an "extraordinary sense of time-arrested clarity." Then, as he tumbled down the mountain, how time stretched.

"First came the thought that I was about to die. The rest was an overwhelmingly clear sense of a multitude of threads that had been leading to this precise moment. Threads such as my head teacher at school, when I told her I was going climbing one weekend, saying, 'You take care, Jim.' My love for my partner Ronwen and our children. Regret at having depended on a borrowed ice axe. The knowledge that for the past five minutes the ice axe hadn't felt right, it had been shouting a barrage of severe warnings at me. The realization that I was about to pay the price for having failed so dismally to spot the signals. And curiosity—wondering if I was going to die, and what it would be like."

He wasn't wearing a helmet. Instinctively, he covered his head with his arms. He remembers crashing, bouncing, and somersaulting down the rocky section, then hitting a shallower and smoother snow slope.

"I thought, *Wow! I'm doing well.* But I knew that there were some cliffs just below, and that if I went over them I'd be finished off. I thought, *Ah, I have to execute a self-arrest with the ice axe. How does one do that, again?*"

He rolled onto his belly, brought the axe up to his shoulder, dug the adze into the snow, and came to a halt. A few more feet, and he'd have been over the edge of the cliffs. His fall—during which he considered the advice of a former teacher, his love for his wife and family, the condition of his borrowed axe, and the details of a self-rescue maneuver—had lasted only a few seconds.

W hat causes that shift in the perception of time? It's a tricky question for scientists to tackle, because the nature of time itself is still so little understood. One of the earliest known discussions of time was conducted by Saint Augustine, an Algerian theologian and bishop who lived in the third century A.D. When we say an event or interval of time is short or long, he asked, what is it that is being described? It cannot be what is past, as that has ceased to be, and what is future is nonexistent. But neither can it be the present, as this has no duration. His answer to the riddle was that what we are measuring when we measure the duration of an event or interval of time is in the memory. So that time itself is something in the mind. And perception of temporal duration is some feature of our memory of an event that allows us to form a belief about its duration.

In the late 1800s, William James developed Saint Augustine's theory. James, a professor of philosophy at Harvard and one of the founders of modern psychology, said that we are constantly aware of a certain duration of time, varying from a few seconds to probably not more than a minute. He called this the "specious present," the prototype of all time that we perceive. The experience of the "present" is specious because, unlike the objective present, it is an interval, having an earlier and a later part. The "real" present must be durationless, without earlier and later parts. But, as science has since discovered, such a "real" present simply can't exist. Taking into account the finite speeds of light and sound, events experienced as present will, in fact, be past.

Making accurate decisions regarding the duration of brief intervals of time, from three hundred milliseconds to ten seconds, is critical to most aspects of human behavior. Contemporary theories of short-interval timing assume the existence of a timekeeper system within the brain, yet identifying this system has been elusive and controversial. The cerebellum, a structure that helps coordinate movement and balance, was long believed to be involved in time perception. In 2001, however, research led by Stephen Rao at the Medical College of Wisconsin challenged this assumption, corroborating earlier suggestions that the basal ganglia, deep within the base of the brain, and the parietal lobe, on the surface of the right side of the brain are both critical areas for the time-keeping system. Rao's research involved fMRI brain scans of volunteers while they were engaged in various listening tasks.

"Activation in the basal ganglia occurred early—uniquely associated with encoding time intervals and suggesting an involvement in processes other than explicit timing," writes Rao.

The basal ganglia's cells contain the neurotransmitter dopamine. Sufferers of Parkinson's disease, who have an abnormal reduction in dopamine, commonly experience problems with time perception, which partially improve when their dopamine levels are increased. Drugs that increase the amount of dopamine, such as cocaine and methamphetamine, seem to speed up the internal clock; so do moments of high stress, when dopamine and other neurotransmitters flood the brain and time seems to stand still or move incredibly slowly.

Nine-year-old David Eagleman was illicitly climbing around on a partly constructed house when he stepped onto some stiff tar paper jutting over the side of the roof, thinking it would take his weight. It didn't, and he fell two stories, landing on a brick patio. During that fall, he experienced the same slowing of time that Jim Buckley described during his tumble down a Welsh mountainside.

"It felt like it took forever," the adult Eagleman recalls. "One of the things that was so interesting subjectively was that in the moment of falling there was no fear, it was calm calculation. Wondering if I had enough time to reach up and grab that bit of tar paper. Wondering if I should turn this way or that as I was falling. At some point I remembered the story of Alice in Wonderland falling down the rabbit hole. I was watching the ground coming toward me and thinking, *This is what it must have been like for her.*"

As he grew up he often thought back to that fall, which left him fascinated by the nature of time. Now a professor at the departments of neuroscience and psychiatry at Baylor College of Medicine, he runs the Eagleman Laboratory, working on what he calls the "temporal binding problem"—trying to understand how the brain meshes sensory information, allowing us to experience different temporal events as simultaneous. If you tap your finger on the table, for example, because light is faster than sound, your brain should register the sight of the tap a few milliseconds earlier than the sound, yet you experience both as simultaneous. His theory for this is that the brain "collects a lot of information, waits, then stitches a story together."

He is also trying to discover what happens in the brain during high-stress experiences, such as falling off a roof, or down a mountain. Does the person's perception of time slow down enough to absorb extra information? William James suggested that time perception is composed of fast "snapshots" of the world, in the same way that a movie is made of fast sequences of still pictures. Could the sense that time is slowing, in high-adrenaline situations, be a result of these "neural snapshots" clicking at a faster rate? Or does the brain "stitch together a story" and details after the event? Or does time itself slow down?

In his search for answers, Eagleman has designed a unique research project. He sets up a 150-foot-high SCAD diving tower, from the top of which his subjects are suspended hanging faceup. On release, they fall backward into a net, hitting it at seventy miles per hour. Eagleman has done this himself, three times.

"It's totally safe," he says, "but it's terrifying. Falling backward, you can't turn yourself. You fall straight down. I needed to put people in a situation where they were terrified for their lives but wouldn't get hurt, so I could test this issue about time, to see if they could see the world in slower motion during such an event."

Eagleman invented a device, the perceptual chronometer, which he also calls the Eagle Eye, small enough to be strapped onto his subjects' wrists. Each of its four tiny LED screens presents numbers in random sequences, alternating between positive and negative images, white on black and black on white. Once the alternation rate reaches a certain speed, it is impossible to read the numbers. Before each subject is attached to the SCAD, Eagleman checks to find the threshold at which they can still recognize the numbers, and sets the alternation rate just slightly faster than that threshold. Under normal circumstances, they would not be able to read the numbers at all. Their task, as they are falling from the top of the SCAD tower, is to try to decipher them.

It was Eagleman's hope that if the world actually slowed down in high-stress situations, his subjects should be able to see the numbers and report them. But out of the twenty-three tests he's run so far, he has found no result. People were not able to read the numbers on the way down. They were not actually seeing the world in slow motion, as he had thought he had done during his fall off the roof. A series of experiments he ran in a laboratory have come up with the same result.

"The world you experience is a construction of your brain," he concludes. "Your brain is a vast universe of an organ that goes through a lot of editing tricks to make the world appear the way it does to you. It can completely separate out different aspects of time experience. We can set something up in the lab so that you think something lasted for a much longer duration, and yet there are no concomitant temporal stretchings with it in other ways."

How does he explain Dean Potter's experience, on his BASE jump into Mexico's *Sotano de las Golondrinas*—the Cellar of the Swallows?

Early one morning in 2003, in the midst of the Mexican jungle, Potter stood on the edge of a limestone sinkhole, the deepest vertical cave in the world. Shaped like an inverted cone, it is between 170 and 300 feet across at the top and 1,200 feet deep, big enough for the Empire State Building to fit inside. Potter had heard the local stories about evil spirits residing in the cave, luring people to their deaths. He knew they weren't true, that only parrots lived there, as well as the swallows, fifty thousand of them, giving it its name.

An hour after dawn, the birds rose en masse from their perches in the limestone walls. A hurricane of wing beats created wind currents around Potter, and the solid cloud of birds blocked out the sun as they spiraled up and out of the hole, heading off for a day's feeding.

It was his turn to fly. Down into the depths of the earth, freefalling for six seconds, accelerating to a hundred miles an hour, before deploying his parachute at the last possible moment. Then floating the rest of the way, steering away from the walls, landing among the sharp rocks, screes, and heaps of guano on the cave floor. Packing up his parachute and getting hoisted back to the surface to do it all again, and again, and again... until the shadows of the surrounding trees lengthened and the first of swallows returned.

Potter was at the Cellar of the Swallows with a support team and a film crew who wanted to record him highlining across the mouth of the hole. During the week they spent there, several of the team jumped with him every day. They jumped even when bad weather moved in, bringing torrential rain and waterfalls that cascaded down the sides of the sinkhole. On the final morning, Potter and his friend Jimmy Pouchert stood together on the floor of the cave after what was supposed to be their last jump. Pouchert wanted to linger there. He gazed at the rushing water, taking in the amplified sounds, the feel of the air. But Potter was restless. He wanted to jump one more time. He got hoisted back up, and grabbed a chute that was already prepared. He didn't know that it had been left out in the rain for a few minutes; that it was partly wet. He put it on. He looked at the layers of mist drifting across the mouth of the hole. He stepped into space.

One second. Humid air rushes against his face and ears. He shoots through cloud, into brilliant light.

Two seconds. He examines floating dust particles lit by the sun.

Three seconds. He analyzes the colors of the walls rising past him: gold and red from the oxides, white from guano.

Four seconds, five seconds. The floor of the cave speeds toward him.

Six seconds. He reaches back to deploy his pilot parachute.

Seven seconds. The pilot chute connects to the main chute and opens it.

Eight seconds. Dry on one side, wet on the other, the chute spins awkwardly. The lines twist.

Nine seconds. He torques his body and kicks his legs, trying to untwist the lines. The cave echoes with Jimmy's thundering voice, "STEER AWAY FROM THE WALLS!"

Ten seconds. He's heading for impact when his lines untwist. Grabbing the steering toggles he makes a tight left turn, away from the wall.

Eleven seconds. He collides head-on with the hoist line. The chute collapses.

Twelve seconds. Folds of material fall over his head and upper body, blinding him. He lunges at the hoist line, grabbing it with both hands.

Thirteen seconds. He hears a zipping noise as rope slices through skin and flesh. His hands blaze with pain. Roaring, he clenches his entire body and stops his slide. Jimmy's voice echoes, "HANG ON."

Fourteen seconds. He's sliding again, the rope ripping through muscle, the pain unbearable.

Fifteen seconds. With every ounce of strength he halts the slide again.

Sixteen seconds. A voice echoes up to him. "YOU'RE TEN FEET OFF THE GROUND, MAN! LET GO!"

Seventeen seconds. He crumples to the earth.

David Eagleman's reaction to this story?

"Amazing."

But he sticks to his theory. Dean Potter, he says, wasn't experiencing a slowing of time as he fell. He was simply in a state of extreme focus.

"He was devoting all the immense resources of his brain toward this one problem. It's something that we almost never do. The brain is always trying to strike a balance between working on different problems at the same time. But there's a mechanism, which under extreme situations allows the brain to take all that processing power and direct it to one thing. The amygdala kicks in and says, *Okay everybody, you're working for me right now.* That's the experience he's describing. You have to put yourself into extreme situations to get your brain to do that. When that happens, you unmask its tremendous resources."

Perhaps there is another explanation. Perhaps, when he was falling, Potter entered what the British author Jay Griffiths calls "wild time." Based in nature and immeasurable by any form of clock, wild time allows us to transcend ordinary temporal limitations. Once, writes Griffiths, most of the world was wilderness, surrounding small pockets of human settlements. Now it's the other way around. Likewise, humans were once surrounded by wild time, until they began to chart time, to clock it, to buy and sell it. As humanity overtook wilderness, so Western society's peculiar time-marking has become the norm and wild time the exception. Only young children live naturally in wild time, but as they grow they are taught to see time as something concrete and defined.

"*Tuesday* is spoken of as if it is made of slate," writes Griffiths, "*deadline* as if it were a wall and *decade* as if it were a water tank. We brick ourselves into a house of time which we then find claustrophobic."

In adulthood, "tamed time" becomes so oppressive that we seek to escape it and rediscover wild time. One way of doing that is by going out into the pockets of wilderness that remain, to find what she calls "the visible picture of wild time."

Griffiths, an urban creature who lives in London, had her first experience of true wilderness, or "nature without audience," on a rafting trip across the Taku watershed, in Alaska and British Columbia. The watershed covers four and a half million acres of volcanic mountains, glaciers, deep canyons, high waterfalls, vast swaths of spruce and pastures covered with sage, alpine strawberries, and juniper. Griffiths was profoundly affected by her journey through it, and into wild time.

"Wilderness is a ferocious intoxication which sweeps over your senses with rinsing vitality, leaving you stripped to the vivid, your senses rubbed until they shine," she writes. "It is an untouched place which touches you deeply and its aftermath—when landscape becomes innerscape—leaves you elated, awed and changed utterly."

Elated. Awed. Changed utterly. A state some would call transcendence. What the psychologist and psi researcher Dean Radin describes as the "luminosity of the experience." It's something that science can't fully explain—how it happens, and why it is so compelling that some people go to remarkable lengths to reach it.

Chapter 4

SUFFERING

As soon as pain gives its precautionary signal…it is time to reduce the speed—some great danger, some storm is approaching and we do well to "catch" as little wind as possible. It is true that there are men who, on the approach of severe pain, hear the very opposite call of command, and never appear more proud, more martial, or more happy than when the storm is brewing; indeed, pain itself provides them with their supreme moments. These are the heroic men, the great pain bringers of mankind.… They are forces of the greatest importance for preserving and advancing the species, be it only because they are opposed to smug ease, and do not conceal their disgust at this kind of smug happiness.

FRIEDRICH NIETZSCHE, *Joyful Wisdom*

When Joe Tasker was at home in Britain, he was all in favor of "smug ease." He loved warmth and comfort, good food and wine. He claimed to dread the thought of being back on a mountain in subzero temperatures, existing on freeze-dried food, with no female company for months on end. And yet, long before I was his girlfriend, mountains were where he spent half his life. The highest mountains in the world, which he climbed without oxygen, putting up new routes and taking outrageous risks. It was how he made his name as one of the world's great mountaineers. It was also something, I suspect, for which he was hardwired.

Joe had told me once about the five sacred mountains of ancient Taoist tradition. Four were located at each corner of the universe, a fifth at its center in China. They connected the terrestrial and the divine. From their peaks, it was possible to survey not just the panorama of the earth but the essence of its spirit. The mountains were guarded by monsters, and only the true adepts of Tao could climb them, in mystical trances they reached through pain, suffering, and self-abnegation. I remember wondering aloud if he was a reincarnated Taoist monk. Joe laughed. One religious vocation had been enough for him.

Both Joe and I had been raised as Roman Catholics. By the time I reached fifteen, I stopped going to communion or confession. A couple of years after that, I turned my back on the church entirely. Joe's break was more extreme. He'd spent all his teenage years in a seminary, training to be a priest. Getting up at the crack of dawn several times a week for Mass in a freezing-cold church. Long days in the classroom, having Latin and the Catechism drummed into him by Jesuit priests. More church in the evenings, followed by hours of homework. Then a little free time in the common room, paging through magazines and newspapers from which pictures of women and any slightly salacious articles had been carefully cut out. "I used to wonder who did the cutting," he once said. "We all wanted that job." And, of course, the celibacy, which, more than anything, eventually drove him from those walls and out into the world.

So why, after all that, did he choose the rigors and self-discipline of high-altitude mountaineering?

I talked to him sometimes about how my apostasy had left not only a legacy of guilt but a spiritual void, an existential loneliness. A "God-shaped hole." I'd patched in bits from a few obscure spiritual traditions, but nothing had filled that hole. Joe claimed he hadn't even tried. For him, there was no God now. There was no life after death. When the end came, it would be annihilation. Life was material, not spiritual. But I wondered, and I wonder still, if his insatiable need to test himself in the mountains wasn't linked to a spiritual void even more profound than my own. If his years in the seminary, the isolation of the life, the mental preparations for the challenges of priesthood, hadn't reconfigured his brain to need privation, to seek it out in order to feel complete, and at peace.

In the months before Joe left on his last expedition, in 1982, he wrote *Savage Arena,* his second book. An account of most of his climbing career, it was also a meditation on what impelled him to climb difficult routes on high mountains, and why it was worth all the suffering. About his 1978 Kanchenjunga expedition, he wrote, "I could not answer my own questions of whether I was here because I really wanted to be or whether I felt I had to drive myself on, no matter the suffering involved....I wondered if climbing one of the world's highest mountains made one a better person, if it would give courage and strength in other aspects of life. Only reaching the top would answer that and I no longer knew what the motivation was which would enable me to put one foot in front of the other when there was only pain, and shortage of air, and no fun or enjoyment."

Suffering, my mother once told me, is a great leveler. It's a good teacher, too. It reminds us of our fragility. It strips away our pretenses. And, some believe, it brings us closer to the divine.

In August 1979, a group of British mountaineers were heading up to the summit of Mount Kenya when they met a man on his way down. All he wore on his feet were woolen socks. He carried a length of hemp rope and a bag containing a small package of food, a thin blanket, a bread knife, and a Bible. In answer to their questions, he described his climbing method: tying the bag to his rope and throwing it over rocks to anchor it, then hacking holds in the ice with his bread knife. He said he had just spent five days on the summit, and that God had sent him there to pray for the world. The British climbers urged him to take care, and carried on. On their descent, they looked in vain for the man. They reported him missing, and search parties went up the mountain but also found no sign. He was presumed dead. A few days later the man was finally located in a village at the foot of the mountain. Ephraim M'Ikiara, fifty-two, a devout Christian and believer in native Kikuyu animism, claimed that this was his third ascent of the mountain.

Suffering has long been a component of many religious traditions, and often practiced in wild, forbidding places. Milarepa, the eleventh-century Tibetan mystic, spent months wandering in the Himalayas, protected only by a thin cotton sheet and living off nettles. Manchurian shamans of the ninth century tested themselves by swimming underneath the ice of a frozen river, between air holes cut far apart in the ice. Missing a hole meant death. The Tamang shamans, or *bombos,* of Nepal completed their initiation with trances brought about by fasting for seven days in a *gufa,* a barrel set high on a pole. In the first century A.D., Simeon the Stylite of Syria spent thirty-three years perched on a high pillar and Saint John of Rila lived much of his life in caves and among tree roots on the slopes of his namesake mountain in Bulgaria.

Early last century, Igjugarjuk, a member of the Caribou Inuit tribe in Northern Canada, was dragged on a sled into the wilderness by his teacher, Perqanaq, and sealed inside an igloo. For a month. In the depth of winter. Igjugarjuk wanted to become an *angakoq,* or shaman, and this was his initiation, which he later described to the Danish ethnographer Knut Rasmussen. During the thirty days of dark solitude he had no clothing, no food, barely any water, and only a piece of hide to lie on. His suffering was so great, he said, that at times he "died a little." But it was only the beginning of a lifetime of fasting and privation, which, he learned, were essential to accessing shamanic powers.

"All the true wisdom is only to be found far from the dwellings of man, in the great solitudes, and it can only be attained through suffering," Igjugarjuk told Rasmussen. "Suffering and privation are the only things that can open the mind of man to that which is hidden from his fellows."

Extreme athletes and adventurers understand the need for suffering; they use it as a means to increase their endurance and as a proving ground for their capabilities.

"When you train," writes high-wire walker Philippe Petit, "you should be outside on a rough coast, all alone. To learn what you must, it is important to have been treacherously overturned by the ocean's salty air. To have climbed back up to the wire with a wild leap. To have frozen yourself with rage, to have been hell-bent on keeping your balance in the claws of the wind. You must have weathered long hours of rain and storm, have cried out with joy after each flash of lightning, have cried cries that could push back the thunder."

As part of his training for long races across Death Valley, in California, where daytime temperatures can exceed 122 degrees Fahrenheit, the ultramarathoner Marshall Ulrich runs on the spot for hours inside a sauna. To prepare himself for his solo climb of Nanga Parbat in 1953, the legendary Austrian mountaineer Hermann Buhl walked around with snowballs in his hands until his skin was frozen, trying to increase his capillary capacity and thus make himself more immune to frostbite. Not so the Mexican mountaineer Carlos Carsolio, who at the age of thirty-three had climbed all fourteen of the highest peaks in the world. As a boy in Mexico, he trained himself to withstand cold and thirst by immersing his hands in ice for long periods and deliberately becoming dehydrated. American alpinist Mark Twight toughened himself for hard climbs by beating his hands against concrete until they bled, and running stairs until he vomited. To become a great climber, he believed, he needed the strong will and hardness that come only from "suffering and being rewarded for it."

Michael Fournier, a French high-altitude skydiver, is reported to be spending periods of time in a thermal chamber chilled to –67 degrees Fahrenheit, and sitting for hours in front of a blank wall, wearing "white noise" headphones. He's doing this as part of his training for what he hopes will be a successful attempt to break Joe Kittinger's 1960 record of free-falling from 102,800 feet (16 miles). In 2008, Fournier plans to climb aboard a ten-ton helium weather balloon tethered on the plains of Saskatchewan in Canada. Once cut free, he will begin a three-hour descent, for twenty-five miles, up to the very edge of space. There, he will step off the balloon and plummet head-first into the stratosphere. While no one can predict exactly what will happen next, scientists on his team believe that thirty-seven seconds into his free fall he will break through the 760 miles-per-hour sound barrier and eventually reach a top speed of 1,113 miles per hour, before wind resistance slows him down. His free fall will last up to five minutes. After his parachute deploys, he will float down for another four minutes and seven thousand feet before touching down on earth. If he gets that far. During the fall, external temperatures will be –148 degrees Fahrenheit; if anything goes wrong with his pressurized carbon-fiber suit, he will freeze to death. No one knows for sure if his specially designed helmet will protect him from the impact of the sonic boom as he breaks through the Mach 1 sound barrier. And if he fails to maintain the correct body position and starts to spin as he falls, the g-forces will rip him apart.

In the race for that record with Michael Fournier is Cheryl Sterns, an aviator who is the current and twenty-two-time U.S. women's parachuting champion. A pilot for US Airways, she holds a master's degree in aeronautical science and was the first female admitted to the U.S. Army's elite parachute group, the Golden Knights. With her short, curly hair and neat, conservative dress style, Sterns looks more like a Sunday school teacher than someone who is prepared to risk being flash-frozen or ripped to bits as she falls from space. She lives in a tidy ranch home on six acres near Fort Bragg, North Carolina, which she shares with her partner, eleven cats, and a dog. It's a comfortable setup, but comfort isn't what moves her. In 1995, she jumped from an airplane 352 times in a single day, shattering her own Guinness world record. Even by her standards, it was a grueling experience. Each time she landed, she had to aim for a small disk, and place one of her heels on it. Then she was usually dragged along the ground by her parachute. Despite five layers of clothes, she says, "In the end, I had no skin left on my rear end."

She'd begun the attempt at five p.m. one evening and by two a.m. the next day she was spent. Every bone in her body ached, her back was seized up, and hands were cramping from holding the parachute lines. She decided to quit.

"But then I thought about having to face the press, telling them that I couldn't continue. I realized that would be harder than just somehow pulling myself together and going twice the speed, and getting my team to go twice the speed with me. So I carried on."

She has no explanation for what happened next.

"Suddenly I stepped out of my body. For the next seventeen hours there was no pain, no cold, no indecision."

When she completed her final jump, journalists surrounded her. They were flabbergasted to find her so full of energy. But when they all left, a strange feeling overtook her.

"I felt myself going back inside my body. Instantly I hurt all over and I couldn't move."

Her team had to carry her to the car, and bend her legs to get her inside it. In the hotel they undressed her, showered her, and then put her to bed. For the next two weeks she had such severe tendonitis in her hands that she couldn't button her shirt.

But for Sterns, it was all worthwhile.

"You have to step outside yourself, to a place where there is no pain. You go beyond the pain, to the next level, where you do things that seem impossible. There's the spiritual part of it. You need that level of pain to get to that place; most people can't push themselves that hard."

Masochism? Some athletes, like the freediver Tanya Streeter, admit that it is. "The masochistic label," she says, "is something I absolutely subscribe to."

Streeter exudes health and well-being. Shiny blond hair falls to her waist. Tiny diamonds glisten in her earlobes. She has perfect teeth, wide blue eyes, flawless skin, and an athletic, well-toned body. Yet she admits that pain, suffering, and punishment have been fundamental to her success as a multiple-world-record-holding freediver.

Underwater, in her skintight suit and huge mono-fin, she resembles a graceful mermaid. But this belies the enormous effort involved in her exacting sport. After inhaling for thirty seconds, she holds that breath for almost three and a half minutes, while diving down in the ocean to a depth of four hundred feet with the help of a line, then swimming back to the surface. The descent takes a minute and ten seconds. On the way she suffers from thoracic filling—her lungs compress to the size of fists, and to avoid collapsing they draw plasma from her blood. When she reaches her target, she grabs a tag, then begins her ascent, which she likens to "a two-minute-and-thirty-second sprint without breathing." During that period her oxygen level drops and her CO_2 increases to the point where her body, in effect, starts ordering her to breathe by creating diaphragmatic contractions, spasms that violently suck her stomach in then push it out again, like the worst type of hiccups imaginable.

Meanwhile, there's the pressure on her ears. She can't "pop" them by swallowing, forcing air into her Eustachian tubes, because she runs out of air volume in her lungs. The result is massive earache.

"If you can't equalize the air space on the inside of your eardrums with the pressure on the outside, they are going to bend in and be on the verge of rupture. It hurts like hell. Past three hundred feet on a dive there can be an ever-increasing pain in the eardrum. It's a sharp, stabbing pain and if you can't pressurize it and you want to go on, you just have to endure it."

Then there's the pain in her muscles, caused by the buildup of lactic acid. It creates burning and extreme fatigue and can literally cripple her. And there are jellyfish stings to contend with.

"When you're on your way down to four hundred feet and beyond and a jellyfish suddenly blazes you across the face," says Streeter, "well, it's not very pleasant."

Tanya Streeter's deepest dive was to 525 feet. On one breath, her heart rate down to five beats a minute, her blood saturated with nitrogen. And how did she feel after that?

"I was at peace. I had achieved my goal. But the idea of some form of punishment being necessary to find that peace has been pretty consistent for me from the beginning."

When she first started free-diving, she had to do serious gym training to get into the right physical shape. Three hours a day, five days a week: the sessions were grueling and she hated them.

"But I had this idea that if I was able to suffer through doing the thing that was so hard for me and that I hated, then I would be able to excel beyond what I thought was possible in doing the thing that I loved. Saturday was my reward day, when I went diving. I would sit on the back of the boat on the way to the dive, and whenever any doubt crept in about whether I could reach the depth I'd set myself, I assured myself that I could do it because I deserved to do it. Because I had punished myself and suffered so much to be able to get there. And when I completed the dive, I'd be rewarded with a sense of inner peace."

Sunday was a day of rest. "Then rinse, repeat, and start all over again."

Lance Armstrong would understand; he refers to his own sport, long-distance cycle racing, as "self-abuse." He describes pain as "self-revelatory," his "chosen way of exploring the human heart." When he was diagnosed with cancer, riding—and suffering—became more important for him than ever. "Cycling is so hard," he writes, "the suffering is so intense, that it's absolutely cleansing. You can go out there with the weight of the world on your shoulders, and after a six-hour ride at a high pain threshold, you feel at peace. The pain is so deep and strong that a curtain descends over your brain.... [T]he effort and subsequent fatigue are absolute. There is an unthinking simplicity in something so hard."

In 1996, when Texas-born Armstrong was twenty-five years old, and a world champion cyclist, he was diagnosed with testicular cancer, which had already metastasized to his lungs and brain. His chances of survival were rated at between 20 and 50 percent. He underwent two operations and aggressive treatments with an experimental form of chemotherapy. A new form of pain, and not one that brought any spiritual peace. "Chemo was a burning in my vein, a matter of being slowly eaten from the inside out by a destroying river of pollutants.... Chemo was a continuous cough, hacking up black chunks of mysterious tar-like matter from deep in my chest.... Chemo felt like a kind of living death."

In between his chemo sessions, he tried to keep up with some level of bike riding, but he became increasingly weak, managing at best only half an hour at a time. One day, as he approached a hill, a woman in her fifties on a heavy bike overtook him, despite his desperate struggle to keep up with her. Eighteen months later, however, he was riding professionally again. In 1999, he won the Tour de France, a three-week event said to be the equivalent of running a marathon a day for twenty days. For Armstrong, it was the first of seven consecutive wins of the Tour de France. In 2005, after the final win, he retired from professional racing. When asked what pleasure he took in riding for so long, he said he didn't understand the question. "I didn't do it for pleasure. I did it for pain.... In fact, if I didn't suffer I'd feel cheated."

And he is not alone. During the 2004 Tour de France race, at the critical point when the leaders break away from the head pack, Jan Ullrich's German teammate Udo Bölts would yell at him encouragingly, "Torture yourself, you bastard!"

The contested winner of the 2006 Tour de France, Floyd Landis, also has a close relationship with pain. He has osteonecrosis, dying bone, in his right hip, caused by the interruption of the blood supply to the femoral head of the hip joint. The condition is very painful. If the dead bone subsequently collapses, the resulting incongruity of the joint, the flattened femoral head like a square peg in a round hole, causes further pain with evolving arthritis. Landis walks with a limp, and finds stairs challenging. He can't cross his right leg over his left. His pain, which he refers to as "grinding...bone on bone," sometimes keeps him awake at night, and when he's cycling up steep hills it becomes excruciating. He kept his condition secret from his teammates and sponsors for as long as he could, and he also hid his plans for a hip replacement after the big race. When the story broke, the *Daily Telegraph* dubbed him "the true king of pain," noting that more than 200,000 Americans receive a hip replacement every year—but that in 2006, only one of them would have completed the Tour de France.

One of six children, Landis was born in Farmersville, Pennsylvania, a strict Mennonite community that forbade modern influences such as television, dancing, movies, and anything that brought glory to oneself rather than God. When Landis started mountain-biking in his teens, he had to wear sweatpants, as shorts were banned. His parents considered that his new passion was taking him away from God. So his father tried to block his training sessions by giving him lots of chores around the farm—digging out the septic tank, painting the barn, fixing the car engine. Landis did all that he was asked to do and then set off on his bike for late-night training sessions. He was desperate to escape the constraints of his community, and the bike was his vehicle. When he was seventeen, he won the junior national mountain bike championship. Two years later, he left home for good and moved to California. But he took the lessons of his teens with him—when life demands a lot of you, respond by giving more than anyone would ever expect.

The participants of the Race Across America, RAAM, obviously agree. At 3,042 miles, from the West to the East Coast of the USA, it is the longest and arguably the toughest annual endurance cycling event in the world. It has no designated rest periods; the clock keeps running from start to finish. To win the race, a cyclist must be prepared to ride for twenty-two hours a day, over mountain passes and through deserts, in blistering heat and chilling rain storms. Every moment not spent pedaling reduces the chance of success, so, while riding, the participants drink, eat, urinate, change their clothing, and apply sunscreen to their skin and Band-Aids to their blisters. Some of them have suffered Shermer syndrome, named after a veteran RAAM participant, a condition in which the neck muscles can no longer support the head. Rumor has it that a few of those afflicted in the past chose to carry on riding with duct tape or a bungee cord holding their heads upright.

The lack of sleep, the constant effort, and the stress of competition take their toll in other ways. The Slovenian rider Jure Robič is a three-time winner of RAAM. His record time for completing the course is eight days, nineteen hours, and thirty-three minutes, during which period he claimed to have slept a total of eight hours. He has a pattern of steadily unraveling during the race. By the second day he starts talking at an abnormally fast rate. By day three he becomes volatile, sometimes getting off his bike and storming back to his support vehicle in such a rage that his crew lock the doors. By day four he loses his short-term memory and has attacks of weeping. Finally, the hallucinations kick in; he sees wolves, bears, Martians, and bandits chasing him with guns. He's been known to leap off his bike to fight with mailboxes that were threatening him.

Perry Stone, a journalist and extreme cyclist who accompanied Robič's support team in 2004, wrote that Robič's suffering "was like he suffered through his skin and emerged a new man, a cleaner man—a justified man."

These may be extreme examples, but even recreational bike racers admit to a relationship with suffering. Justin Harvey, from Whistler, British Columbia, competes each year in the Samurai of Singletrack race, which takes place in his local mountains. It lasts for two days, with about six hours of cycling and five thousand feet of climbing each day, on remote forest trails, negotiating rocks, tree roots, and some terrifyingly steep gradients. Harvey doesn't stop at feed stations— ahead of the race he plants water bottles and food in the woods along the route. And his rest periods? "I stop for thirty seconds max each time. Jump off, grab the water bottle, jump back on."

Every year, organizers make the race harder. But still they turn participants away. And Harvey isn't surprised.

"These are the days that stand out in life. You have to dig deep in those events, to cope with the amount of stress and physical discomfort. You get to know yourself in those instances when you are digging so deep to continue."

His favorite rides are the spontaneous ones. Like the morning he and some friends set out at three a.m. from Whistler and rode to the top of Black Tusk Mountain, crossing a big pass on the way, in the dark. Four and a half hours of hard riding, through woods on rocky rutted trails, in the dark, before breakfast. Then the reward: freewheeling down as the sun rose.

It would be easy to disappear on the vast areas of mountain slopes around Whistler. For Harvey, this is an important part of the equation.

"Being out in the woods, challenging the natural environment— you have to be self-sufficient out there, able to get yourself out of a bad situation if necessary. It's a great adventure. But the spiritual part—that's much bigger than the physical."

As in mountain-bike racing, the number of runners signing up for ultramarathons is increasing exponentially, and is now over seventy thousand a year. An ultramarathon is classed as any race more than the 26.2 miles of a marathon, but usually they are much longer. They include the 3,100-mile Sri Chinmoy, held each year in New York on a one-mile loop, and the annual Trans America Footrace, which is three thousand miles long and run in sixty-four consecutive daily stages of about forty-five miles each.

The sport of ultramarathoning has deep roots. In 1861, Edward Payson Weston made a bet with a friend over the upcoming presidential election. The terms were that the loser would walk from Boston to Washington in ten straight days, arriving in time to see the inauguration of the new president. Weston lost the bet. He began his 478-mile walk on February 22, and quickly settled into an average pace of three miles an hour. He walked through snow and driving rain. He slept for no more than six hours at a time, sometimes at the side of the road, in barns, or on kitchen tables in farmhouses. As word spread of his adventure, he was often cheered on by crowds of admirers. He made it to the Capitol at five p.m. on March 4, too late to see Abraham Lincoln sworn in, but in time for the inauguration ball, where he received a congratulatory handshake from the new president.

Weston's walk, and the fame it brought him, spurred him on to bigger goals. In 1867, he walked 1,200 miles from Portland, Maine, to Chicago in twenty-six days. Two years later he walked 1,058 miles through snow-covered New England in thirty days. He started competing with professional "pedestrian walkers" in six-day events, held in stadiums in New York and London, eventually beating Britain's best walker when he covered 550 miles in six days. He carried on testing himself all his life—when he was seventy-two, he walked across North America from Santa Monica, California, to New York City in seventy-six days. He never stopped preaching about the merits of walking; automobiles, he said, were bad, making people lazy. He was still walking up to twenty-five miles a day when, in his early nineties, he was struck down by a taxicab in New York, an accident which cost him the use of his legs. He died two years later, in his sleep.

By then, a bicycle with a chain, sprockets, and air-filled tires had been developed, and in 1902, the first Tour de France was held. Its success, along with the opening of Route 66 linking Chicago and Los Angeles, inspired an American entrepreneur to set up a new endurance event in the USA—not cycling or walking but running across the width of the continent. In 1928, the inaugural Cash and Carry Pyle United States Transcontinental Race was held. It was run in eighty-four stages of approximately thirty-seven miles each, with a route that took participants through the Mojave Desert and across the Rocky Mountains. According to H. Berry, a journalist covering the event, they faced "standing snow, driving hail and sandstorms," as well as desert heat and steep, rough terrain, all of which served to quickly weed out the weaker runners—of the 199 who started, only 55 crossed the finish line in New York.

"For a brief period of time," Berry commented, "they provided Americans with a belly laugh at the insanity of their endeavors."

But maybe their endeavors weren't so insane. Research done by

Dr. Tim Noakes, a professor of human biology at the Sport Science Institute of South Africa, indicates that humans evolved as endurance animals. With the greatest ratio of leg length to body weight of any mammal, our skeletal design favors running and walking. We are one of the few mammals to use the sweating response as a primary means of dissipating body heat. And while our peak sprinting speed is poor compared to many other mammals, our endurance capacity is better than most.

"Elite marathon runners can sustain running speeds of 5.6 meters per second for more than two hours," writes Noakes. "This compares to sustained running speeds of about 5.1 meters per second in [one of the migratory] African antelope[s], the wildebeest and...the postal horses that traditionally carried the mail across the United States before the coming of the railroad...The only mammal consistently able to outperform humans over very prolonged distances is the Husky dog, which in freezing polar conditions can comfortably run 1,700 km in 8 days, for example during the Iditarod sledding race held annually between Fairbanks and Nome, Alaska. But in hot conditions humans will usually outlast even the dog which is also limited by the absence of a sweating response and the inability to lose heat rapidly when running in hot conditions."

In prehistoric times, these attributes were crucial for human survival. Since the development of mechanization, we rarely need to test the limits of our evolutionary design. Some of us, however, consciously chose not just to test, but to push at those limits.

Every year, organizers of the annual Western States Endurance Run in California have to turn down more than half the people who apply for it. Not because they don't meet the physical requirements to enter a hundred-mile, thirty-hour race through rugged mountainous terrain, including a climb of 2,550 vertical feet in the first four and a half miles. Only because the Parks Service limits the number of participants to 369.

Runners also fight for a place in the North Pole Marathon. Numbers of participants in this race are limited by aircraft capacity constraints, and a fee of 11,900 Euros. The race Web site instructs would-be entrants to ask themselves the following questions: "Can you handle the extreme cold? Do you want to push yourself to the edge?" Lots do. In March 2006, fifty-four people started the race, and finished it, running over ice floes in temperatures that dipped to –9 degrees Fahrenheit.

Evolutionary impulses notwithstanding, why would anyone subject themselves to this sort of punishment?

Kirk Johnson frequently asked himself that question while he was training for the 135-mile Badwater Race. The nonstop race crosses Death Valley, goes over three mountain ranges, and ends at 8,360 feet on Mount Whitney. It's held each July, when daytime temperatures can hit 129 degrees Fahrenheit in Death Valley and the blacktop on the road radiates up into the runners' feet at temperatures close to 199 degrees Fahrenheit. It's considered one of the most demanding extreme running races in the world. Only ninety people are allowed to compete each year. The quota is always full, with a waiting list.

The physical challenge of running across Death Valley called to Johnson as a "portal" into another realm of experience. "If there was a place where human limitation—but also the limits of explanation and reason and science—should hit the wall, this was it," he writes. "Badwater was a perch from which I could look for the definitions of what we are, what makes us stop and what makes us go. Maybe spirituality wasn't quite the word for what I sought. But I was enough of a believer, or a seeker at least, to think that there might be a way—through the unfathomable postapocalyptic wilderness of racing in Death Valley—to reach the veil and touch something beyond me and my life. A place where misery and transcendence were so deeply intertwined it could not be without meaning."

After fifteen hours of running through searing heat, night came as a blessing.

"The world was surprising and filled with eye-opening wonder, and the simple act of moving through it had become a source of joy. Above me the sky was enfolded from horizon to horizon with stars, more than I had ever seen. Meteors were as regular as metronomes, as regular as my footfalls on the road and the Milky Way, cutting a swath across everything, was a road, too. The heavens above mirrored my little world below. I would follow the Milky Way, or Highway 190, it didn't matter. All that counted was that I was moving."

Marshall Ulrich, a fifty-five-year-old all-around athlete from Colorado, has run Badwater thirteen times and won it four times. He's made a total of nineteen crossings of Death Valley on foot, including his solo "quad crossing": four times back and forth, nonstop, towing a modified baby jogger filled with water, ice, spare clothes, and weighing more than two hundred pounds, for seventy-seven hours and forty-six minutes. He's also run a total of 116 ultramarathons, each one an average of a hundred miles. He's completed twelve expedition-length adventure races—nonstop, multiday, multiactivity events that involve canoeing, kayaking, climbing, and biking, as well as running. The most famous of these, the Eco Challenge, has been held nine times, and Ulrich has completed every one. Just for good measure, he climbed the highest mountain on each continent, in only three years. And in 2008, he plans to run across America.

Ask Ulrich about the physical pain involved in all this, and he shrugs it off. It's the sleep deprivation that's the hard part. He knows why it's used as a form of torture. During the second Eco Challenge he was existing on fifteen minutes of sleep a night, for five nights in a row. "It can be disastrous," he says. "You lose all but 20 percent of your reasoning powers." During one Eco Challenge race, he was kayaking from Martha's Vineyard to Newport Beach when he became convinced that a spillway over a large dam lay just ahead of his group's boats. There was no dam. "But I could hear the water rushing over it," he says. "We all heard it."

When they got to Newport Beach, they had to portage their kayaks, a process that took two carries. In normal circumstances, getting from one end of the beach to the other would have been simple, but when he set out for the second carry he realized he was lost. He just stood there, shaking his head in confusion. "It was painful to even think," he says. "But it was worst for Tom Possard, one of my team members. When he got home, he didn't recognize his wife."

All this suffering, he believes, has a profound purpose. "It elevates our senses. It allows us to tap into other resources. There are times when I reach special places in my mind and body. Afterward, I think, how can I get back to that place?"

Wendy Sternberg, a professor of psychology at Haverford College in Pennsylvania, is interested in discovering how athletes like Ulrich, who push themselves to the edge, experience pain. Pain is perceived when nociceptors, tiny sensory organs at the end of neurons, detect damage and send signals via the dorsal horn in the spinal column to certain areas of the brain. The response is a cascade of neurotransmitters, including endorphins, enkephalins and dynorphins, natural painkillers that are collectively known as endogenous opioids. These opioids, the body's own narcotics, bind to receptors distributed throughout the brain, modulating reactions to painful stimuli.

When Sternberg subjected her volunteers to mild torture—zapping their fingertips with a heat-emitting light and immersing their arms in ice-cold water—she found they endured pain differently at different times. Immediately after they'd competed in running, biking, or kayaking races, they could stand the pain for much longer than they could two days before or two days afterward. Her results suggest that the brain can control the influence of pain transmission by neurons through "stress-induced analgesia," which dulls the signals sent during moments of great stress, danger, or competition, allowing athletes to extend their limits far beyond what they thought possible.

Sport psychologists have long exhorted that pain can be a valuable driving force, and have used recent findings by scientists such as Sternberg to encourage athletes to improve performance by "embracing" or "associating" with pain rather than trying to distract themselves from it. And scientific research is now showing that pain itself can be pleasurable. While it has long been known that the brain produces its own form of relief in response to painful stimuli, recent studies have shown that this relief is actually produced by the reward pathway. The engine of the reward responses is the nucleus accumbens, which, in certain brain-imaging techniques, is seen to "light up" during pleasurable sensations and which is linked to the release of dopamine. In 2001, experiments done at the Massachusetts General Hospital showed a link between pleasure and pain. The work was led by David Borsook, associate professor of radiology at Harvard Medical School. While undergoing fMRI, his volunteers had their hands gently heated by small pads up to 115 degrees Fahrenheit. This produced a burning feeling without actual skin damage. As expected, the resulting sensations activated well-known circuits in the center of the brain, which release natural painkillers. But just before this occurred, the images showed activity in the nucleus accumbens—the area that usually responds to rewards. These studies indicate the existence of a single, subconscious system in humans that responds to a continuum of emotions from pain to pleasure.

Interesting as these findings are, they don't explain why suffering brings Lance Armstrong his "higher purpose" or Tanya Streeter her sense of peace. Or why the link with the natural world is so important. Long-distance fell-runner Richard Askwith writes of his chosen sport, "The man who is truly at home in the mountains...can see that our selves can never be entirely divorced from our surroundings; and the man who is lucky enough to live among beautiful hills and who enters into an intimate relationship with them is also deeply in touch with himself."

To have such an intimate relationship, Askwith claims it is vital to get "cold, or wet, or lost, or exhausted, or bruised by rocks or covered in mud.... The point is not the exertion involved, it's the degree of involvement, or immersion, in the landscape. You need to feel it; to interact with it, to be in it, not just looking from outside. You need to lose yourself—for it is then that you are most human."

The physical pain of long-distance running, he believes, focuses his brain on the central concern for which it originally evolved—survival. All other anxieties fall away. He calls this "reconnecting with your inner animal." And this reconnection brings him special rewards. After completing the Borrowdale Fell Race in England's Lake District, he lay down in a mountain stream to cool off.

"Never have I felt such comfort," he writes. "The smooth stones beneath, the gentle massaging of the current, the feel and scent and taste of the sweetest fresh water. But the view too seems supernaturally perfect: dappled, liquid shadows in the foreground, and visible through a gap in the leaves a line of green mountains shining beneath a clear sky. This, I tell myself, is England at its best. And I am immersed in it."

To most human beings, prolonged solitude is a hard form of suffering. Throughout history, however, and in every culture, it has been used as a tool to delve into the spiritual aspects of our being. "[Solitude] is different from loneliness," writes the Irish author John O'Donoghue. "When you are lonely, you become acutely aware of your own separation. Solitude can be a homecoming to your deepest belonging."

Bob Kull from Vancouver wrote a Ph.D. thesis on solitude and its physical, psychological, emotional, and spiritual effects. For his research he spent most of the year 2000 on a small uninhabited island off the southern coast of Chile, a hundred miles and ten hours by water from the nearest settlement. His only companion was a cat, which the Chilean park service urged him to bring along, so that it could taste and test shellfish before he ate them.

Kull had lots to occupy his time. He had to build and maintain his cabin, hunt and forage for food, keep up with his reading and note-taking, and stay healthy. A crucial part of the process, however, was to "sit in mindful meditation in wilderness." Staying still in order to quiet his mind.

In the journal he kept during that year, he describes how the wild buffeting of the wind around his little cabin often made the "existential dread always lurking in the shadows" rise up before him: the dread that man's ultimate destiny is to be alone and to suffer. Out in the wilderness, he became intensely aware of death, and the impermanence of all things. Being so alone, vulnerable to weather, wild animals, and the pressures of extreme solitude, sometimes he recognized panic bubbling up. He'd looked deeply into himself before, on long meditation retreats, but this was different.

"In a controlled retreat setting, a teacher can guide students through personal difficulties, but in solitude you must face your fear alone," he writes. He concludes that it was a worthy exercise. "Suffering is such a deep part of living for all of us that if we try too hard to avoid it, we end up avoiding life entirely."

Tenzin Palmo spent thirteen years in solitude, in a cave at 13,200 feet in the Himalayas. She was born in 1943 as Diane Perry, to a spiritualist mother who held weekly séances at the family house in London, England. When Perry was eighteen, she came across a book on Buddhism. A year later she traveled to India, and at twenty-one she was ordained as a novice Tibetan Buddhist nun and given her spiritual name. For the next seven years her home was a monastery in Lahoul, at 11,000 feet on the Tibetan border, in a valley cut off by ice and snow for three quarters of the year. Then she heard about the cave, an hour's walk above the monastery. She decided to go into retreat there.

With the help of villagers from the valley, she bricked up the front and sides of the cave, and built a small food storeroom inside. She put in a door and window. She installed a wood-burning stove. She made a patio where she could sit and contemplate the spectacular view. From outside, the cave resembled a pretty little house, but its living space was only six feet square, with a ledge along one wall that served as a bookcase. It was dominated by a two-and-a-half-foot-square "meditation box," where she slept, sitting up, every night for the next thirteen years. The inside of the cave was always cold and dank, but even in the worst conditions she only ever lit her stove once a day, at noon.

During one winter, there was a particularly ferocious blizzard. Drifts built up against the door and the outside wall. She was trapped, running out of oxygen. Accepting that she was going to die, she began praying to her teacher, asking him to help her through the stages of death. When she was in deep meditation, she heard his voice—calm, clear, and loud: "Just tunnel out!" So she got a saucepan lid and did what many a climber has done when trapped in a snow hole—she started to dig her way to air and light.

Tenzin Palmo believes we're not on this earth to be comfortable. We're here to learn and grow, she says, and facing problems and challenges is an essential part of growth and knowledge. To discover the nature of our mind, and what lies beyond it, takes a lot of work and training—there is no easy route. Which is essentially what every extreme athlete would say about their sport.

Unlike Bob Kull and Tenzin Palmo, however, extreme adventurers find spiritual growth not by sitting still but through physical action linked to a concrete goal. In the preface to *Annapurna,* Lucien Devies writes, "Man overcomes himself, affirms himself and realizes himself in the struggle toward the summit, toward the absolute. In the extreme tension of the struggle, on the frontier of death, the universe disappears and drops away beneath us. Space, time, fear, suffering no longer exist. Everything then becomes quite simple. As on the crest of a wave, or in the heart of a cyclone, we are strangely calm—not the calm of emptiness, but the heart of action itself."

When Reinhold Messner was making his solo climb of the north side of Everest, in 1981, he recognized inactivity as his greatest enemy. Lying at 19,600 feet on the East Rongbuk glacier, he contemplated the coming climb.

"I know the dangers that await me up there: crevasses, avalanches, mist and storm. I know, above all, of my own weaknesses: exhaustion, fear, loneliness. With inactivity my self-understanding, my self-confidence shrink. Perhaps that is the reason why I so wonder at the hermits.... It is hardest to endure the desert in idleness."

Of his climb without oxygen up the world's highest mountain, he writes, "Each action becomes a triumph, an ordeal.... Whatever it is that drives me is planted much deeper than I or the magnifying glass of the psychologists can detect. Day by day, hour by hour, minute by minute, step by step I force myself to do something against which my body rebels. At the same time this condition is only bearable in activity."

Something Robert Falcon Scott would have understood. As Professor Noakes shows in his comparative analyses of the energy expenditure of athletes in various events and activities, none can compare with that reached by the polar explorers of the early twentieth century. He claims that the greatest human performance was achieved by the Antarctic sledding expedition led by Robert Scott in 1911–1912. Scott chose to "man-haul" his sleds, rather than use dogs like his competitor Roald Amundsen, because, he wrote, "in my mind, no journey ever made with dogs can approach the height of that fine conception which is realized when a party of men go forth to face hardships, dangers and difficulties with their own unaided efforts, and by days and weeks of hard physical labor succeed in solving some problem of the great unknown."

Scott and his men set off from McMurdo Sound on October 24 and reached the South Pole on January 18. On their return journey, they were within eleven miles of a supply depot when frostbite forced Scott to stop walking. His team opted to stay with him, dooming them all to die. Noakes argues that "by man-hauling essentially for 159 consecutive days, the last 60 of which were in extreme cold, for a total of 2,500 kilometers [1,553 miles], the feat of Scott and his colleagues is one of the two greatest human performances of sustained physical endurance of all time." The only performance to equal it, he states, "is that of Aenas MacIntosh and Frank Wild, members of Shackleton's ill-fated Trans-Continental Antarctic Expedition of 1914–1916, who between 1 September and 18 March man-hauled for 2,513 kilometers in 160 days."

Another great epic of that time was Shackleton's expedition to Antarctica aboard the *Endurance.* According to an unsubstantiated story, to find a crew he placed an advertisement in a London newspaper: "Men wanted for hazardous journey. Small wages, bitter cold, long months of complete darkness, constant danger, safe return doubtful. Honor and recognition in case of success."

Inspired by this story, in 1961 the British explorer Harold Tilman placed an advertisement in the *Times* to find men to accompany him on a sailing expedition. "Hands wanted for long voyage in small boat. No pay, no prospects, no much pleasure." He got twenty replies, and from them recruited the three men he needed.

Maybe there was something else he and Shackleton could have offered, less quantifiable but equally of value: the spiritual rewards of suffering.

In 1992, my husband and I arrived in New Delhi, India, intending to spend six weeks on the River Ganges, kayaking between Haridwar and Varanasi. Almost everyone we met in the city tried to dissuade us. We would get sick from the polluted water, its rotting corpses, and from the food we ate along the way. We would be attacked by the hordes of bandits roaming the flood plain, robbed of all our belongings, our throats slit. Although we tried to shrug off the warnings, we set off feeling anxious and unsettled.

It was pre-monsoon season, and the river had shrunk to a maze of channels, like a vast, knotted skein that snaked tortuously across a huge flood plain, up to ten miles across in places. With all the bends in the river, and channels that just petered out, often we ended up having to backtrack, paddling for hours in the direction we'd just come from. When barely submerged sandbanks ensnared the boat, we had to get out to push it free, sometimes sinking up to our thighs in quicksand. For the first week, the weather was cold and wet. At night, we camped in mud, kept awake by howling hyenas and worries about bandits. A man, rifle raised, had chased us when we ignored his command to come ashore: we were no longer shrugging off the warnings we'd heard in New Delhi.

Day after day, we paddled past cremations. Hindus believe that the Ganges embodies a goddess, Holy Mother Ganga, who has the power of spiritual and physical renewal. To be cremated on the banks of the river, or to simply decompose in its waters, is a direct road to heaven, a way of bypassing all the painful cycles of death and rebirth. Bodies, naked and smeared in ghee, lay atop burning piles of dung and wood. If the wind blew in the wrong direction, flakes of ash from the fire landed on the decks of our kayak and caught in our eyelashes. Our nostrils filled with the smell of sizzling human hair and fat.

When we stepped ashore, our feet crunched over the charred remains of human bones. We grew accustomed to these, but not to the floating bodies. After bumping into a few, we learned how to spot them from a distance—by the cloth they were wrapped in ballooning up above the surface like a pillowcase, or by the wild dogs swimming out to snack on the rotting flesh. Some we couldn't avoid: the elderly man, his skin yellow and bloated, part of his face eaten away; those all but concealed by the water, with just the buttocks sailing by or the feet and splayed toes floating above the surface; the young girl whose body a dog dragged ashore to chew on, its teeth crunching through her bones, a sudden flick of its head flipping her frail corpse over.

In some places the presence of bandits forced us to seek refuge in encampments of rough fishermen, drunk and armed to the teeth. Once, when the warnings of banditry grew especially intense, we spent an entire night paddling on the river. Some of the channels were so narrow that we found ourselves a few feet away from bonfires surrounded by flickering figures. Fishermen? Bandits? We didn't know. But we knew that if they heard us they would take fright and fire off their guns. We drifted past, breath held, our backs rigid with tension, praying we wouldn't run aground. The night seemed endless, but when dawn finally crept across the sky we saw a village ahead. Pulling ashore on its outskirts, we sat on the earth, our faces turned to the rising sun, stiff and cold but filled with elation, strangely glad for the long, hard night that was behind us.

Whenever we came across villages, or encampments of holy men, people there offered us hospitality, and a place to stay—a room in a mud house, a straw hut where rats ran over our legs at night. They brought us beakers of water to drink—their sacred water, straight from the river. We couldn't refuse it, nor could we turn down the food they offered, even when the rotis were made from lumps of dough turned black by the mass of flies crawling over it.

Each day left us utterly spent. Every night I went to sleep wondering if I'd be awakened by cramps ripping through my guts, or by the muzzle of a gun in my face. But villagers and holy men kept insisting that we were pilgrims, because we were traveling on the holy river, to a holy place, in a boat that was red, the holy color of Hinduism.

"Your pilgrimage will protect you," they promised. "It will purify what you eat and drink, it will save you from the dangers ahead."

As the days and weeks went by, I began to believe them. The river was protecting us; we were traveling on a stream of her grace. I was enchanted by the elemental quality of the rituals enacted along her banks. Handfuls of her water held up to the rising sun. Libations of milk offered to her. The faithful bathed in her, drank from her. They prayed with deep devotion to Mother Ganga, who swept away life each year as she flooded, then gave it back in the rich sediments left behind when her waters receded.

Like the Hindus, every morning I held my nose and fully immersed myself three times in the river to receive the blessing of Holy Mother Ganga. I also maintained a strictly vegetarian diet. I was never sick. But Dag, against all my advice, ordered meat in a restaurant in Alhallabad. And suffered violent gastrointestinal pain for forty-eight hours.

When finally we reached Varanasi, leaving Mother Ganga was a huge wrench. I was part of the river now, and she was part of me. My final offering to her was a banana-leaf boat, filled with marigold heads and burning camphor. Crouching on the bottom step of a ghat, I laid it on the surface of the river. Six weeks earlier, I had taken part in my first *puja* with a cool detachment. Now, as I watched the current catch the little boat and carry it away, I offered my thanks to Mother

Ganga for our safe passage. Our voyage along the river had turned me inside out, challenged and exhausted me on every level. Yet it shines in memory as one of the most memorable experiences of my life—an accidental pilgrimage that forced me to step beyond my Western sensibilities and, for a time at least, into a place of magic.

Chapter 5

ONLY CONNECT

In the body of the world, they say, there is a soul. And you are that.

JELALUDDIN RUMI, "A Great Wagon"

I t was six a.m. They pitched their tent on tussocky grass and lay down inside it, fully clothed. All around them, as far as the eye could see, stretched the vast wilderness of northern Alaska. They'd been on the move throughout the long, light Arctic night, marching across the tundra with sixty-pound packs on their backs. They set their alarm for two hours ahead; they couldn't afford more sleep, afraid of losing all trace of the herd.

For three months and 650 miles, Karsten Heuer and Leanne Allison had been following the Porcupine caribou herd on its annual spring migration. Setting out from Old Crow, in the Yukon, they had tracked the animals across frigid rivers, through snowstorms, and in freezing conditions. They had lived with constant underlying fears—of bear attack, of getting sick or injured in such a remote place—but now, with the onset of summer, what concerned them most were the clouds of relentless flies. The flies were bothering the caribou, too, and they were ramping up the pace, anxious to escape the buggy coastal plain and reach higher, windy areas.

Since leaving its wintering grounds, the herd, 123,000 in number, had been moving in groups: pregnant females in the lead, bulls and young juveniles behind. Now, with the young born and the flies buzzing, all the groups were due to gather for the race to higher ground, a sea of animals known as the post-calving aggregation. To keep up, Heuer, a wildlife biologist, and Allison, a filmmaker, took short naps between nine-hour marches, fueling themselves with hurried snacks. Traveling around the clock, for days on end, they reached their limits of sleep deprivation and physical exhaustion, then pushed past them.

Their goal was to bring attention to the threat that oil and gas development posed to the calving grounds of the Porcupine caribou, revered by the indigenous Gwich'in people as "the sacred place where life began." Their plan was to record the stresses and struggles of the animals on their long annual migration and to report on how the proposed drilling would add to these difficulties, and endanger the future of the herd itself. They intended to come back with stories about a physical journey, and physical events. But as the trip went on, they changed from being observers to participants. Strange things began to occur, things that went against Heuer's scientific training, his rational, analytic background. Like the dreams that began a few days into the post-calving period, when the couple were on the move most of the day and night.

"We hadn't seen any bulls on the trip yet," Heuer recalls. "We had a nap and when I woke up I turned to Leanne and said, 'I think we're going to see our first bull today.' I described what I'd seen in my dream: one bull, big velvet antlers, and a ridge with a green slope behind, boulders in the front. We had to get going, so Leanne hopped out of the tent and started packing. A few moments later she came back in, her face full of surprise. She pointed behind her. There was the first bull, just as I had described it to her, the exact scene. A rocky hill in the foreground, a green slope behind it, and a lone, velvet-antlered bull walking between the two, following a boulder-strewn ridge."

Two days later, it was Allison who dreamed the future. They had been walking, post-nap, for about ten minutes when the biggest group of caribou they'd seen to date came up behind them.

"From a distance they looked like heat waves. The light was surreal, the wind was stirring up sand and gravel from the river bed below, covering the whole mountainside. Leanne turned to me and she was out of her skin with excitement. She said, 'I just dreamed this, while we were napping!'"

If that had occurred at the beginning of the trip, Heuer would have been skeptical. But now there was no question.

"It started happening more and more. We'd wake up from these sharp, clear dreams, we would describe them to each other and then they would happen."

Heuer and Allison believe it was the rigors of the journey that led to their dreams and the other inexplicable events that began to unfold. The isolation, the danger from bears, the exposure to the elements, the sheer, unrelenting hard work of carrying heavy packs over difficult terrain. The space and the silence.

"In the modern world you need distractions and layers of protection and ways of blocking things out in order to survive," says Heuer. "On our trip, it was the opposite. It wasn't until those layers and blocks and filters had gone that these things began to happen."

Like the thrumming. Heuer is sure it was always there. But they'd ignored it, screening it out as you would the faint gurgling of the fridge in your kitchen. It was during another rest period that Heuer finally acknowledged it. More a vibration than a sound, it rose up through the ground, through their whole bodies. A strange melody that was coming from everywhere, that faded in and out. It wasn't made by hooves—that was a sound they were familiar with. It was deeper, some infrasonic resonance, oscillating on the lower edge of human hearing. Allison picked it up, too. She first located it on either side of a group of caribou moving toward them. In an instant the thrumming was gone, replaced by "a chaos of snorts, huffs and tendon clicks as the nearest animals closed in."

They began listening for the thrumming, concentrating hard.

"It was the kind of intense focus you have in your fingertips when you're gripped on rock halfway up a really difficult face climb," says Heuer. "With that intensity of focus we could tap into it. Our ears felt like huge gramophone horns. Over a period of listening we could put some rough direction on it."

They began using the thrumming, rather than tracks on the ground, to guide them to the herd.

"It's one thing to hear the thrumming," Heuer muses. "It's another thing to acknowledge it, and it's yet another thing to believe it to the extent that you're going to expend this energy and effort following something that you couldn't say for sure truly exists. To be guided by something like that, and to be rewarded for your faith—you begin to see the world as an incredibly compassionate place. Instead of being constantly fearful and insecure, if you drop all your barriers and filters and protective walls and truly open up, the world will take care of you."

Heuer describes the sensory awareness they reached in the Arctic as "a vague memory of belonging." It's the memory, he believes, from the time before we learned to separate the possible from the impossible. The state of being at one with the world and secure within it.

Like his son, Zev, who, at eighteen months old, embraced sticks and talked to rocks and who, as a three-year-old, says hello and good-bye to rivers. A state, Heuer maintains, we all once enjoyed, and the loss of which leaves us "yearning for that state of belonging and seeking it out in different ways."

American rock athlete Lynn Hill has a direct route to that state: up a sheer, sun-warmed granite face.

"When I'm climbing," she says, "I have an immediate sense of adapting to the forces and forms of the natural world. I love the touch and feel of rock, the aesthetics of rock, the plants and animals I see. For me, climbing is a communion with nature."

Wesley Bunch, a mountain guide with Exum, in Wyoming, finds that communion in deep, fresh snow.

"Skiing powder—you can't get more spiritual than that. You have this sensation of being weightless and flying, you feel the g-forces. You jump into big air and you land in feathers. You feel snow cascading around you. The visuals, the speed, the wind flashing past your ears—you're always gasping, grabbing at your heart, going, Oh God, it's so beautiful out here!"

For Clay Hunting, it's in the ocean, riding a wave. After a decade of ice climbing, and after nearly losing his best friend in a climbing accident, Hunting returned to his first love, surfing, which he discovered on a trip to Australia in his teens.

"With surfing you're in a mobile environment," he says, "You're harnessing the energy of the wave to propel you forward. Catching a wave—that wall of energy that has traveled so far—just at the right moment, and riding it for a few seconds, it gives you a feeling that doesn't compare to anything else."

Hunting now lives on the exposed side of Nootka Island, on the far west coast of Canada. It's a wild, remote spot, part of the "Grave-yard of the Pacific"—so named because of all the ships that have been pushed ashore in storms and smashed to pieces on its rocks. From the surf lodge he runs with his wife, he can gaze across the ocean that stretches away, uninterrupted for thousands of miles. He spends hours doing that—when he's not surfing the Web for weather and wave conditions worldwide.

"Last fall we had a beautiful swell come in all the way from between the Antarctic and New Zealand," he says. "There was a massive storm down there and the power of nature pushed this swell thousands of miles to us. We were on our boards, waiting for it. The connectedness we felt was not just to the ocean. It was also to the thunderclouds that had gathered so far away. To all the different elements driving a huge amount of energy into the ocean and giving us these waves. Surfing them, we were connected to the energy of the whole planet."

Climbing, skiing, surfing, snowboarding. Why should it take so much effort to reach a sense of belonging in the world? Because, according to cultural historian Morris Berman, the "ecstatic merger" with nature, which was once part of the Western worldview, has been lost. That loss leaves a state of alienation and suffering, "a sickness of the soul." For some people, it's a sickness that can only be treated by going out into wild places, making themselves vulnerable to nature and doing things that seem insane, unacceptable. Things that help to sate not only their hunger for adrenaline, but also their need to feel at home in and at one with the world.

Until the seventeenth century, the Western world's view of nature was a place in which everything—rocks, trees, ocean, rivers, sky—was alive. This view was largely shaped by the ancient Greeks, who believed in the concept of *anima mundi,* a "world soul" that held the stars in place, was responsible for the movements of the planets, and was diffused through everything in nature. Human beings were not alienated observers of the cosmos, but integral participants in its drama, and the earth was a single living entity, containing all other living entities, which were all interrelated.

Aristotle, whose thinking greatly influenced Western intellectual history, claimed that every object had a soul, not in the supernatural or religious sense, but rather as an invisible model that gives an organism its purpose, that pulls matter to its full reality. The soul of a plant, for example, would attract the developing seedling toward the mature form of the plant. Aristotle called this process *entelechy*—"the end which is within itself."

He described three levels of souls. Plants had only one level: nutritive. Animals had an additional animal soul, which integrates sensations, coordinates movements, and underlies instincts and the ability of the body to regenerate or heal itself. Humans had a third level, the rational or intellectual soul, concerned with language and thought. The three souls weren't separate, but folded into a larger psychic system that pervaded the whole body. All of nature, then, was alive and everything within the world participated in the life of the cosmos. Man was part of nature, nature was part of Man. This "participating consciousness," as Berman calls it, gave rise to a "psychic wholeness" that held sway until the paradigm shift of the scientific revolution.

In 1619, René Descartes, a young French soldier and philosopher, was lying in a stuffy room in a small town along the Danube, thinking about the nature of the universe. Suddenly he had a vision of a mechanist universe, a whirling vortex in which all organisms were machines and everything was based on mathematics. Descartes' dream, which he claimed was channeled to him from an angel, and the writing he embarked upon as a result of it, irrevocably changed the West's reciprocal relationship with the world. Nature no longer had soul, only behavior. Modern man now had to find his own purpose in the universe, and perceive ways to control the mechanistic world of nature. This became the foundation of modern science. The old holistic view of man being part of nature, at home in the cosmos, was, and still is, discounted as a romantic illusion. In the early 1900s the German sociologist Max Weber claimed that this process, *die Entzauberung der Welt*—the "demagnification of nature," was one of the defining characteristics of the modern world.

On the West Coast of Ireland, farmers carefully till around the pre-Celtic standing stones in their fields, wary of disturbing the power they believe resides there. Catholics leave offerings at ancient holy wells, which were once pre-Christian sites, and collect the water for its curative powers. These remnants of belief in nature's magic are manifestations of what author Simon Schama calls "the memory of generations." He argues that our impressions and values of nature add up to "a tradition built from a rich deposit of myths, memories and obsessions." Elements cited as evidence of a strong connection with nature in indigenous cultures—sacred mountains, rivers of life, spirits of the forest—are in fact all around us, shot through our own culture.

"Neither the frontiers between the wild and the cultivated nor those that lie between the present and the past are so easily fixed," he writes. "Whether we scramble the slopes or ramble the woods, our Western sensibilities carry a bulging backpack of myth and recollection."

Even in the most urban settings, myth and recollection abide in commonly held superstitions. In a Vancouver restaurant, my waitress, a young woman with piercings, tattoos, and spiky hair, accidentally knocked over the salt shaker as she was clearing the table. When some salt spilled out, she took a pinch of it between two fingers and flung it over her shoulder. "I've had a bad day," she explained. "I don't want to make it worse." The belief that spilling salt brings bad luck is an ancient one, dating back to when salt was a highly prized commodity. A part of the earth, essential for life.

It is this age-old backpack of beliefs that causes climbers to take talismans to the mountains with them, to fend off bad luck. For Slovenian alpinist Tomaz Humar, it is the shoe his son wore when he was a baby; for the Seattle-born climber Steve Susted, it was one of his daughter's teddy bears; for Ed Viesturs, the first American to climb the world's fourteen highest mountains without oxygen, it is his "*ju ju bag*" that contains an old postcard from his wife, a lucky playing card, and the hospital bracelets his children wore at birth.

In the Himalayas, Sherpas employed on mountaineering expeditions refuse to start climbing until they have performed a *puja,* a ritual of prayer and offerings to the spirits of the mountain, petitioning them for good weather and the safe return of the team. Western climbers often take part in these *puja*s, as Stephen Koch did before setting off on his attempt to ski down the North Face of Everest in 2003.

Koch's plan was to climb the nine-thousand-foot face in a single, thirty-six-hour push, without fixed ropes or supplementary oxygen. Then he would descend the mountain by snowboard, via the vertiginous Hornbein Couloir and Japanese Couloir, two linked gullies and notorious avalanche chutes. Only one other person had attempted to do this. The previous year, Marco Siffredi, a French ski mountaineer, climbed the mountain then descended to the lip of the Hornbein Couloir. The Sherpas with him later reported that when he pushed off on his snowboard, conditions were good, he was rested, and he had a full bottle of oxygen on his back. He was never seen again.

Now Koch sat in Everest Base Camp, waiting for the weather to clear. Ten days earlier, with photographer Jimmy Chin and their support team of Lakpa Dorge Sherpa and Kami Sherpa, he had climbed to the base of the Japanese Couloir. While they were taking a break, they heard a sound "like an auto wreck" followed by a loud booming. Above them, a massive serac—a hanging block of glacial ice—had collapsed. Helpless, they could only watch as it sped down the slope toward them, breaking into fridge-sized pieces. Its trajectory missed them by yards, but the air blast was so strong that Chin was thrown to the end of his rope. Unnerved, and already close to their turn-around time, they decided to head back to Base Camp.

While they waited for a break in the weather, Koch, Chin, and their Base Camp manager Eric Henderson made daily visits to the little shrine they had created in a corner of the cook tent.

"The Sherpas were first up and they would light incense in there," says Koch. "We would do it later in the day. It made us feel good to have a place of worship. We all had a few different things that we had put in there, personal things that meant something to us. It was tied into the *puja* ceremony, asking that we would be brought back safely."

On August 30, just after dark, Koch and his team set off for another attempt.

"The four of us were unroped, climbing solo with axes and crampons. It felt so free. Around midnight the moon appeared over the ridge and cast this huge silvery path for us to follow. It was beautiful climbing."

By morning, things had changed. The knee-deep snow was becoming dangerously sloppy and unconsolidated. By nine a.m. they were still 6,581 feet below the summit. Koch made the judgment call to turn around. While the rest of the team began to climb down, he strapped on his board and rode several thousand feet of the "steep, deep powder" on Everest's North Face.

"Despite the setbacks and disappointment, it was still a dream come true," he recalls. "Strapping on the board and saying, okay, no more fighting gravity, now I'm going to flow with the world. And that flow, that connection, is deeply spiritual."

On reaching Base Camp, he went to the shrine, his "place of worship," to give thanks for his safe return. Whom or what was he thanking?

"The energy of the mountain," he says. "The spirits on the mountain. The mountain gods."

Gods and mountains have a long relationship. Moses received the Ten Commandments from God on the slopes of Mount Zion. The ancient Chinese believed Mount Tai Shan was the son of the Emperor of Heaven, and channel of communication between humans and God. The twelve principal gods of the Greek pantheon resided on the top of Mount Olympus. All mountains in the Himalayas are considered holy, and many are named after the deities of the Hindu and Buddhist pantheons, like Chomolungma, Goddess Mother of the World, which the British renamed Everest. Mount Kailash, in Tibet, is the most revered. For Hindus it is home to the god Shiva. Followers of Bon, a form of Tibetan Buddhism, believe it is the seat of the sky goddess Sipaimen. Jains revere it as the place where the first of the twenty-four Tirthankaras attained liberation. All three traditions see it as the earthly manifestation of Mount Meru, the spiritual center of the universe.

For millennia, Buddhist and Hindu ascetics wandered the world's high ranges. Modern mountaineers are following in their footsteps, and going even higher.

"We have always honored the high places because we sense them to be the home of gods," writes the late Rob Parker, a climbing filmmaker and cave-diver. "In the mountains there is the promise of...something unexplainable. A higher place of awareness, a spirit that soars. So we climb...and in climbing there is more than a metaphor; there is a means of discovery."

Climbing history indicates that it's wise not to offend the mountain gods. In the 1800s, G. W. Traill, an early explorer of Nanda Devi, the highest mountain in India, became blind while attempting to cross a pass on its southwest flank. Local people attributed his affliction to the wrath of the goddess Nanda, said to reside at its summit. Traill only recovered after making offerings at a temple dedicated to the goddess in the hill station of Almora. When another early explorer, Adolph Schlagintweit, tried the same pass, he and three of his men suffered epileptic fits. The porters believed they had been possessed by Nanda, but because Schlagintweit had made offerings at the temple before setting out, they all recovered.

On August 26, 1936, the day that British explorers Harold Tilman and Noel Odell made the first ascent of Nanda Devi, forty people drowned in the nearby village of Tharali after monsoonal rains caused a river to flood. Reports in an Indian newspaper claimed the wrath of the goddess had been aroused and that she had avenged the violation of her sanctuary, "blindly but terribly."

Dr. Charles Houston, now in his nineties, is the only surviving member of that climbing team. Illness prevented him from going to the summit, but he still counts the expedition as one of the greatest experiences of his life. He remembers hearing about the drownings, but does not believe they were linked to the climbers' actions.

"We climbed Nanda Devi with the utmost respect and gratitude," he says. "There was no violation. Our climb was a tribute to the mountain."

Six decades later, Jamling Tenzing Norgay sought the divination of a Tibetan Buddhist lama, Chatral Rinpoche, about the forthcoming climbing season on Everest. Jamling is the son of the man who, in 1953, with Edmund Hillary, was the first person to stand atop the world's highest mountain. It had long been his ambition to follow in his late father's footsteps, and now, in early 1996, he had been invited to join an IMAX expedition on Everest. But the rinpoche was not encouraging. "Conditions do not look favorable," he said. "There is something malevolent about the mountain this coming season."

Jamling sought a second opinion. The predictions of Geshe Rinchen Sonam Rinpoche were more muted. There would be obstacles and difficulties, he said. The season looked bad but "not entirely unfavorable." He advised Jamling to make offerings to the mountains. On a day selected by the astrologer of his wife's family, Jamling had 25,000 butter lamps lit at the base of the Great Stupa of Boudhanath in Kathmandu, to ask the gods for the safe passage of his expedition. He brought with him to Everest blessed strings to tie around his wrists and onto his climbing equipment, a pouch of blessed rice to sprinkle onto the mountain when he felt afraid, and a protective amulet of paper inscribed with astrological designs and religious symbols, to wear next to his skin. During his upbringing in the States, Jamling had rejected most of his family's Buddhist beliefs, but now he began to readopt them. He knew the dangers that lay in wait on Everest; he needed all the help he could get.

Jamling reached the summit of his mountain and came back safely, but others didn't. Some of the "obstacles and difficulties" predicted by Geshe Richen Sonam Rinpoche materialized as a storm that engulfed Everest on May 10–11, claiming nine lives. In the aftermath, Jamling has thought seriously about the power of lamas, whose connection with the earth and its gods, he now believes, allows them to make accurate divinations.

"The averages would confirm that those who defy a high lama, especially when the lama has done a divination, are putting themselves at grave risk," he writes. "Sherpas occasionally climb, travel or engage in activities that their lamas advise them against, and in most cases I'm aware of they have met with misfortune. With such a high correlation between poor divinations and bad luck, I don't think our caution in such matters can be ascribed to mere superstition."

According to Pascal Boyer, a professor of psychology and anthropology at Washington University, the belief that everything in nature has a spirit capable of interacting with humans persists because the human mind has evolved over many millennia to be receptive to such ideas. It is highly plausible, he claims, that in the unpredictable and often threatening environment of the Pleistocene, it was adaptive for our ancestors to attribute conscious agency not only to animals, whether as predators or as prey, but to everything that impacted their well-being and survival. Thus they invested the elements, mountains, oceans, and rivers with spirits that needed to be appeased.

In modernized societies this is no longer necessary. We understand animal behavior, we know how storms form and why avalanches occur. We realize that walking under ladders doesn't trigger misfortune, nor does wearing a talisman protect us from harm. Why is it, then, that so many people still cling to their superstitions? What they are engaging in, says Boyer, is behavior resulting from "an evolved precaution system," which causes them to feel, in certain situations, that they must take action to guard their safety or ensure their success. The action sequences they choose, which appear intuitively appropriate, come from what he calls an "evolutionary precaution repertoire."

"Common to all domains," he writes, "is the important fact that compulsion does not require any explanation. People feel they must perform the ritual...deviation from the established pattern is intuitively construed as dangerous, although in most cases the participants have or require no explanation of why that is the case."

Could there be another explanation, one not motivated by fear or compulsion? Is it not possible that, like Karsten Heuer's little boy, we can all converse with the earth? Climbers, for their survival, must develop a close relationship to their environment, sharpening their senses to take in everything that is going on around them. They have to study the patterns of weather, wind, and snow, to know the features of rock and ice. Attention—to every detail—develops keen intuition, a connection to the surrounding landscape. Given the intensity of the connection—a matter of life and death—maybe speaking to rocks and giving offerings to the mountain spirits comes naturally under such circumstances.

But developing that close connection with the earth takes lots of practice. The early Polynesians were deeply attuned to their world. By the fourth century B.C., they had formulated highly sophisticated navigational techniques to find their way through sixteen million square miles of ocean and the islands dotted across it. By minutely studying wave types and directions, they detected swell patterns, noted their changes, and worked out where land lay. They saw that ocean swells became refracted as they passed around islands, generating cross seas downwind of the island. They noticed the lines of flotsam that accumulated where opposing currents meet, and observed that flying fish always headed into the current on reentering the water. They calculated the speed of their craft by watching bubbles and patches of passing foam on the surface of the sea. They realized that clouds over low-lying islands were visible long before the island came into view. They used the flight paths of sea birds at different times of the day as an indication of the distance from land. Such navigational lore was considered secret, restricted to a select few, and imbued with spiritual significance. Between 300 A.D. and 1200 A.D., with the help of a band of highly skilled navigators and their ritual priests, Polynesians laid claim to a territory stretching from Hawaii in the north, Easter Island in the east, and New Zealand in the southwest.

Their expertise did not go unnoticed by the European explorers who came in their wake. In 1769, Captain Cook asked a Tahitian ritual priest called Tupaia to accompany him on his voyage of discovery south. In addition to being a brilliant navigator, Tupaia performed rituals to make the winds blow favorably, and he guided the *Endeavour* to New Zealand, Australia, and finally to Batavia, in Java, where he died of a fever.

Wanting to negate Polynesian claims on territory in the South Pacific, colonial powers insisted their landfalls were a result of being blown off course, not deliberate exploration. At the same time, they prohibited sailing without compass or mechanical instruments in Tahiti and the Marquesas. Consequently, the skills and credibility of Polynesian navigators went into a rapid decline. Those skills might have disappeared forever had it not been for David Lewis, a British adventurer born in 1917. He spent years in the South Pacific, researching and recording the ancient navigational techniques, and sailing 13,000 miles under the instructions of the few surviving Polynesian and Micronesian navigators. As a result of his work, the Polynesian Voyaging Society was created. In 1976, its members brought one of the last remaining traditional navigators, Mau Piailug, from his home in the Caroline Islands to Hawaii. From there, in a replica of an ancient voyaging canoe, Piailug and a crew embarked on a 2,400-mile voyage to Tahiti, using the old navigation techniques. The canoe arrived at the time and location predicted by Piailug, even though he had never navigated those waters or voyaged that far before.

Our ancestors have taught us to read the elements," says big-wave surfer Brian Keaulana. "There are so many different signs that the ocean, the skies, will communicate to you, if you know what you are looking for." Keaulana also talks about his relationship with the ocean, one that brings balance to his life. "The ocean feeds me, consoles me, relaxes me. It's a place of work, a place of pleasure. It's my life's blood."

World champion freediver Tanya Streeter agrees. She understands what the ocean is communicating to her.

"This is where I'm completely protected, where I do the thing that I do better than anything else in my life.... I'm not judged in the ocean. It's the only place I can strip down to my essence, and accept myself and my performance and capabilities."

Freedivers do what other extreme adventurers regard as *truly* extreme—descending to great depths in the ocean on one breath, or lying facedown in a swimming pool and holding their breath for up to the world record of eight minutes. They do this by rediscovering and harnessing the mammalian dive reflex, something they believe exists in each of us as a memory from when humans were aquatic

animals. When the reflex kicks in, a diver experiences the physiological changes that occur when mammals—be they whales, dolphins, or,
potentially, humans—hold their breath and dive deep in the sea. The
heart rate slows, the veins constrict to increase the blood supply to the
lungs, the red cell blood count increases, and the thorax fills with plasma
to prevent the lungs and chest from collapsing under the pressure.

Leading up to a dive, Streeter claims she's not nervous about going
so deep, or about whether or not she'll survive. She's more scared of
failing in front of the TV cameras or finding out she's not as strong as
she thought she was. "But as soon as I get into the water those feelings
evaporate. I hear myself saying that this is the place I can do anything
I want to do, where I've never failed."

For Streeter it's a relationship that goes back to her childhood in
the Cayman Islands, where the ocean was her best friend, a sanctuary from family problems. When she was nine years old, she was sent
to boarding school in England. Leaving the ocean after holidays was
always wrenching.

"The last thing I would do before I left would be to go into the
water wearing a mask, exhale, and lie on the bottom looking at the way
the light plays on the sand. That was my ritual, saying good-bye to
the ocean. It never occurred to me that it might be a long time to lie
underwater or that it was an odd thing to do. I remember popping my
head up and my mom screaming from the beach that we were going
to miss our flight."

Saying good-bye to her family at the airport, she never cried. But
when the plane took off, it was a different matter. "I would fall apart
the second the plane was high enough for me to look down on the
sea. It was awful. I would curl up at the window and promise myself I
would come back."

Even now, when she leaves Cayman for her home in Austin, Texas, she feels that same sense of loss. "It's my sea. I can dive elsewhere but it's never the same as your own little patch of ocean."

When she's on a boat heading out to or returning from a dive site, she finds a secluded place where she can sit and "communicate" with the ocean. "It's not praying...I'm not asking for anything. I'm just conversing somehow. If it's an important or a tough dive, and I'm successful, after I surface I go back underwater again almost immediately, without my mask on. I get very emotional. And I've had moments when I consciously make a promise to the sea. The protection I feel in the ocean is a very clear message to me and a clear understanding of what my responsibility is, to help protect it in return. I know what a gift it is, to be able to spend my life and my talents this way. I chose to repay the gift through the environmental work that I do. That's what I promise."

David Abram argues that being in conversation with the natural world is an essential skill, now lost by most people in the West. Abram is an ecologist, an anthropologist, and a sleight-of-hand magician. He began learning magic skills in his teens, and put himself through college by working as a house magician at Alice's Restaurant in Massachusetts. Midway through his studies, he spent a year traveling through Europe as a street magician. By the time he decided to return to school, he had become interested in the link between magic and medicine, and subsequently traveled extensively in Indonesia, Nepal, and Sri Lanka, connecting with traditional medical practitioners, most of whom regarded themselves as magicians. For them, magic wasn't about entertainment. Still, though the end results were different, the means were very similar to those employed by Western magicians.

"When a magician is successful in making a stone vanish and then plucking it back from thin air," says Abram, "it leaves us without any framework of explanation. We are suddenly floating in that open space of direct sensory experience, actually encountering the world without preconceptions, if only for a moment. The magician is one who frees the senses from static holding patterns that they are held in by assumptions, by outmoded ways of thinking and by the styles of speech and discourse."

Sleight of hand, he discovered, first originated in the work of shamans, whose modus operandi is to alter people's perceptions. The shamans and healers that Abram met believe they are intermediaries between their human community and what he calls the "more-than-human world" of animals, plants, rocks, water, weather—everything in the surrounding environment. Their job is to ensure a balance between these two communities, offering prayers, praise, and respect to the more-than-human world in appeasement for humans using it as a resource. Such magicians are "boundary keepers," ensuring a two-way flow between these realms and preventing or breaking through barriers that shut out the "more than human" powers from our awareness.

In the West, then, the real role of magic has fallen by the wayside. During our rush toward modernization, writes Abram, mankind has lost "the humility and grace that comes from being fully a part of [the] whirling world....the poise that comes from living in storied relationship with the myriad things, the myriad beings that perpetually surround us."

It is essential, he says, for mankind to recover its ancient reciprocal relationship with the natural world, not by going back to old ways, but rather by coming full circle, "grounding our new knowledge in older forms of experience, uniting our rational, reasoning sides with a more sensorial way of being."

A way of being he discovered by accident. While hiking through a canyon in Bali, Abram got caught out by a severe rainstorm that caused a flash flood. The cave in which he took refuge soon became a prison when a waterfall began cascading down the hillside, sealing its mouth. His initial nervousness at being trapped turned to fascination when he noticed a number of spiders had begun weaving their webs across the mouth of the cave, right in front of the wall of water. For hours he sat mesmerized by the complex, overlapping patterns forming between him and the torrent. Suddenly, he realized that the curtain of water had become totally silent. He tried to hear it, and couldn't. "My senses," he writes, "were entranced." Night came, the rain fell relentlessly. Yet Abram was neither cold nor hungry, "only remarkably peaceful and at home." Stretching out on the mossy floor of the cave, he slept deeply. When he woke, the sky was clear, the canyon was awash with sunlight, and the webs were gone.

Those spiders were his introduction to the spirits and the magic that he believes are part of nature.

"It was from them I first learned of the intelligence that lurks in nonhuman nature, the ability that an alien form of sentience has to echo one's own, to instill a reverberation in oneself that temporarily shatters habitual ways of seeing and feeling, leaving one open to a world all alive, awake, and aware."

Karsten Heuer and Leanne Allison have experienced that echo, that reverberation. Four months into their journey, they found themselves literally immersed in the Porcupine caribou herd. Earlier in the migration, the animals had kept their distance, always staying at least a hundred yards away from the two humans. Now there was a change. Caribou passed within a few paces of them. A calf lay down within arm's length and fell asleep. One day, after walking for five hours, Heuer spoke to his wife, who shortly before had been right behind him. When she didn't answer, he turned to discover she'd fallen back to do some filming. In her place was a caribou bull. Heuer faced forward again. When a pair of hooves stepped into view, he told himself to keep walking, hoping "that the rhythm that had taken me to the edge of this moment would carry me in." Antlers appeared, the bull pulled alongside him, head and neck bobbing in time with his stride. Two more males drew up alongside the creature. Heuer was in the herd, a bull among bulls.

"I could hear, smell and feel them as their nostrils whooshed, bodies sweated and brown eyes rolled up and down, inspecting me as I in turn inspected them," he writes. "Everything else had been shed—my false sense of security, my hubris, my mental clutter— and what it allowed me to do in that moment was simply relax. The bulls seemed to sense this: their eyes softened, their breathing quietened, and for a brief suspended moment we moved in unison, heartbeats and footsteps mingling while we inhaled each other's exhaled breaths."

Was this an example of Abram's "storied relationship?" Heuer implies as much. "There were times when the caribou did seem to be acknowledging us and curious about us," he says, "and curiosity is defined by yearning for interaction."

Toward the end of the journey, the couple would sometimes get out of the soggy tundra by veering away from the caribou and climbing a ridge. More often than not, they found animals following them.

"I doubt they were seeing us as part of the herd," says Heuer. "But over time our body language, our very gait changed and began to approximate theirs. We were walking in a loose-limbed way. We weren't bothering to protect ourselves from the elements. When it rained we got wet, when we crossed a river we just kept going and let our clothes dry on our backs as we walked. We stopped trying to be perfectly comfortable and in doing that we truly did become comfortable. I'm sure that was apparent in the way we moved, and that this communicated some level of comfort to the caribou. There was something about us that said, these are things that belong here so we don't need to avoid them. That becomes an incredibly satisfying feeling. That is when the sense of oneness creeps in, when you feel like you fit in totally with your surroundings."

Rupert Sheldrake, a plant biologist, offers another explanation for the ease that developed between the caribou and the two humans: communication through what he calls morphic fields. Sheldrake studied at Cambridge and Harvard. He is a former research fellow of Clare College, Cambridge, and of the Royal Society. For seven years he worked on plant development in India. Then he stepped out of the traditional scientific box to develop his theory of morphic fields and morphic resonance.

The universe is not governed by laws, says Sheldrake, but by evolving habits of nature. Through natural selection, animals inherit the successful habits of their species. These habits become instincts and grow up within nature through areas of influence called morphic fields. The habits act as a kind of memory in nature by patterns of vibratory activity influencing subsequent similar patterns, a process Sheldrake calls morphic resonance. To explain it, he uses the metaphor of sympathetic vibration.

"If you have a stretched string and you make it vibrate, another string will start vibrating in sympathy. If you put down the sustaining pedal on a piano and put your head inside and go *Ooooo,* the piano will say *Ooooo* back to you—you've set the strings in resonance."

Sheldrake notes that the ancient Greeks believed the magnet had a soul. So did William Gilbert, an Elizabethan scientist who in 1600 published the revolutionary *De Magnete,* in which he showed that the earth has an immaterial magnetic force. Gilbert also credited the earth with a soul, or anima, which rotated the planet around its axis. The scientific revolution, Sheldrake believes, "drained the soul" out of the world, but magnetism remained a mystery that no one could explain. It wasn't until 1831 that Faraday replaced the old idea of the soul with the new idea of the field and field lines of force that exist around material bodies. In the 1920s, Einstein extended the field theory to gravitation, a field which coordinates and holds together the whole universe, taking over from the *anima mundi,* the world soul of ancient Greece. Quantum matter fields followed, and then fields were introduced into biology in the shape of morphogenetic fields, which organize the development of plants and animals. The British biologist C. H. Waddington claimed that morphogenetic fields have attractors in them: in an oak tree, for example, is the form of the mature oak attracting the seedling toward it—Aristotle's *entelechy.*

"In effect," says Sheldrake, "the vegetative soul was reinvented as the morphogenetic field. Everything the soul did before, the field did now. We've recovered a sense of the living universe through modern science and field theory."

If the morphic field, like a magnetic field, is within and around the body, can that field be detected? It seems possible. Everyone has had the experience of feeling uncomfortable when a stranger stands too close to them. In one of Sheldrake's experiments, blindfolded subjects walk between several people placed randomly along a space. Most of his subjects sense when they are passing someone, which, according to Sheldrake, means they are picking up on their field. He has the same explanation for why, if you stare fixedly at the back of someone's head, they will often turn around. And for why a flock of birds in flight or a large shoal of fish all seem to change direction at the same moment. It's to do with field phenomena, and, according to Sheldrake, with minds extending beyond brains across these fields, to touch other minds.

Is interspecies communication possible? Sheldrake believes it might be, and he is conducting exhaustive experiments into the communication between humans and domestic pets. In one of these experiments, captured on film, two sets of researchers simultaneously monitor the behavior of a dog in a house and the movements of its owner, several miles away in an office. As the owner prepares to leave her desk for the day, the dog, which has been sleeping all afternoon, suddenly wakes up. The closer the woman gets to the house—walking out of the office, driving along the highway—the more agitated the dog becomes until, as she's about to turn the car into her road, he's barking in excitement.

In the July 2007 issue of the New England Journal of Medicine, Dr. David M. Dosa, a geriatrican at Rhode Island Hospital, writes about Oscar, the pet cat of a local nursing home, Oscar has gained a reputation for signalling when patients are near death by curling up with them on their beds—something the usually aloof cat would not normally do. After more than twenty-five correct "predictions," doctors and nurses at the home now pay heed to Oscar's actions. If he is found on a patient's bed, they call in that person's family.

These may seem like wild theories, but they have parallels in traditional beliefs. In Borneo, the Penan people believe that trees bloom when they hear the call of *karnkaputt* birds. Birdcalls from one direction bring good luck, from another bad tidings. A hunting party will turn back if it hears the cry of a bat hawk.

Before setting off on their long journey, Heuer and Allison spent some time in the Gwich'in settlement of Old Crow. The people there told them to pay close attention to their dreams. And they related stories from past generations. How there was a time when people talked to caribou, and caribou talked back.

"So all these mythical possibilities were explained to us before we started the trip," says Heuer. "But they were couched in Gwich'in legends and myths and at the time my response was, That's your native shtick and I've got mine and they don't quite line up, but I respect it. Then, five months after we set out, there we were, two white people who grew up in Calgary, communicating with caribou."

At the end of their journey, the couple spent a week in Old Crow. On a number of occasions they gathered in the community hall to share stories.

"There was a sense of relief among a lot of people. They said that our stories were just like the stories they had heard from their elders. That the cadence and rhythm of our speech was so much like that of their parents and great- and great-great-grandfathers. It showed us that the wisdom they thought was being lost as older generations died out could be accessed again. It's in the land. It's with the caribou."

During their journey, Heuer and Allison's worldview changed. They realized that there are things science can't explain. They began to see nature as magical. They learned to watch the earth for signs, listen with their whole bodies and spirits, and let themselves be guided by what they could feel, rather than what they saw or heard. This shift in consciousness enabled them to establish a dialogue with the animals, whose difficulties they shared. In a journal entry, Heuer wrote, "A part of me still wants to question, to know exactly how and why—[but] it is smaller than before, a voice that's scarcely audible amid the overwhelming urge to surrender and accept. It is the act of moving that has brought me here.... The miles, the weather, the bears and the uncertainty, hammering every extraneous thought, action, question, phone number and song from my head. Cleansed, I am on the edge of something, some other realm of knowing, being pushed and pulled through the same physical world but in a different dimension of time and space."

PART THREE

Indeed: there is a Mystery Zone out there, beyond the edge of the human world, in the backcountry, the empty skies and waters of the planet.

ROB SCHULTHEIS, *Bone Games*

Chapter 6

REMEMBERING THE FUTURE

"I don't understand you," said Alice. "It's dreadfully confusing!"

"That's the effect of living backwards," the Queen said kindly. "It always makes one a little giddy at first—"

"Living backwards!" Alice repeated in great astonishment. "I never heard of such a thing!"

"—but there's one great advantage in it, that one's memory works both ways."

"I'm sure mine *only works one way," Alice remarked. "I can't remember things before they happen."*

"It's a poor sort of memory that only works backwards," the Queen remarked.

LEWIS CARROLL, *Through the Looking-Glass*

When he spotted his friend in the departure lounge at Heathrow Airport, Jim Duff sensed something was wrong.

"Nick was as pale as a ghost," he recalls. "He looked really gripped. I asked him if he was okay and he said, *Jim, I've got a terrible feeling that I won't be coming back from this trip.*"

As the doctor on the 1978 British expedition to climb K2, the world's second-highest mountain, Duff thought his duties would begin only when the team, led by Chris Bonington and including Joe Tasker, Peter Boardman, and Doug Scott, arrived in Pakistan. He expected stomach ailments, sprained muscles, and high-altitude sickness. He didn't expect a case of pre-expedition nerves—especially from Nick Estcourt, an experienced mountaineer with an ebullient personality. Duff prescribed a couple of stiff brandies from the bar.

"This was only my third Himalayan expedition," he says. "I didn't really listen to what Nick was telling me. A year or so later, I would have told him to rip up his plane ticket and go home. Before you've had these intuitive experiences, you don't really trust them."

During the long march into Base Camp, the two men shared a tent. One morning, Estcourt woke up and recounted a strange dream. He had been caught in an avalanche and was buried under deep snow. He was looking down on the scene and Doug Scott was in the debris, poking among blocks of ice, searching for him.

"He said he knew it was Doug," says Duff, "even though he looked like a snow groomer. We laughed about that. I wrote about his dream in my journal, and I drew a little cartoon of a snow groomer with Doug's face on it. I didn't take it seriously."

A couple of weeks later, Duff was at Camp 1, along with Bonington. Earlier in the day, Estcourt, Scott, and a Hunza high-altitude porter, Quamajan, had left to start ferrying loads up to Camp 2 in support of the lead climbers, Tasker and Boardman. It was a perfect afternoon, the wind calm and the sky clear. Duff was outside his tent, relaxing in the sunshine, when a thunderous boom ripped through the peace of the day. Above and to the right of the camp, an avalanche was pouring over some ice cliffs and down the slope leading to Camp 2.

"It was enormous," says Duff. "A mega-avalanche. I've never seen anything that scale, before or since."

Bonington picked up his camera and started taking photos; he was sure the three load-carriers were out of the line of avalanche. Duff felt differently.

"I screamed at him to stop. I told him that one of our lads was in there. I just knew."

Crossing the slope, Doug Scott had been in the lead. While he broke trail, Estcourt and Quamajan rested and shared a cigarette. Quamajan was second on the rope, but just before he set off, Estcourt insisted on trading places. Scott had reached the far side, and Est-court was halfway across, when Quamajan heard a cracking sound and saw the top of the slope fracture into giant jigsaw pieces—the sign of a dangerous wind slab avalanche. He saw the whole slope start to slide. He saw Estcourt overwhelmed by huge blocks of ice. He tried to hold the rope that attached them—later, the burn marks on his hands would attest to his struggle. Meanwhile, on the other end of the rope, Scott was whipped into the avalanche, cartwheeling back-ward. Suddenly, he landed hard on the slope. The rope had snapped. Beneath him, the mass of snow and ice poured down four thousand feet to the glacier, taking Estcourt with it.

The team called off the expedition. Next day, at first light, they all headed back to advance base. Scott and Duff went first.

"We got down to the glacier," says Duff, "and Doug unclipped from the rope and started stomping around in the avalanche debris, searching for traces of Nick. I was worried about him being out there, unroped. I was sitting on my haunches, calling to him to come back, when suddenly I thought—*This is Nick's dream. It's exactly what he described to me.*"

Duff is a physician, a scientist, but he's convinced that Estcourt had an awareness of his impending death. That he tapped into some level of consciousness where the future was revealed.

Every night, when we fall asleep and dream, we slip into another form of consciousness. Our bodies lie paralyzed, while our minds wander of their own accord, creating dramas, bending time, and dispensing with our "waking" understanding of space and causality. In our dreams we can fly, astral travel, shape shift, meet with the dead. Things that are impossible become possible, until, of course, we wake up and realize that it was all a fantasy created by our mind.

In the thirteenth century, the Persian poet Rumi wrote,

Part of the self leaves the body when we sleep
and changes shape. You might say, "Last night
I was a cypress tree, a small bed of tulips,
a field of grapevines." Then the phantasm goes away
And you're back in the room.

But what if it wasn't all a fantasy? What if dreaming *is* a channel into other levels of experience? Oneiromancy—the interpretation of dreams to tell the future—has a long history. Priests of the Egyptian god Horus recorded dream interpretations on papyrus texts written around 1250 B.C. Scraps of these texts still exist, and show various dreams as being simply "good" or "bad" omens. Scripts written on clay tablets—cuneiform—that date back to 669 B.C. and were part of the library of King Assurbanipal of Assyria, tell the story of the legendary Gilgamesh and his recurring dreams, which were interpreted by his mother, Ninsun. What is believed to be the first full text on dream interpretation, *Oneircocritica,* was written by Artemidorus, a Roman who lived in Greece around 140 A.D. The Roman philosopher Cicero considered the possibility that dreams could be precognitive. "The soul in sleep," he writes, "gives proof of its divine nature."

In ancient Greece, physicians received training on how to use patients' accounts of certain types of dreams, called prodromal, which they believed helped to diagnose their ailments. Centuries later, in the 1900s, the Russian psychiatrist Vasily Kasatkin, of the Leningrad Neurosurgical Institute, studied over ten thousand dreams recalled by twelve hundred subjects over a forty-year period. He discovered that illness is often associated with dream recall, particularly with nightmares, and that the dreams can sometimes pinpoint the location and severity of an illness before it is medically diagnosed. Such dreams, he believed, are caused by internal physical stimuli, external stimuli, and social environment.

Prodromal dreams are still accepted by some medical practitioners as signals of what is going on in the body, before the symptoms become obvious and diagnosable. Daniel Schneider, a psychoanalyst and neurologist, calls them an "early warning system," suggesting that our body cells send chemical messages to our para-conscious mind to give alerts on the state of our health.

Research has shown that we can dream during all stages of sleep—from the "waking stage" as the body prepares for shut-down, through drowsiness, light sleep, and deep sleep, but most intensely during REM, or rapid eye movement, sleep, when there is heightened cerebral activity. Studies of brain activity during REM sleep and neuropsychological studies of brain-injured patients both point to a specific neural network for dreaming, but it has not yet been definitively mapped, nor is its functioning clearly understood.

Analyses of dreams collected in sleep laboratories, college classrooms, and dream diaries suggest that while some dreams contain puzzling scenarios or images, most are concerned with everyday life, set in familiar places with a cast of known characters. Although many cultures throughout time have considered dreams to be highly symbolic, the psychologist and dream researcher David Foulkes calls into doubt the idea that dreams have any psychological purpose in waking life. Dreams, he believes, are a reasonable simulation of the waking world, an enactment of everyday activities and interests—what Freud called the "day residue." There is no mystery. The dream is an accidental event that can be used by the dreamer to carry some heavier emotional weight. Most people remember only a tiny percentage of their dreams, and a dream-derived idea or a message most probably came to the dreamer at the moment of awaking or on reflection of the dream.

In 1998, the British alpinist Andy Parkin was at the base camp of Mount Hunter, Alaska, with French alpinist François Marsigny, waiting for the weather to clear so that they could attempt a new route on the North Buttress. One night he had a dream that he was at the foot of the mountain, getting ready to climb it, but he didn't want to go up. He knew someone had been buried in an avalanche on its slopes and that it was too late to help them. He awoke feeling deeply troubled. Later that morning the weather improved but Parkin's dream had left him so ill at ease he insisted they wait another day.

In the afternoon, planes started landing on the glacier, bringing climbers on their way to Denali. A newly arrived Italian climber struck up a conversation with Parkin and Marsigny. Parkin asked him if he had any news from Europe.

"Do you know Chantal Maudit?" he said. "She died on Dhaulagiri."

Maudit was a French mountaineer. Several years earlier, she and Parkin had been lovers, and since then they had stayed close friends. He knew about her expedition to Dhaulagiri, and he'd been feeling that something wasn't right. In shock, he listened to the Italian explaining how she had been found dead in her tent, which had been partly buried by an avalanche. Either that had killed her, or she'd been asphyxiated from stove fumes.

"I hated the guy," says Parkin. "He was talking about her as if she was just another climber. François said, 'Are you all right?' It turns out he already knew, a couple of guys from another team had told him a few days before, but he was waiting for the right moment to break the news to me. I couldn't speak. I was standing there thinking, *Is this the dream?*"

Adrian Burgess claims that normally he never remembers dreams, but there are two that he recalled on waking, and that still remain vivid in his memory. The first was when he was climbing Nanga Parbat in 1990. He had joined up with a small New Zealand team whose members, he quickly discovered, were disorganized and inexperienced. Despite recent heavy snowfalls, they seemed unconcerned about avalanche danger. During one foray up the mountain they started crossing a terrifyingly unstable slope, until Burgess insisted they turn back. A few nights after that incident, he was sleeping in a camp at 21,000 feet when he had what he describes as "a visitation" from Catherine Freer, a climber who had died on Mount Logan three years earlier. Burgess had never climbed with Freer, but they had become friends while working for the same window-cleaning company in Colorado. At the time, she was planning her trip to Logan with Dave Cheesmond, a Canadian climber. Burgess recalls her racing off each lunchtime to make phone calls about the trip and returning "psyched." She and Cheesmond both disappeared on the mountain.

"I knew her quite well, but I hadn't thought about her for ages, and I certainly wasn't thinking about her on Nanga Parbat," says Burgess. "And then I had this dream, this vision. It's Catherine, and she's saying, *Adrian, you're with the wrong people, get the fuck out of there.* It really made a mark on me."

Early the next day, he packed up and left the expedition. Shortly afterward, the rest of the team went up the mountain. A storm moved in and they were hit by a big avalanche. They all survived, but only just. "They were very, very lucky," says Burgess.

His other memorable dream was a happier one, and also linked to the days when he had cleaned the windows of high-rise buildings in downtown Denver. It occurred in 1993, when he was in Patagonia, on his way to climb Cerro Torre with a small team. Eighteen years earlier, he had successfully climbed another mountain in the area, but now, at forty-five, he was wondering if he was still up to the challenge.

"We were finding a route across a glacier," he recalls, "and I was looking up at this mountain, thinking, *This is a serious deal.* I was tense about it all."

One night, when they were bivouacking on the glacier, Burgess dreamed about the Dalai Lama. Burgess's wife, Lorna, is an immigration lawyer based in Salt Lake City, who has done a lot of pro-bono work for Tibetan organizations. When the Dalai Lama first came to Salt Lake City, the couple was invited to all the "inner sanctum" functions.

"I've been within ten feet of His Holiness," says Burgess. "I've heard him talk for hours, in person." Now he had an encounter with him of a different kind.

"He was swinging on a rope, like he was cleaning windows with me in Denver. He was swinging in and out of these windows in his maroon and yellow robes, going *Everything's fine! Everything's great! Things are looking good here, Adrian. Yoo-hoo!* I woke up in the morning with a glow about me, and I thought, *This is going to work out.* And it did. It was a perfect expedition."

After the expedition, Burgess flew back into the States on Thanksgiving. He got home to Salt Lake City in time for dinner with Lorna and two of their Tibetan friends. After the meal, Lorna suggested that they should each tell a Thanksgiving story. Burgess recounted his dream.

"I said I knew everything was going to be okay in Patagonia because I had this dream of His Holiness swinging in and out of windows in his robes going *Yoo-hoo!* Their eyes were popping out."

Dr. Montague Ullman, a psychoanalyst and psychiatrist at the Maimonides Medical Center in Brooklyn, New York, has led some of the world's most extensive laboratory research on dreams. He disagrees with Freud and David Foulkes that dreams are simply a processing of the "day residue."

"Why, we might ask, is there a need in the first place for a day residue to trigger the content of a dream?" he asks. "Why do we need reminders from the outside that there is something to be attended to?"

If looked at from a biological point of view, the REM stage, with its physiological underpinnings located in the brain stem, is considered an older and more primitive form of sleep than the non-REM stages. Thus, according to Ullman, it would seem logical to connect it with more primitive survival needs.

"In both waking consciousness and dreaming, a scanning process sensitive to novelty is going on, but under very different circumstances," he writes. "Awake and embedded in a social matrix, we scan a limited horizon. Asleep and dreaming, we are very much alone. We have taken temporary leave of that social cushioning, and as a consequence, we are potentially at greater risk. We now have to be open to a much wider scanning process, one capable of registering a range of possible disconnects from the most subtle to the most threatening."

While awake, mountaineers of Adrian Burgess and Andy Parkin's caliber are keenly tuned into their environment, picking up on every nuance. In sleep, then, according to Ullman's ideas, they should be able to do the same, but to a much more powerful degree. This, says Ullman, gives a hint of how dreams might be conduits to paranormal powers.

"If we take psi effects seriously, this is so, regardless of whether the source of the disconnect lies close at hand or is distant in time and space."

Perhaps this explains John Porter's dreams of falling rocks at Annapurna Base Camp in 1982. Porter, originally from New Hampshire, was on the mountain with Alex MacIntyre from Britain and René Ghilini from France. Their plan was to establish a new route on the South Face of Annapurna, climbing as light and as fast as possible. No camps on the mountain to bail out to if things turned nasty. No fixed ropes. No backup if anything went wrong.

For training, they spent eighteen days doing first ascents on several surrounding peaks. When finally they returned to their base camp, storm clouds were gathering over the summit of Annapurna. The climbers hunkered down to wait out the weather. Porter was sharing a tent with MacIntyre. They had met a decade earlier at Leeds University, where Porter, already an experienced climber, was studying for a master's degree after fleeing from the Vietnam War draft. MacIntyre, eight years his junior and studying law, became Porter's apprentice. They climbed together in the Alps, then headed for the Himalayas, where they did the first ascent of Bandaka and the South Face of Changabang. They traveled through South America, climbing lots of routes as lightweight as possible. For three years they went their separate ways, before reuniting to attempt Annapurna.

"By then," says Porter, "Alex had become the master climber and I was working hard to keep up with him."

A fiercely ambitious climber, MacIntyre was willing to push at outrageous limits. But there was one thing that always unnerved him in the mountains: falling rocks.

"A lot of people I know have agreed on that," said Porter. "Alex always had this huge fear of rocks. I saw it on other climbs. We were all a bit stupid, we'd get in these bombardments of rockfall, and go, *What the hell,* but Alex would have a really violent reaction. He'd be quivering. It was something he had to struggle to control."

Night after night at Annapurna Base Camp, as Porter was drifting into sleep, he would hear the rockfall. Stones clattering down cliffs. Boulders crashing and bouncing along the glacier, toward their tent.

"I'd suddenly sit up, fully awake, and realize it was totally silent out there, apart from the usual creaking and groaning of the ice underneath us. There were no falling rocks. Yet I *had* heard them. I had several of these half-dreams, and frankly I was totally spooked."

He didn't tell MacIntyre about the dreams because he didn't want to unsettle him any further. Clearly, something was already bothering his old friend. He was restless. He seemed homesick. He wasn't his usual cheery self. But they didn't talk about that, either. Later, Porter would discover that MacIntyre's behavior had been equally uncharacteristic just before he left home. Usually he had no trouble with farewells. He'd saunter off, turning for a final wave, his wicked grin, twinkling eyes, and mop of raven-black ringlets giving him an air of boyish invincibility that he clearly believed in, and that reassured those who loved him. This time though, for weeks before his departure, he kept telling his girlfriend, Sarah Richard, that she shouldn't worry about him while he was away, that it wasn't *this* mountain that would kill him.

"He said it so often," she recalls, "I really began to worry."

In a farewell letter, he wrote to her, "Remember that whatever happens, I'll always love you."

She didn't go to the airport with him. But his mother, Jean, did. She was puzzled when, after saying good-bye, he turned around and came back to her, urging her to look after Sarah and his sister, Libby.

Good weather moved in over Annapurna. The team had their window of opportunity. But Porter was struggling with a stomach bug, and a deepening sense of unease.

"I just wasn't in a state to climb, either physically or psychologically. I told the guys to go ahead and have a quick look at the route. I was hoping that by the time they came back I'd be better and then we could all go for the summit."

MacIntyre and Ghilini left Base Camp carrying only one ice screw and two rock pegs, a couple of bivouac bags, and a minimum of food and water. Porter tracked their progress through a telescope. At 24,000 feet, they came to a rock wall that proved too difficult for them to ascend. Retreating a little way, they set up their bivouac on a ledge. Next morning, as Porter watched them get ready to leave, suddenly the lens of the telescope filled with something blood-red.

"I thought, *What is it?* Then I realized it was one of them shaking out a bright red bivvy sack. But I was completely unnerved."

Later that day, he watched them descend a couloir. He was concerned about their position, because the sun had been hitting the face for hours, loosening the snow and ice above them. But they were only a thousand feet from the relatively safe ground at the bottom of the face, and he presumed that they had decided to take the risk rather than sit out in the open for a second night.

"They were both crossing a gully," Porter recalls. "I lowered the telescope to clean a speck of dust off the lens. When I raised it to my eye again, René was alone."

A single stone had flown down the South Face of Annapurna, with an unerring aim for MacIntyre. It smashed into the back of his head. His limp form tumbled more than five hundred feet down the slope. When Ghilini reached him, he was dead.

Had MacIntyre sensed the approach of his own death? Were Porter's dreams a foretelling of the accident? Porter has an open mind on these questions. "I think the starting point for any sort of weirdness is life itself," he says. "If we're here, then it seems to me that anything is possible."

Montague Ullman considers the unique features of dreaming as analogous to some aspects of quantum mechanics. He likens the opposite states of waking and dreaming consciousness to the dual nature of an electron and how its nature shifts depending on how it is being measured, manifesting as either a particle or a wave.

"Awake we are in the particle mode facing a world of discrete objects," he writes. "Asleep and dreaming we are coping with the internal resonant wave-like feelings seeking to embed themselves in symbolic imagery."

Another mystery in quantum mechanics is non-locality, the instantaneous transfer of information from one particle to another through no known physical means. The same phenomenon appears to occur in dreams. The telepathic dream spans space; the precognitive dream spans time.

"While awake," Ullman writes, "our view of ourselves is one in which we stress our autonomy, our individuality, our discreteness. We define our own boundaries and we try to work with them. What I'm suggesting, and which is not at all novel, is that our dreaming self is

organized along a different principle. Our dreaming self is more concerned with our connection with 'all' others."

In other words, energy and mass being interchangeable ($E=mc^2$),
awake we are mass, asleep we are energy.

Ullman has a hunch that our ability to pick up information from
the future is related to the importance of maintaining a connection to
our human and natural environment. Such powers are "a surface out-
cropping of this underlying sense and need for unity, a kind of deeply
hidden connective tissue available when other connective strate-
gies fail."

Could dreams, then, act as early warning systems? A type of prodromal dream for adventurers? In 1984, Cherie Bremer-Kamp was
working as a nurse in the intensive care unit of a San Francisco hospital, and planning a winter climbing expedition to Kanchenjunga
with her husband, Dr. Chris Chandler. She was looking for someone
who could accompany them in the role of base camp manager, when
it occurred to her that a coworker, Lori Orlando, would be the ideal
person. Orlando wasn't a mountaineer, but she was fit, strong, and
driven, with good organizational and people skills. She was intrigued
by the idea of taking part in an expedition and quickly agreed. To
ensure she knew what she was getting into, Bremer-Kamp and Chandler fed her a steady stream of information, including the medical
problems that might arise on the mountain: a whole gamut of altitude-
related illnesses ranging from headaches, shortness of breath, weak-
ness, and lassitude to pulmonary and cerebral edema. She studied the
information assiduously, and met regularly with Bremer-Kamp after
work to discuss questions and concerns.

One evening, when they were both about to end their shift,

Orlando asked Bremer-Kamp if they could go somewhere quiet to talk. She told her that she'd had a disturbing dream. In it, she had seen three people near the top of the mountain. Two were climbing together, the third was close by, under some rocks, apparently guiding the others in some way. There was a communication problem: the climbers were shouting at each other but not making themselves understood. And they were falling a lot, down the mountain slopes. There was a problem with gloves, being dropped or lost. As Orlando finished recounting the dream, she blurted out, "Cherie, you've got to do something about your hands. Promise me."

Bremer-Kamp refused to take the dream seriously. She and Chandler planned to be on the mountain with one Sherpa to help them to establish their lower camps, but they would head to the top alone. There would be no third climber. They always carried extra gloves with them. And when their hands got cold, they could warm them up under their armpits. It was their feet, she told Orlando, that they worried about most. She omitted to say that she was having her own unsettling dreams. In one she had been avalanched on the mountain. Buried in snow, she floated out of her body and looked down to see herself and Chandler, holding each other, embraced in death.

Once they got to the mountain, their plans to climb alone changed. Their sirdar, Mongol Sing, was a young Hunza man who had worked with other foreign expeditions. Previously, Sing had only climbed to 20,000 feet, but at the start of the trip he did well, helping to establish a camp at 23,000 feet. When he asked if he could join them on their summit attempt, they agreed.

They spent fifty days on the mountain, waiting out storms and suffering punishing cold. Finally, they reached a high point of 26,000 feet. But on the morning of their summit bid, Chandler started coughing up blood. His movements became uncoordinated. He told

Bremer-Kamp he had gone blind. They knew his coughing meant the onset of pulmonary edema, and that his blindness was a symptom of cerebral edema. Every mountaineer dreads getting one or the other of these ailments, and Chandler had been struck by both. His only hope was to get lower down the mountain, as fast as possible, but he could barely walk, or even stand unsupported. Terror sent a surge of adrenaline through Bremer-Kamp's body, cutting off blood to her extremities, and causing her fingers to freeze. She pulled off her gloves. Her hands were "white and marble-like." When she clapped them together, they made a hollow, clunking sound.

For hours, Bremer-Kamp and Sing tried to get Chandler lower. They stumbled, slid, and fell; their progress was painfully slow and by nightfall they had only descended a thousand feet. They dug out a platform in the snow for Chandler, and Bremer-Kamp tried to settle him into a bivouac bag. He was confused and afraid; he started to panic. Struggling out of the bag, he stood up and tried to run. His feet got tangled up in the bag, and he keeled over. His breathing stopped. Bremer-Kamp tried frantically to revive him, with mouth-to-mouth resuscitation, and by banging on his chest with her frozen hands. But Chandler was gone. She lay down next to him on the slope, pressing her body against his motionless form. She wanted to go with him. To join him in death on the mountain. Just like in her dream.

Had she lain there much longer, fully exposed to the freezing temperatures and biting wind, the dream would have been realized. But something else began to tug at her attention. A "subtle presence" that gradually she felt more strongly. She recognized it as her two small children, standing beside her, solemnly watching the scene. She sensed how much they needed her, to guide them through the years ahead. She turned toward them, leaving Chandler to continue his journey alone.

She spent the night shivering in her bivouac sack, ten feet away from Chandler's body. Once she heard him coughing, then calling her name in a strange, echoing voice. She sat up, startled and afraid. Staring through the darkness, she saw the still form of Chandler's body, half-sitting, half-lying on the snow. It hadn't moved. The voice, she believes, came from the "tunnel," his passage from life to death.

Lying down again, she thought about the countless strands of experience that had brought her to this place, this moment in time. Suddenly she remembered one strand. The hospital in San Francisco. Lori Orlando, her big, dark eyes troubled, her voice insistent as she recounted the details of a dream.

"There are three people on the mountain. One person is sitting by himself under some rocks while the other two are climbing down alone.... Your hands, Cherie. You've got to do something about your hands."

By morning her hands were frozen into "rigid claws," and her arms, legs, and feet were stiff with cold. She hadn't the strength to bury Chandler, or drag his remains down the mountain. She left him where he was, and began the long struggle to get herself and Sing to safety. Sing was nearly paralyzed with fear, and at times she raged at him for his lack of experience, venting her despair and anger on his stumbling form. It took them three days and nights to reach Camp 1. Setting up belays, Bremer-Kamp often grew frustrated with her wooden fingers and just took off her gloves to tie knots. Her hands felt neither cold nor pain; the nerves in her fingers were dead. All the way, she felt Chandler's presence. He was watching, giving her strength and comfort.

Orlando had been anxiously waiting at the camp; her relief on seeing the approach of Bremer-Kamp and Sing was soon over-whelmed by grief when she learned that Chandler was dead. But she immediately set to work, trying to warm up and treat the climbers' hands and feet.

"I was pretty dazed," says Bremer-Kamp. "But I kept thinking, *Oh my God. We lived out Lori's dream. I've got to talk to her about it.*"

When Bremer-Kamp eventually raised the subject of the dream, however, Orlando claimed not to know what she was talking about.

"I think she was frightened by it, and blocked it out," says Bremer-Kamp. "It took her the longest time to vaguely remember our conversation in the hospital."

Bremer-Kamp has never forgotten it. Her maimed hands and feet constantly remind her. The frostbite she suffered was so bad that all her fingers and a third of each foot had to be amputated. Mongol Sing lost parts of several fingers and toes. Not long afterward he returned to the mountains, only to be killed in an avalanche while working for a British expedition.

For years, Bremer-Kamp was haunted by Orlando's dream, and the fact that it contained a warning.

"I spent a lot of time with this whole thing about the dream coming true. That I had this knowledge. Why didn't I act on it? There was a lot of struggle and self-examination around that. Pivotal to accepting what happened was understanding that yes, there is a grand plan. It was like our decision to take Mongol along with us at the last minute. It seemed to us like a complex decision. But the dream knew all along."

Soon after the expedition, Orlando disappeared from Bremer-Kamp's life, so she's never been able to further discuss the premonition with her. Does she herself have any explanation for the dream, and the "visitation" of her children?

"Maybe, somehow, everything is happening at once, the past, the future, the present," she muses. "So you're able to skip from one realm into the other."

Doesn't time move like an arrow in one direction, irreversibly from the past, through the present and into the future? The obvious answer seems to be yes, supported by everything we see and intuit in the world around us. But ideas about time have always been in a state of flux. Medieval man understood two types of time—that of the human realm flowing from the past to the future, and God's time, which is all eternity, with no before or after. In the 1600s Isaac Newton developed his theory of absolute time, which "by its own nature flows uniformly on, without regard to anything external." This held sway until, in the early 1900s, Albert Einstein introduced his special and general theories of relativity and the concept of space-time, a fabric that can be bent, stretched, or compressed. During the same period, a new branch of science was emerging—quantum physics, which studies the behavior of matter at atomic and subatomic scales. One of its founders, Max Planck, speculated about the beginning of the universe, when measurement of its density and heat required incredibly small scales of distance, energy, and time. His attempts to quantify this became known as the Planck scale. The Planck length is the shortest anything can get, and the time it takes for a photon to cross it at the speed of light—about 10^{-43} seconds—is known as the Planck time. In the 1950s, the physicist John Wheeler said that Planck's theories made nonsense of ordinary notions of measurements. If Planck was right, he writes, "So great would be the fluctuations that there would literally be no left and right, no before and after. Ordinary ideas of length would disappear. Ordinary ideas of time would evaporate."

Half a century later, physicists are still puzzling over the implications of the Planck scale. According to recent theories, space and time are not a smooth continuum but are made up of grains, or quanta. Quantum mechanics allow all particles of matter and energy to be described as waves, infinite numbers of which can exist in the same location. So, according to Carlo Rovelli, a French physicist, if time and space consist of quanta, they could all be heaped together in one dimensionless point. At the atomic level, time would disappear.

Does any of this help to explain people apparently being able to see into the future? Most scientists would say conclusively that it doesn't. But Einstein, for one, remained opened to mystery. In 1955, when his close friend Michael Besso died, he sent a consolation letter to Besso's family. "Now he has departed from this curious world a little ahead of me," he wrote. "That means nothing. People like us, who believe in physics, know that the distinction between past, present and future is only a stubbornly persistent illusion."

On an early summer evening in 1984, Ed Webster, a twenty-eight-year-old climbing guide, was chatting with his girlfriend, Lauren Husted, in the apartment they shared in Boulder, Colorado. An avid rock climber, Husted was determined to improve her skills, and was already leading some of the routes she did with Webster in their local mountains. But Webster's ambitions were soaring higher than hers; that evening, he confided his dream of joining a Himalayan expedition. Of climbing Everest.

"I was telling her it was the one thing I really wanted to do," he recalls. "Suddenly she burst out crying and said, 'I'll die before you go to the Himalaya.' I was like—what? I was hugging her, trying to calm her down, but then she got hysterical. She was really losing it, sobbing, rolling on the floor, and I was like, *God, what is wrong?* I kept trying to comfort her, reassuring her that I'd be really careful if I went on an expedition. Finally she turned to me and said, 'I will never be able to tell my dad how much I love him and how much he's done for me.' "

When she calmed down, Webster wiped away Husted's tears, and they talked of other things. Though puzzled by her outburst, he didn't question her further about it.

The following weekend, on the first anniversary of their relationship, they went climbing in Black Canyon, on the Gunnison River. On their very last pitch, when they were two hundred feet below the rim of the canyon, Husted announced that she wanted to free-solo the rest of the climb, without ropes or any form of protection. The day before, they had argued fiercely after she'd made a similar request.

"She had been bugging me about wanting to solo up this crack at the top of the climb," says Webster. "I told her it was a lot harder than it looked and that we had to rope up. She kept insisting she could do it and in the end I got annoyed, and told her that she didn't have a choice. I took the rope and tied the end of it into her harness. I led the pitch, and it was even harder than I expected, eighty or ninety feet high and about 5.8. When we got to the top, she said, 'Well, it was probably a good idea that we roped up.' "

This time, though, it was an easier pitch, a traverse across a series of ledges. Husted was adamant that she wanted to climb it solo. Again, Webster tried to dissuade her; as a climbing guide, with more experience, he felt responsible for her. Eventually, against his better judgment, he gave in.

"She kept saying she'd be fine, and not to worry about her. I was tired and dehydrated. I didn't want another argument. In the end I just threw up my hands mentally and said, 'If you think you'll be okay, let's just do it.' "

Webster went first. Husted was twenty feet behind him. She wore the coiled rope around her neck and chest; he carried the rest of their equipment. He reached the last ledge. The end of the climb was just a few moves away.

"Almost there!" he called to her. "Are you okay?"

"I'm fine, I'm coming," she replied.

Webster watched her reach for the next handhold, a small outcrop of rock. He watched her put her weight on the hold without testing it. Before he could call a warning, the rock broke loose. Husted fell backward, tumbling down the wall of the canyon, out of Webster's sight. He stared at the space she'd left behind.

"It was unbelievable," he says. "Horrifyingly unbelievable."

Frantically, he scrambled to the top of the canyon, then descended via a gully to where Husted lay. Her limbs were splayed out at odd angles. She was unconscious, her breathing was labored, and she was bleeding from several wounds. Some passing hikers ran to get a rescue. But Husted was beyond help. As the sun sank behind the canyon wall, she died in Webster's arms.

Breaking the news to her family was the most difficult task of Ed Webster's life. He called from a pay phone, his girlfriend's blood still on his clothes. Her father answered. Webster could hear laughter in the background—they were having a party in the house, to celebrate Father's Day.

"I had to tell him that his eldest daughter had just died. I will forever hear his cries, echoing in the back of my head."

Just as he will forever wonder about Husted's premonitions. A few months after her fatal fall, he was invited to join an expedition to the Himalayas. By the end of that year, he was climbing on Everest.

Living backward.

Chapter 7

STRANGE INTUITIONS

What [intuition] lacks in precision, it makes up in immediacy. It comes into play when our vital interest is at stake. It pierces the darkness of the night in which our intellect leaves us.

HENRI BERGSON, *The Creative Mind*

M argo Talbot was hiking up to the start of a climb in the Canadian Rockies with her boyfriend, when suddenly she had a strong sense of foreboding.

"I said to him, 'You're going to think I'm crazy but I feel like if I go on this climb today I'm going to die.' We turned around and went back to Canmore. The next day, a woman went up to the route with two male friends. A huge section of ice fell down, and killed her. It happened exactly where we would have been climbing."

It's not uncommon in her world to hear of people who have insisted on turning back on a mountain because of an uneasy feeling. Or of sensing something disastrous—an avalanche, a rockfall—just before it happens.

In 1986, John Porter was fast asleep in his tent at Camp 1 on K2, where he was part of a British expedition to climb the Northeast Ridge. In the middle of the night he suddenly found himself sitting upright, all senses alert.

"I thought, *What's going on, why am I so awake?* The next thing, there was this almighty *Ka-WOOOHMP* and a huge bit of Angel Peak was racing down toward us."

The falling serac missed the camp—but Porter still wonders what it was that alerted him to it, seconds before it sheared off the mountainside.

A feeling, a hunch, a sixth sense—often these are described as intuition. The word comes from the Latin *intueri*—"to look within"—and the Oxford English Dictionary defines it as "immediate apprehension by the mind without reasoning." Carl Jung described intuition as the perception of realities that are unknown to the conscious mind, and said it was one of our four basic functions, along with sensing, feeling, and thinking. It appears to be accessed in different ways: through sudden clear thoughts, through emotions, and through physical sensations. In North America we say we have a "gut feeling" about something; in Japan the term for using one's intuition translates to "stomach art."

While scientists have yet to understand what intuition is and how it works, many people take it very seriously, and use it as a tool that provides information about themselves, other people, and their environment. In 1992, Peter Vegso, the head of HCI, a struggling publishing company, met a writer trying to sell a book of motivational essays, for which to date he'd received scores of rejection letters. Vegso had a good feeling about the writer, and a hunch that he should buy his work. Without even looking at the manuscript, he agreed to publish it. His hunch proved right. The book, *Chicken Soup for the Soul,* went on to sell more than 70 million copies, in thirty-five different languages, and turned HCI into one of the largest publishing houses outside New York. Vegso still follows his gut feelings. He doesn't believe in five- or ten-year plans. He believes in intuition. And he's not alone. A survey conducted in May 2002 by the executive search firm Christian and Timbers revealed that of 601 executives from the Fortune 1000, a list of the top revenue-earning American companies, 45 percent admitted they relied more on intuition than on facts and figures in running their businesses.

Behavioral psychologists class intuitive thinkers as creative, alert, confident, informal, spontaneous, and independent. Such people are not afraid of their experiences and are open to new challenges. They can live with doubt and uncertainty. This is also a comprehensive profile of extreme risk-takers, in both business and adventure.

"When you're entering an area where the unknowns are high and experience is important," says Howard Gardner, professor of cognition and education at Harvard University, "if you don't rely on intuition you're cutting yourself short." And if you're an extreme adventurer, you might be dead.

In the summer of 2000, American climbers Timmy O'Neill and Miles Smart were in the wilds of Pakistan, attempting a one-day speed ascent of Trango Tower, a dramatic granite pinnacle over twenty thousand feet high. They were simu-climbing—attached by rope but climbing at the same time, rather than one leading a pitch while protected by the other. It is a method that offers more speed but gives far less protection in the event of a fall.

They reached a ledge high on the route. Smart looked at the sheer wall looming above them. Turning to O'Neill, he said, "I have this strong feeling that we should go down."

O'Neill didn't question him. They immediately turned around.

"Did I believe in his sense of foreboding?" says O'Neill. "I don't know. What I thought at the time was, he was tired, we still had a long way to go, he was concerned about getting to the top at night, and getting stuck. We had hardly any food or water with us, we were lightly dressed and had no bivouac gear. If a storm blew in, it could have killed us. So I respected his desire to go down."

The following day they went back up the wall.

"There we were, high in the Himalayas, as remote as it gets, climbing in rock shoes," O'Neill recounts. "We were pared down to the minimum in one of the most barren, inhospitable environments in the world. It was sketchy. Earlier in the day, ice had been falling past us, from where the sun was hitting it higher on the face. But we were kicking ass, pumped up, yelling at each other about how we were about to do the first one-day ascent of this peak."

O'Neill had almost reached their previous high point. He was climbing on smooth rock that offered only tiny cracks into which he placed "stoppers," aluminum nuts attached to loops of wire. He wedged each nut into a crack, and attached a small webbing stirrup to the loop. These stirrups became his footholds, on which he balanced precariously, high-stepping from one to another. For protection, he was clipping into the stoppers with his "daisy chain," a webbing strap sewn across at two-inch intervals, which was attached to his harness. Smart was still jumaring up the last pitch, so O'Neill's only other point of protection was the anchor that his rope was attached to, a hundred feet below.

"I was on an incipient parallel crack, very hard to free-climb," says O'Neill. "I placed a stopper, stood up on it, put another one in, stood on that. I had to move fast, I was like a frenetic spider running up the rock. I saw a piece from the previous day's climb that Miles had left in. I clipped into it with my daisy chain. I didn't test it. I thought it was fixed. As I put my weight on it I felt it pull out of the crack."

He fell twelve feet to a narrow ledge, bounced off it, and flew past Smart. As he sped through space, he wondered if the anchor his rope was attached to would hold, and stop his fall, or shear out of the rock, sending him thousands of feet to his death. It held.

Did he also consider the fact that he fell from very close to the point where Smart had his premonition the previous day?

"No. And I didn't sense anything before I fell, except the danger I was in. I was thinking that I should be on belay. I was having an inner dialogue—run the belay, run the belay. I didn't do it. I made the decision to forgo it and keep going for the sake of speed."

His big failing, he says, was not to listen to his intuition, that "inner dialogue." As well as being a climber, O'Neill is a white-water kayaker, a highliner, a BASE jumper, and a paraglider. In all of these activities, he pushes his limits. And relies on his intuition.

"It's the exposing of the nerve so that when something happens you feel it immediately and react. You need the same rawness whether you're highlining or free-soloing or about to drop in on a Class Five rapid. I use my intuition so much, it's on my desktop, a common application that I open all the time. I use it to read and assess a rock face or a river or the wind. It's almost like telepathy. Intuition is part of your aura. Your vibe. It's more of an essence than empirical evidence."

The pilot and high-altitude skydiver Cheryl Sterns calls her intuition "an angel that sometimes sits on my shoulder and talks to me." When it speaks, she's learned to listen.

"I had a problem once with my Cessna airplane," she says. "I was on the ground and I should have been taking off but I had a gut feeling, my guts were literally churning, something was telling me that I shouldn't go. I kept trying to persuade myself to just take off, but inside I was getting torn up. Something was bugging me really badly.

So I put down a lot of money to get a really good mechanic to come and check out the plane. He found a serious maintenance problem with the wing. If I'd flown, it would have come off within one or two hours. The guy I'd bought the plane from hadn't had it rebuilt properly, but there was no way you could have known that unless you went inside for a really in-depth check."

Was there something subliminal that Sterns was picking up—a faint noise or some slight reverberation in the wing registering with her at the subconscious level? She doesn't know. It was simply a feeling, one she can't explain and doesn't question.

Rupert Sheldrake suggests that intuition could be a type of early warning system, built into our biological system, which prepares us for emergencies with inner cues. He has a large database of stories from people who sensed something disastrous was going to happen and acted upon it—such as hitting the brakes of a car just as the vehicle in front crashes or swerves out of control. He believes this is a common phenomenon in fast sports, like downhill skiing, when people are responding too fast to actually see what is happening and react to it by the normal means.

In the wild, animals use such "early warning systems" all the time, responding to changing weather conditions, deciding where is safe to go hunting, and figuring out how to avoid predators. Natural selection ensures that the most intuitive animals will thrive and survive longest. Before Karsten Heuer and Leanne Allison set out from the settlement of Old Crow on their long trek to follow the Porcupine caribou, some Gwich'in elders told them that caribou have the ability to predict the future. Some years earlier, they said, the caribou had set off as usual on the fall migration, across the Porcupine River near Old Crow and south to their wintering grounds below the tree line. In late October, suddenly they all returned. They went north across the river and stayed there as winter came on, as if they were start-ing the spring migration. Everyone in Old Crow was perplexed. This had never happened before. Two months later, in January, there was an unusual warming trend. Heavy rain fell and everywhere south of the Porcupine River, including the caribou's usual wintering ground, was encased in an unbreakable glaze of ice. The animals couldn't dig through to get to lichens and grass. There was a high mortality rate among moose. The area the caribou had gone to a couple of months before, however, was spared the rain; they were able to get to their food. They survived.

For thousands of years there have been accounts of animals antici-pating natural events, particularly earthquakes. In 373 B.C., rats, snakes, and weasels were reported fleeing the Greek city of Helice, days before it was flattened by an earthquake. Since then, stories have been recounted of both domestic and wild animals behaving strangely in the days before a quake—chickens stop laying eggs, bees leave their hives, catfish flail about in the water, dogs bark for no reason, cats run away, horses kick at their stable doors. In 1974, more than a million people were ordered to evacuate the city of Haicheng, in Lia-oning Province, China, because of a rare series of small earth tremors coupled with wide-scale reports of strange animal behavior. Within hours, there was an earthquake of 7.3 on the Richter scale. Ninety percent of the city's buildings were destroyed, and, over the whole area, a total of two thousand people were hurt or killed—far fewer than if the city had been populated at the time. A year later, another earthquake struck the city of Tang Shan; despite similar geological and animal signs, no evacuation was called for, and more than a quar-ter of a million people perished. The Chinese Seismological Bureau now welcomes reports of unusual behavior in animals. Ashan Zoo in Liaoning Province and a network of zoos in Shanghai run animal seismology programs, keeping close watch on the inmates for any changes in their usual patterns.

After the Asian tsunami in December 2004, Rupert Sheldrake collected accounts of animals' behavior shortly before the catastrophe. Elephants in Sri Lanka, Sumatra, and Thailand were seen to leave coastal regions and head for higher ground. At Galle, in Sri Lanka, some dog owners said their pets had refused to go for their morning walk that day, and at Ao Sane beach in Thailand dogs went running up to hill tops. A villager in Bang Koey, Thailand, said that a herd of buffalo were grazing by the beach when they suddenly lifted their heads and stared out to sea, their ears upright.

Theories proposed by scientists to explain such phenomena include animals being able to pick up ultrasounds emitted as microseisms from fracturing rock deep in the earth, and being sensitive to variations in the earth's magnetic fields, which occur near the epicenter of earthquakes. These changes activate the fear centers of their brains, sending them into flight mode.

Can humans also pick up subtle signals of environmental changes? After a massive earthquake and tsunami hit the Solomon Islands in early 2007, there were reports of children from the village of Gizo, near the epicenter of the quake, uncharacteristically deciding not to go swimming that morning, and fishermen suddenly turning for home in their dugout canoes because of the "strange currents" they noticed in the ocean. In both instances, these intuitions saved their lives.

"Intuition is about our body translating the energy it picks up," says Marlene Smith, a veterinarian and a mountaineer who lives on Vancouver Island. "Animals listen to those physical messages, but most humans reason them away."

In 1974, Smith was in the Russian Pamirs, climbing Lenin Peak with a Dutch expedition. They were at their high camp, preparing to go for the 24,000 foot summit, when Smith had a panic attack. "It was around five o'clock one morning," she recalls. "My whole being was screaming at me, that I had to get off the mountain. There was no apparent reason for it, but I couldn't control the fear, I was like an animal, I just had to flee."

As she threw her gear together, the rest of the team tried to dissuade her, saying it was only the altitude, and the prospect of going for the summit, that was making her afraid. But she wouldn't listen. She raced down the mountain, and only when she reached Base Camp did her panic subside.

Early the next morning, she was roused from sleep by an unnatural silence. Not far from Base Camp there was a group of shepherds, and usually, at daybreak, their dogs were barking and howling. But now there was a strange stillness. Not just among the animals, but in the atmosphere, the air. "It was almost as if the river had stopped flowing," says Smith.

She was dozing, half in and half out of sleep, when the ground began to rock.

"I remember thinking that I was in a boat. Then I snapped awake, and heard people shouting from the other tents, *Earthquake, earthquake!*"

She was outside in a flash. "The mountain was swaying," she says. "We could see the avalanches popping off all over its slopes. By then, the dogs were barking like crazy."

The earthquake was 7.8 on the Richter scale. The ice and snow it shook off Lenin Peak trapped scores of climbers. Then a storm moved in. It was four days before the rest of Smith's team could descend to safety. Thirteen climbers perished on the mountain, including an entire team of eight Soviet female climbers.

During an exploratory expedition to K2 in 1938, Dr. Charlie

Houston was trekking from Base Camp up the glacier that is now called the Baltoro, along with a British climber, Norman Streatfield, and three Hunza porters. They had reached nineteen thousand feet and were walking along a fairly flat section of the glacier, which was about two miles wide, when they heard some strange sounds that seemed to come from the top of the mountain.

"It was not wind, and it was not avalanche," says Houston. "It was not creaky ice or any of things you usually hear in the mountains. This sounded like howls or moans. We all heard them."

The porters were afraid. They said the sounds were made by a yeti, and that it was warning them to get out of that place. They wanted to turn back, or to hurry on as fast as they could. Houston and Streatfield shrugged this off as superstition.

"We didn't pay much attention. We didn't believe in the yeti. But the porters were insistent; they said the sounds were a warning that this was a very dangerous place for us to be. They made us hurry."

Over the next few days, as they looked for a route to the summit, Houston thought no more of the sounds. But on their way back to Base Camp, when they reached the point where they had heard the howling, they saw that an avalanche had come down from Broad Peak, sweeping clean across the glacier.

"It had been enormous," said Houston. "If we'd stayed there after we'd heard the sounds, we would have been wiped out."

Houston is a scientist, renowned, among other things, for his work on high-altitude medicine and for building an early model of the artificial heart. He's a rational thinker. What did he think about the whole incident?

"The sounds were not a hallucination. Hallucinations are common higher up, we know a lot about them, we know that they are due to high-altitude cerebral edema. This was something different. We all heard the sounds. The porters warned us. The avalanche happened. These are the facts. I can't explain them."

I n 1985, Carlos Carsolio was climbing Nanga Parbat with a Polish team, attempting the south spur of the Rupal Face, the biggest mountain wall in the world. Conditions were dreadful, with blizzards so dense that often the men lost sight of each other. Throughout the ascent they communicated by two-way radio, and their conversations were recorded by people at Base Camp. Before they reached the top of the face, their food and fuel ran out. During their desperate descent, they all felt very close to death.

Back at Base Camp, as they recovered from the ordeal, they listened to the recordings of their conversations. They were shocked. The Polish climbers spoke no Spanish and Carsolio spoke no Polish, so normally they conversed in English. During the final part of their ascent, however, and on the way down the mountain, they had all been speaking in their native languages. Listening to the tapes, the Poles couldn't understand Carsolio and he couldn't understand them.

"But when we were up there we had understood each other perfectly," says Carsolio. "We had opened some channels, to another level of communication."

Carsolio believes it was a form of telepathy, which, like other paranormal phenomena he has experienced, happens under conditions of focus, fear, and suffering.

"When a climb was not so demanding I never had these experiences. But when it was really extreme, especially when you were on the edge of dying, somehow in that moment, *Poof!* The channel is open."

According to Rupert Sheldrake, telepathy—gathering information from others in real time, even at a distance—is a form of intuition. He claims there are two main types of telepathy. The first is thought transference, which usually occurs between people who have some sort of bond, are spatially fairly close, and aware of the other's presence. The second is typified by "distress calls" between people who have a very strong bond.

The term "telepathy"—*tele* = distant, *pathy* = feeling—was coined in the 1880s by Frederic Myers, a fellow of Cambridge University and one of the founders of the Society for Psychical Research. He defined it as "the communication of impressions of any kind from one mind to another, independent of the recognized channels of sense."

His work was developed in the 1930s by Professor J. B. Rhine, who became interested in the paranormal while he was doing graduate work in biology at Harvard University. Dissatisfied with both materialistic scientific philosophy and orthodox religion, he was longing to investigate "any challenging fact that might hold possibilities of new insight into human personality and its relations to the universe." Then he attended a lecture by Sir Arthur Conan Doyle, about his experiences with spirit mediums after the death of his son. Rhine had found his "challenging fact."

Rhine was skeptical by nature. With his wife, who was also a biologist, he spent years looking through data collected by the American Society for Psychical Research, "trying to sort out the occasional grain of truth from the unusable chaff that makes up the great part of spiritualistic writing." Eventually he landed a post in the psychology department of Duke University, where he became involved in a study of telepathy and clairvoyance.

Rhine was determined that the newly created field of parapsychology should be a regular laboratory science, using rigorous experimental methods. He designed a program of scientific study into the ability of people to access information through channels other than the five known senses, calling these channels extrasensory perception—ESP. He and his colleagues invented the Zener cards, each displaying one of five symbols: a circle, a cross, a square, a star, and three wavy lines, which are matched to random numbers. For a telepathy test, after the pack is shuffled, the subject has to guess the sequence of the cards while an experimenter looks at them. For a precognition test, the subject tries to guess the sequence before the pack is shuffled.

Many years later, the astronaut Edgar Mitchell became interested in the idea that spiritual and physical realities meet in paranormal phenomena. During the *Apollo 14* mission in 1971, he used Zener cards in secretly arranged telepathic experiments with a group of collaborators in Florida. At prearranged times, twice on the way to the moon and twice on the way back, he matched each Zener card with a random number, then concentrated on the symbols for fifteen seconds while his collaborators—two research physicists and two psychics—attempted to intuit the same sequence. Of the two hundred sequences Mitchell completed, forty correct matches was seen as the probable result if left to chance. Two of the recipients matched fifty-one sequences correctly, which greatly exceeded Mitchell's expectations.

When news of the experiments was leaked to the press, there was negative reaction. An American hero, involved in activities that smacked of the occult! Mitchell was unfazed. Paranormal experiences, he said later, were "no more amazing or mystical than the phenomena of a creative thought spontaneously arising in the mind. We all experience the latter and accept it as natural, but we have not all experienced the former and thus such events seem bizarre."

In the 1960s, Montague Ullman and his colleagues carried out laboratory tests on dream telepathy, working with sleeping subjects in soundproofed laboratories. When a subject entered the REM stage of sleep, a sender—sometimes up to forty-five miles away—tried to transmit images. Toward the end of each dreaming period the subject was awakened and asked to recall her dreams. Based on a technique called "meta analysis," widely used in medicine, in which the results of many different studies are combined, the hit rate of the dream telepathy trials was 63 percent, compared with 50 percent expected by chance.

A decade later, the Ganzfeld telepathy tests were developed. A subject lies in a relaxed state while someone in a different building looks at photos and tries to transmit the images telepathically to the subject, who is asked to verbalize the images she is seeing in her mind. The success rate expected by chance is 25 percent. Of all the Ganzfeld experiments conducted between 1974 and 1985, the success rate was 37 percent, with an even better score occurring when the sender and receiver knew each other well.

Despite these figures, such experiments are regarded with much skepticism by the mainstream scientific community. Yet, claims Rupert Sheldrake, they are among the most rigorous and heavily monitored fields of research in the whole of science.

"The experiments have proved repeatable," he says. "They have been independently replicated in several different countries; they are continuing to give impressive results. The effects are fairly small, but nevertheless they are clear, showing big odds against chance."

His comments are backed by the work of Dr. Jessica Utts, a statistician based at the University of California. In 1995, Utts was hired by the American Institute of Research to examine the results of two decades of government-sponsored experiments on psychic phenomena, particularly remote viewing, done on behalf of the CIA. She was impressed by the thoroughness of the methodology, as well as by the results. According to Utts's meta-analysis of the studies, in remote viewing the subject could identify the target correctly 34 percent of the time.

"Using that standard applied to any other area of science," she writes, "it is concluded that psychic functioning has been well established. The statistical results of the studies examined are far beyond what is expected by chance.... The magnitude of psychic functioning exhibited appears to be in the range between what social scientists call a small and medium effect. That means it is reliable enough to be replicated in properly conducted experiments with sufficient trials to achieve the long-run statistical results needed for replicability."

Even if tests such as Ganzfeld indicate that telepathy does appear to happen, they don't shed light on how it happens. Rupert Sheldrake believes he might have an answer for that with his extended-mind theory. The mind, he says, stretches out beyond the brain through a system of mental fields that link organisms to their environment and to each other. While he admits that this is highly speculative, with no scientific proof to back it, he states the importance of developing a theory of the "extended mind" rather than just accepting the conventional view of a "contracted mind" inside the skull.

"Mental fields go beyond, through, and interface with the electromagnetic patterns in our brain," he writes. "In this way mental fields can affect our bodies through our brains. However, they are much more extensive than our brains, reaching out to great distances in some cases.... With a mental field...we have a medium for a whole series of connections between us and the people, places and animals we know and care about—with the rest of the world, in fact."

Telepathy, says Sheldrake, is a natural phenomenon, a normal channel of communication between members of a social group who are bonded to each other in some way.

"When two people come into contact and establish some mental connections (perhaps experienced as affection, love, even hate), their morphic fields in effect become part of a larger, inclusive field. Then, if they separate from each other it is as if their particular portions of the morphic field are stretched elastically, so that there remains a 'mental tension' or link between them."

It would be hard to find two people who know each other better, and have interacted with each other more in stressful situations, than the identical twins and Himalayan climber partners Alan and Adrian Burgess.

"When we were younger, Adrian and I tuned into each other a lot," says Alan Burgess. "Like when we were on Dhaulagiri, just the two of us, in 1981. We didn't have walkie-talkie radios with us. We got to the top at one in the afternoon and we descended in a storm. It was really tricky going down, and it took us six hours. We were totally in tune. We didn't have to shout across to each other. There was no panic. And yet there was reason to panic, at over 26,000 feet in a storm with any other people so far away."

The twins don't believe they were in telepathic communication on the mountain. Being so in tune, they claim, was the result of years spent in the mountains together, developing "a well-oiled climbing team," rather than anything paranormal.

Other stories they recount, however, point to something that goes beyond good team work. Like the time Adrian was skiing off piste in the Alps, caught a twig in his downhill ski, and had a bad fall.

"The fall ripped my right anterior ligament," he says. "I was in agony. This was long before Alan and I could telephone each other often, and there was no e-mail back then. When I finally spoke to him, I found out he had torn his left anterior cruciate during that exact same week, while cross-country skiing."

What did he think this meant?

"Basically, that neither me nor Alan could ski well enough," laughs Adrian. "But it *was* weird. We were both limping, one on the left leg and the other on the right leg."

Alan has another story. "I climbed Logan once without Adrian. I was on the Southwest Buttress, going alpine-style. We didn't have radios with us. The guy who had flown us into the mountain did a flyby to check on us. He went over the place where he thought we should have camped and saw that there had been a big ice collapse. We had left there by then but he didn't know that, and he reported us missing, presumed dead. Some press contacted Adrian; this was the first he heard of it. They asked him for a comment. Apparently, he paused and said firmly, 'Alan is not dead.' End of discussion. Another time, a few years ago, I was guiding a group and we were trekking toward the Kumbu Valley in Nepal. When we were at about eighteen thousand feet, a storm dumped six feet of snow in thirty-six hours. So we didn't arrive in the Kumbu on time and there were rumors that we'd been avalanched and I was dead. Adrian found out when a climbing magazine called him and asked if he'd heard from me. They told him the rumors and said that nine times out of ten, when you get rumors like these, they are true. Again, Adrian thought about it and said, 'No, he's not dead.' He just knew that, for sure."

In other words, if Alan had been in great distress, and approaching death, his brother would have picked up on it through the "distress call" type of telepathic communication, which occurs between people who have very strong bonds.

Patricia Culver, from Vancouver, British Columbia, describes how she and her husband, the mountaineer Dan Culver, discovered a telepathic connection when he failed to return from a climb in the Coast Mountain Range, in 1994.

"Dan had only gone out climbing for the day, and I was expecting him back for dinner," she says. "When it got to nine o'clock and he wasn't home, I began to really worry. I started thinking about all the things that could have happened to him, and before long, I was pacing the apartment in a panic. To calm myself I sat down and tried to meditate. Suddenly this whole wave of information came in from Dan. There was nothing audible, just a feeling that he was saying, 'I'm okay, I'll call you tomorrow.' I still wasn't sure, I was worried all night. The phone rang next morning. It was Dan; he explained that they'd run into bad conditions, it got dark, and they decided the safest thing to do was bivouac. He said, 'By the way, did you get my message?' He told me that around nine thirty the night before, when he was settled into the bivouac, he concentrated all his thoughts on me and told me he was okay and that he'd call in the morning as soon as he could get to a pay phone. And I said, 'Yup I got it!' It was astonishing to us that it worked."

In January 1997, Tony Bullimore was two months into the Vendée Globe around-the-world singlehanded yacht race, when his boat, *Exide Challenger*, was overturned by storm waves in the Southern Ocean. Bullimore was trapped for almost five days under the hull. When the news came through that the upturned boat had been spotted in huge seas, most people held out little hope for his survival. But his wife, Lalel, insisted he was still alive. She said it was something she could feel in her stomach. Kneeling by her bed in the middle of the night, she started to communicate with her husband. He told her the storm had been terrible, that the boat had rolled over, that he was inside the hull. He said he was warm enough, and that he had food and water. They talked until he said he was tired, and had to sleep for a while. She made him promise he'd wake up.

The following day she talked to him again. "Oh Lal, I'm in a mess," he told her. "It's wet. The boat won't stop rolling. I'm cold."

She told him to hang on, that a rescue boat was on the way. "You're a tough little man, Tony Bullimore," she encouraged him. "Don't you dare go and leave me behind. Don't you dare."

By the next day, Bullimore was drifting in and out of consciousness. Lying in the freezing water, staring into the darkness, he had a sudden vision. An Australian warship was on its way to him. He saw it churning through the waves. He saw a small boat being lowered. He heard people hammering on his hull, trying to make contact with him. He saw himself diving, swimming under the boat then up to the surface. Twenty-four hours later, that is exactly what happened.

Of all telepathic phenomena, that between mothers and babies is perhaps the most widely reported. In nursing mothers, breast milk becomes available for babies through the "let-down reflex," a physiological process mediated by oxytocin, a hormone produced in the pituitary gland. When "let down" occurs, the mother often feels a tingling sensation in her breast, and her nipples begin to leak milk. It is usually stimulated by hearing the baby's cry, but many nursing mothers claim that it can happen when they are too far away to hear the child.

"There is a strong natural-selection element in this bond between mothers and babies, which occurs in all mammals," says Rupert

Sheldrake. "When mammalian mothers are out of earshot of their babies, if they can pick up on their needs and respond to them, the babies have a better chance of survival."

Leanne Allison still feels a strong telepathic connection with her son, Zev, who was born two years after she and Karsten Heuer completed their expedition to follow the Porcupine caribou herd. On that trip, they believe, the rigors of sleep deprivation, physical effort, and intense concentration opened them up to a magical realm, where they could see into the future and were in communication with the caribou. Allison claims the experiences she has had with Zev are just as powerful and mysterious.

"If Zev's getting into trouble in another room, I always get a sense of that. When he was a baby he slept with us in our bed and I always woke up moments before he did, with a strong sense of what he needed."

Mainstream scientists explain this as a physiological component that we share with other mammals. Built into the sleeping state are periods of cortical arousal producing an alertness to certain external stimuli—so, even when deeply asleep, the mother has an auditory channel open, tuned into her infant. But Allison believes it's about more than that.

"There is no greater opportunity to be more animal than when you're giving birth. And mothering—it's not carrying a sixty-pound pack for months or dealing with the rigors of documenting a wilderness trip, but the energy required, the unrelenting nature of it, the sleep deprivation—there is a similar intensity. And from that comes a similar level of intuition."

Michael Thalbourne, a psychologist at the University of Adelaide, has suggested that people who believe they have powers such as telepathy and precognition might simply be accessing information stored in their subconscious. He calls this process "transliminality"—when information in the subconscious "leaks" through to the conscious mind after being stimulated by something in the environment. Such subconscious information, he believes, can be interpreted as psychic abilities.

He designed a questionnaire to measure transliminality, asking subjects if they have ever had a heightened awareness of sights and sounds, and if they feel they ever received some sort of "special wisdom." In 2002, researchers at Goldsmiths College, University of London, tried to demonstrate his theory, using computerized Zener cards. The subjects sat in front of a screen displaying the back of a card and pressed one key to choose which of the five Zener symbols they thought was on the other side, then another key to turn it over. Unbeknown to them, before the card's back was shown, its face was flashed on the screen for 14.8 milliseconds, too fast for most people to register. But some participants appeared to subconsciously pick up on the clue, as they scored better than chance at predicting which symbol would appear. They also turned out to be the people who scored best on Thalbourne's transliminality questionnaire. This, he says, demonstrates how access to subconscious information can give the appearance of and belief in the powers of psychic abilities. His conclusion is that the better someone is at tuning into their subconscious, the more likely they are to believe in the paranormal.

Such people also seem to be better at perceiving patterns in apparently chaotic images—such as images of the Virgin Mary in the rust on a metal fence or on the brick wall of a Tim Horton's building. Peter Brugger, a neuroscientist at the University Hospital in Zurich, Switzerland, has done research on people who can perceive patterns in apparently random images or noise. He thinks they are committing what statisticians call a Type 1 error, perceiving a pattern when none exists. A Type 2 error is when someone fails to recognize a pattern when it does exist, because they are too skeptical. Brugger points out that pattern recognition is a vital skill, allowing us to recognize camouflaged predators or familiar faces. From an evolutionary perspective, he says, it is safest to err on the side of gullibility. "If you miss the tiger hiding in the grass, you're dead. If you're always seeing tigers, you're running away a lot, but you're not dead."

In the account of his epic climb of Annapurna, Maurice Herzog writes, "There is a supernatural power in those close to death. Strange intuitions identify one with the whole world."

For Shaun Ellison, this intuition came through a look exchanged with one of his best friends and a fellow BASE jumper. BASE is an acronym for the type of objects the participants use as their "exit points": buildings, antennae, spans (bridges), and earth (cliffs). Ellison, who was already an accomplished skydiver, took up the sport in his thirties. His first jump was from a 460-foot-high bridge in Twin Falls, Idaho. He went on to jump from the top of buildings and electric antennae. Then he graduated to cliffs in the Alps. BASE jumping, says Ellison, is very different from jumping out of a plane.

"When you exit an aircraft at fourteen thousand feet, everything on the ground looks flat, buildings look the same as fields. You have no dimension of height. You crack your chute open and then it's hang time, when the ground is coming slowly toward you. But with BASE jumps, because you are closer to the ground, and you're tracking and moving away from the object you've jumped from, the ground is zipping by beneath you and it's more like flying."

It's far more dangerous than skydiving, too. If the jumper has the wrong body position, when the canopy opens it can spin and swing him into the object—which might be okay if it's a bridge, but not if it's a big building or a cliff.

"Most accidents happen because people are scared," says Ellison. "Their body position is wrong, they're panicking, they open the parachute early. You've got to fight your demons to the point that when you exit you're calm."

Ellison, now in his early forties, has trained some of the most high-profile BASE jumpers in Britain, but he shuns the limelight himself. He doesn't seek publicity or big sponsorship. He doesn't prop up the bar telling people about his exploits. In his house there isn't a single photograph of him BASE jumping, skydiving, or climbing.

"I don't do any of it for those reasons," he says. "The gains of risking my life are far higher than that."

For him, those gains are spiritual. And because of this, he's no longer interested in jumping from man-made objects.

"Running along a bridge and throwing myself off it onto a tarmac road—there's a massive difference between that and jumping big cliffs in beautiful places. You can't compare the rewards. The connection with nature gives me the third dimension that makes it worth risking my life jumping off a cliff."

In 2003, he went to Baffin Island in the Arctic for his biggest BASE-jumping challenge—The Beak, a cliff more than three thousand feet high. With his companions he flew in a small plane to the remote settlement of Clyde River. From there, some Inuit guides took the group on a six-hour trip by Ski-Doos to the opening of Sam Ford Fjord. They arranged to pick them up in three weeks, and then zoomed away. When the sounds of their engines had faded in the distance, Ellison found himself in an otherworldly landscape. A frozen sea, with huge granite cliffs rising sheer from it for thousands of feet. A ringing silence. And brain-numbing temperatures of −35 degrees Fahrenheit.

On the first day of their trip, Ellison twisted his knee during a climb. For the next week, while his friends were ascending and then jumping off granite spires, he was forced to rest at Base Camp. But he didn't mind too much—he sat quietly, absorbing the majestic surroundings and the total isolation. Eventually, when his knee felt strong enough, he joined his friends to climb The Beak. He reached the top. He let the others jump first. He was in no hurry.

"I stood there for twenty minutes on my own. I knew that if something went wrong, there was no way I could get help. Our radio didn't work anymore. And even if it did, no helicopter could get in there for five days. That knowledge made the jump I was going to do more intense. Yet I was so calm. To say that you're calm just before running off a three-thousand-foot cliff sounds like madness, but it isn't. I was opening myself up to the environment, to nature, to the energy around me. It felt incredibly peaceful."

He jumped. He dropped at a rate of 120 miles an hour, the noise in his ears like a jet engine accelerating. He remembers the experience as "euphoric."

"I was on a different plane, where there were things going on around me, channels opening that are closed in day-to-day life. That's the key to BASE jumping, to learn how to be on that plane in free fall, to stay in that beautiful place. Because once you land, you zap back into reality."

One of Ellison's teammates on Baffin Island was his close friend Duane Thomas, a New Zealander. A year later they were in the Swiss valley of Lauterbrunnen, a mecca for BASE jumping because of the twelve excellent "exit points" on top of its cliffs. Thomas was going to jump in a "wing suit," which incorporates large webs of material under each arm and between the legs, allowing the jumper to literally fly, tracking horizontally from the exit point and lengthening the time of the free fall. A negative aspect of this is that the low fall rate and accelerated horizontal speeds can fool the jumper into believing he is higher than he actually is. Thomas had done fifty jumps in his wing suit from aircraft, and two from a hot-air balloon, but this was to be his first from a cliff.

Ellison and Thomas were assisting two other athletes, Leo Holding and Tim Emmet, on their first BASE jumps in the mountains. They had all just gone off a 1,600-foot cliff and were on the valley floor, packing up their parachutes. Holding and Emmet were learning how to pack, so the process was taking longer than usual. Suddenly Thomas became impatient. He decided he would go on ahead of them to the cliff from where he planned to do his wing-suit jump.

"Just before he got in the car, I went over and shook his hand," Ellison recalls. "It just wasn't something I'd normally do. As a rule, he'd get in the car and say, 'See you later,' and I'd say, 'Right, have a good one.' But something made me go over and grab his hand."

Thomas also reacted in a way that was also totally out of character. He stared fiercely at his friend and snapped, "Don't ever look at me like that again."

Ellison tried to laugh it off. "You okay, mate?" Thomas didn't respond. He got into the car and drove away.

Holding and Emmet were keen to follow Thomas and watch the whole jump.

"I kept saying, 'No, let's keep packing, we can see the start of his jump from here,'" Ellison recalls. "I was really insistent. 'No, we're not going to watch the whole thing.'"

They saw Thomas run off the exit point. Then he went out of sight. Seconds later, Ellison's cell phone rang. It was one of their team, yelling down the line. Thomas had opened his chute far too late. He had hit the ground with a terrible, fatal force.

When your eyes lock on those of another person, says Ellison, sometimes what you see is a mirror of yourself. *Don't ever look at me like that again.* Thirty minutes after Thomas uttered those words, he was dead. Ellison believes he had a premonition of his friend's death, that it showed in his eyes, that Thomas saw it, and that it confirmed what, at some level, he already knew.

"Duane was scared of nothing. Normally when he was BASE jumping he would suit up, turn around, say to the guy filming, 'Are you ready?' and just run off. But on that day it took him five or six minutes to psych himself to get off the cliff. I believe he knew something wasn't right."

When Thomas was still at a reasonable altitude, both the man videoing him from the top of the cliff and his team on the ground saw him reach back to deploy his parachute. They saw his hand on the pilot chute. But he just left it there. Instead of pulling it open, he continued to free-fall. People started yelling at him, "PULL! PULL!" When he did so, it was too late.

Maybe he was mesmerized by the sense of really flying, tracking through air. Maybe he was waiting for the ground rush that you get with ordinary BASE jumping. But his hand was there, ready, and he didn't pull. A man who had already done several hundred BASE jumps. What happened?

"Something went on in the lead-up to that jump that wasn't normal for Duane," said Ellison. "His wife said he got hardly any sleep the night before. There was what he said to me, and then his hesitation at the exit point. You could put it down to nerves but I don't believe it was just that. I believe that he had a premonition, and so did I. I think we were both tapping into other levels of consciousness."

An early warning. Ignored. A Type 2 error—fatal.

Chapter 8

SPIRIT FRIENDS

*We must accept our reality as vastly as we possibly can; every-
thing, even the unprecedented, must be possible within it. This
in the end is the only kind of courage that is required of us: the
courage to find the strangest, most unusual, most inexplicable
experiences that can meet us. The fact that in this sense people
have been cowardly has done infinite harm to life; the experiences that are called "apparitions," the whole so-called "spirit"
world, death, all these Things that are so closely related to us,
have through our daily defensiveness been so entirely pushed out
of life that the senses with which we might have been able to
grasp them have atrophied.*

RAINER MARIA RILKE, *Letters to a Young Poet*

The little black elf was sitting on the wing, facing him. With one
hand it was playing with the canard, threatening to pull it in the
wrong direction and send the plane into a downward spiral. Don't
worry, it assured Dick Rutan. You've already died. You fell asleep and

crashed into a mountain. You're in transition between life and death, this is normal. Relax, go to sleep now, come with me.

Rutan had been flying for over twenty-four hours, shuttling back and forth over Owens Valley in the Sierra Nevadas in a tiny experimental plane, trying to set a closed-course distance record. It was his first long-range flight. After working on the plane for most of the night, he had set off at dawn. The plane had no autopilot, so he was required to maintain a state of constant concentration. He had ten more hours to go.

Part of his brain urged him to lay his head on the control panel, close his eyes, and let the elf take over. Another part ordered him to take control. He wiped his face with a cold rag, he sniffed smelling salts, but the elf remained. And soon he had more company.

"I saw a spacecraft," recalls Rutan. "It was big and complicated with little gray men looking at me from its windows. When I turned my head to see it better it would pull up and go away. If I looked straight ahead I could see the spacecraft in my peripheral vision, with all its intricate details. There were airplanes as well, dogfighting me from behind, and a big battle going on down on the ground. I could hear beautiful loud organ music. I had no idea what the hell was happening."

This occurred in 1979. Has he come up with an explanation since then?

"I don't believe in any spiritual crap," he says bluntly. But his journey, he notes, took exactly the same number of hours as Charles Lindbergh's 1927 nonstop transatlantic solo flight in the *Spirit of St. Louis*. During that flight, Lindbergh was also visited by what he described as "phantoms."

"When I'm staring at the instruments," he wrote, "during an unearthly age of time, both conscious and asleep, the fuselage behind me becomes filled with ghostly presences—vaguely outlined forms, transparent, moving, riding weightless with me in the plane.... These phantoms speak with human voices...they are friendly, vapor-like shapes without substance, able to vanish or appear at will, to pass in and out through the walls of the fuselage as though no walls were there....I feel no surprise at their coming....Without turning my head I see them as clearly as though in my normal field of vision."

Lindbergh believed these visions were "emanations from the experience of ages, inhabitants of a universe closed to mortal men." They spoke to him, helped him with his navigation during the hardest part of the flight, then disappeared.

In 1986, Dick Rutan completed the first nonstop flight around the world, in the *Voyager* aircraft. When the *Voyager* was empty, it weighed only 939 pounds. At takeoff, it was loaded with seventeen tanks of fuel, increasing its weight by ten times and compromising its fragile structure. Rutan spent nine days in the air, flying 26,366 miles, usually working in two- to three-hour shifts with his copilot Jeana Yeager. Resting between shifts was difficult, as the cockpit was the size of a phone booth, too small for either of them to comfortably lie down. Storm fronts, including the six-hundred-mile-wide typhoon Marge, forced them to change direction a number of times. The controls were precise, needing careful monitoring, and Rutan was constantly anxious about the possibility of a total systems failure. A week into the flight, on the leg from Africa to Brazil, he opted to fly the plane throughout the night while Yeager tried to catch up on rest. After hours of flying, he was looking out at the oceanscape when he had the sense of his mind closing down.

"It was as if part of my consciousness turned off. I looked at my right hand, the hand I controlled the airplane with, and I had no idea what it would do. I knew the control stick was there but I had no idea what it did or what any of the other controls and the systems of the plane were for. And I didn't care."

Something broke through: a fleeting feeling of alarm. He turned to speak to Yeager, who luckily woke and heard him just as he passed out.

"Moments like that, and seeing the elf on the wing, they scared the heck out of me. I had to know why these things happen, so that I could deal with them on long flights."

He contacted scientists who were doing research on jet lag, circadian rhythms, and long-duration man-machine interface. He learned about the break-off phenomena—a disassociative reaction that occasionally happens to pilots flying at high altitude, thought to be caused by a combination of low sensory input and the visual confusion of a deep blue sky above and the lack of a marked horizon. Open-ocean kayakers have described a similar sensation, a "kayak dizziness" experienced when sea and sky merge and they lose sense of what is up and down. For pilots, however, it's far more extreme. According to a report by the RAF Institute of Aviation Medicine, about two-thirds of the pilots who experience break-off are not particularly bothered by it. Some say they enjoy the sensation it brings, of utter remoteness from the world. Others have been disturbed by it, reporting that they felt the aircraft was balanced precariously, "on a knife edge" or "on a pinhead," and could easily drop from the sky. One described leaving his body, floating out to the cockpit and sitting on the wing, from where he watched himself fly the aircraft.

"These pilots can be treated by reassurance," says the report, "but only if they make their fears known."

So, by implication, there may be many more who, unlike Rutan and Lindbergh, haven't admitted to their visitations by elves, spacemen, and other types of phantoms.

. . .

The spirit who appeared to the seafarer Joshua Slocum was not from another world but another age. In May 1895, Slocum departed from Boston aboard his thirty-four-foot sloop *Spray,* intent on becoming the first person to sail single-handedly around the world. Three years later he achieved his goal, but not before he had been faced with some surprises. After his first twenty days at sea, he reached the Azores, in the mid-Atlantic, where he quickly became a local celebrity. When he set sail again, local people saw him off with gifts of freshly made cheeses and plums just picked from the tree. He knew there were many lean days ahead. He ate his fill, and more.

Barely a day's sail out of the Azores, he was reefing the main sail to prepare for a building storm when cramps began to rip through his belly. He stumbled below deck, and soon the pain was so intense that he writhed helplessly on the floor of the cabin, slipping in and out of consciousness while the boat sailed on, unattended.

When finally he roused, *Spray* was tossing like a cork, its timbers creaking against the great force of the waves. Glancing through the hatch he saw an angry sky, careening at odd angles. And silhouetted against it, a figure. He sat up. He was on this boat alone! But there *was* a man, tall, wearing a red cap cocked over one ear. He stood firmly at the helm, legs spread, counterbalancing the bucking of the boat. How did he get here? From a pirate ship? That made no sense; coming alongside in such conditions was impossible.

As if sensing Slocum's eyes upon his back, the man turned around. Dark complexion, black hair, a long mustache, and clothes from a different age. He smiled, doffed his hat in greeting, and introduced himself as the pilot of Captain Columbus's ship, *Pinta,* which, he said, was not far ahead. *Don't worry, I am your friend. I've come to guide you. You've been ill, a bad fever. Never good to eat a fresh white cheese unless you know who made it. By tomorrow you'll be fine.*

He turned back to the helm, cranking it hard into a wave that towered high above the masts of the sloop. They surfed down it, into the deep trough, only to be yanked skyward by the next wave. The pilot sang as the rollers bore down relentlessly. Slocum's fever returned; he hallucinated that they were passing a pier where careless draymen were tossing small boats onto the cabin roof of *Spray.* He screamed a warning to the boats' owners, but neither they, nor the figure at the helm, paid him any heed.

When he woke again, his fever and cramps had abated, the sun was high in the sky, and the decks of *Spray* had been swept clean of everything movable by the storm. The pilot, too, was gone. The boat was racing across the sea, unguided. Slocum held up his sextant and made a reading. She was on course! And she had made ninety miles in the night. Gratitude toward the old pilot flooded through him, followed by annoyance—why hadn't he taken in the jib?

The wind dropped and the sun came out. Slocum stripped off his clothes, spread them on the deck to dry, and lay down next to them. Soon he was dozing.

"Then who should visit me again but my old friend of the night before," Slocum later recorded. " 'You did well last night to take my advice,' said he, 'and if you would, I should like to be with you often on this voyage, for the love of adventure alone.' Finishing what he had to say, he again doffed his cap and disappeared as mysteriously as he came, returning, I suppose, to the phantom *Pinta.* I awoke much refreshed, and with the feeling that I had been in the presence of a friend and a seaman of vast experience."

. . .

One of the earliest accounts of a spirit friend was penned in the fifth century B.C. by Herodotus, a Greek historian. He wrote that when the Persians invaded Greece, landing at Marathon, an Athenian herald called Pheidippidēs ran for two days to Sparta, a distance of 150 miles, to request help against the enemy. Near the top of Mount Parthenium, he saw an apparition of the god Pan, who told him to remind the Athenians of how he had assisted them in the past, and to ask them why they had forgotten him. This vision spurred Pheidippidēs to run even faster to reach his destination and deliver Pan's message.

Marshall Ulrich has run a similar distance—135 miles, on the Badwater Ultramarathon, across Death Valley and up Mount Whitney, California—thirteen times. He's run it in daytime temperatures that hit 130 degrees. His fastest speed, in 1993, was thirty-four hours. During that race, as he neared the top of Mount Whitney, he saw hundreds of green lizards flowing down the path, like a river. In 1999, on the second day of the race, he saw a woman roller-blading a hundred feet ahead of him.

"She was wearing a sparkling silver string bikini," he recalls, "and she was skating her ass off. She kept turning to wave at me—she was gorgeous. I didn't even blink—I was thinking, *I'm liking this!* I kept that hallucination going for over ten minutes."

His attempts to conjure her up again failed, but two hours later a one-winged 747 airplane pulled up so close to him that he could see passengers waving at him through portholes.

Hallucinations and visions are usually attributed to some kind of temporary or permanent neurological malfunctioning. People who suffer seizures within the prefrontal or temporal lobe sometimes report "sensed presences," or flashes of mystical rapture. Medical historians have suggested that religious visionaries such as Saint Teresa of Avila, Joan of Arc, Saint Paul, and Joseph Smith, the founder of Mormonism, suffered from seizures. The Russian novelist Feodor Dostoevsky had a rare form of temporal lobe epilepsy termed "ecstatic epilepsy." During the last twenty years of his life, he kept detailed records of 102 seizures, describing the feeling of being in "full harmony" with himself and the whole world, which he experienced a few seconds before each attack. Such ecstasy came at a cost, as his post-fit symptoms, which lasted up to a week, included "heaviness and even pain in the head, disorders of the nerves, nervous laugh and mystical depression."

The Canadian psychiatrist Dr. Robert Persinger, head of the Behavioral Neuroscience Program in Laurentian University's department of psychology, has tried to prove the connection between hallucinations and temporal lobe activity. He developed a helmet that shoots electric currents into specific regions of the brain, generating a low-frequency magnetic field and creating micro-seizures. When currents are aimed into the temporal lobes of his research subjects, they sometimes report dreamlike hallucinations, and sense a "spectral presence" in the room.

In his original experiment, conducted under double-blind conditions, forty-eight men and women were subjected to partial sensory deprivation and exposure to weak, complex magnetic fields across the temporal lobes. Subjects who received greater stimulation over the right hemisphere or equal stimulation across both hemispheres reported more frequent incidences of presences, fears, and odd smells than did the subjects who received greater stimulation over the left hemisphere.

As the left hemisphere of the temporal cortex is, according to Persinger, the seat of our sense of self, he posits that the spectral presence is actually a transient awareness of the right hemispheric equivalent

of the left hemispheric sense of self. While such a "transient awareness" is rare in normal life, he believes it might be caused by periods of distress, psychological depression, and certain drug-induced
and meditation states. The experience of a presence, he believes, is "a
resident property of the human brain, and may be the fundamental
source for phenomena attributed to visitations by gods, spirits, and
other ephemeral phenomena."

Phenomena such as the ghost described in T. S. Eliot's famous
poem, "The Waste Land":

Who is the third who walks always beside you?
When I count, there are only you and I together
But when I look ahead up the white road
There is always another one walking beside you
Gliding wrapt in a brown mantle, hooded
I do not know whether a man or woman
—But who is that on the other side of you?

Eliot's lines were inspired by the experiences of Shackleton, Crean,
and Worsley, as they made their epic crossing of South Georgia Island
in 1916. Shackleton had set out for the South Pole with the goal of
making the first crossing of Antarctica, to reach the South Pole.
Although he knew the odds were against success, he must have had
little inkling of the horrendous saga that lay ahead. Six months after
sailing from London, and a day after first sighting the continent of
Antarctica, his ship *Endurance* became trapped in pack ice. It drifted
with the floe for several days, down to the 77th parallel, where it sat,
frozen in place, throughout the dark Arctic winter. In late October,
the pressure of the ice began to break up *Endurance,* and Shackleton
ordered his men to abandon ship.

They set up camp on the floe; a month later, as it melted, they watched their ship sink into the freezing waters. By December, they had established Patience Camp on another ice floe that drifted south until, by April 1916, they were in sight of Elephant Island. Piling into three lifeboats, they headed for a protected beach. From here, Shackleton and five crew set sail in one boat to South Georgia Island, a voyage of seventeen days and eight hundred miles across the storm-bound Southern Ocean. Their goal was to reach the whaling station, where they knew they would find help, but they were forced to land on the far side of the island. So, Shackleton, Crean, and Worsley traversed its mountainous interior, trekking and climbing, finding their way across glaciers and crevasses, going nonstop for thirty-six hours with only a short length of old rope and an axe to assist them. It is a feat that modern-day mountaineers regard with awe. How did they survive this?

"I know that during that long and racking march," Shackleton writes, "it seemed to me often that we were four, not three."

Delusional or not, he believed this presence guided them to safety, and that an account of it should be included in the record of their journeys.

Shackleton's writing about his mystical experience made him the darling of the spiritualist and revivalist movements that flourished after World War I. While Captain Scott's name had been invoked to inspire young men to go to the trenches, Shackleton's experience was a comfort to those suffering losses in that war, that the dead were out there, and reachable.

They're still out there," writes modern-day polar explorer Peter Hillary. "I still see them come and go.... And I still don't know what to do with them. Isn't that how it is for everybody?"

In 1998, Hillary, from New Zealand, embarked on a three-month journey across the Antarctic, along with Eric Philips and Jon Muir. They planned to follow in Captain Scott's footsteps to the South Pole, and then to walk and ski all the way back—a round trip of eighteen hundred miles, completing the journey on behalf of Scott and his men, who perished on the ice in 1912. It was not to be: at the South Pole they called for a plane, and flew out. Later, Philips would publicly accuse Hillary of "emotional instability" and cite this as a major factor contributing to their decision to end the expedition. Philips himself would then seek out a psychologist to help combat the demons plaguing him from the trip.

By day five of the journey, they had begun crossing the aptly named White Island, through a blizzard so intense they could see no farther than their outstretched arms. Each of them hauled a heavy sled weighing 440 pounds, which to Hillary felt like "pulling out a tree." When they stopped to rest, sitting on the sleds and sipping hot drinks from flasks, the blizzard quickly built up drifts around their knees.

Day after day, for hours on end, they shuffled forward, through a white world. Hillary had flown planes at night and descended mountains in storms; he knew how disorienting these experiences could be, but this was far more intense.

"Imagine skiing down a slope in a whiteout," he says. "At the bottom you turn to stop, but because you're so disoriented you fall over. On a polar trip, that's a permanent state. Day in and day out, you've got streaming spindrift blowing over you. Everything is white with occasional grayish smudges—a crevasse, a team member ahead. It's like being inside a moving mass of cotton wool."

Soon, the hallucinations began. As he trudged on, he found himself in lush river valleys, on mountains, in a supermarket, aboard a sailboat. Then the visitors arrived. Climbing friends—like Jeff

Lakes, who had died of altitude sickness on their K2 expedition in 1995. Most frequently, his dead mother.

It was twenty-three years since he had last seen her, at a bus station in Kathmandu. His father, Sir Edmund Hillary, had evolved from being the world's most famous climber, the conqueror of Everest, to a champion of social welfare in Nepal, facilitating the construction of schools, clinics, hospitals, and airstrips. To concentrate fully on this new role, he had moved the family to Kathmandu for a year.

Out on the ice, Peter Hillary recalled his mother taking him and his friend to the station, when they were leaving to go traveling in India. He saw her driving them through the narrow, crowded lanes of Kathmandu, past temples and cows foraging in the gutters. He saw her slim figure leading the way through throngs of people to find their bus. And, as the bus pulled away, blaring its horn, he watched her standing and waving her arms in big, generous arcs.

"I looked over my shoulder," he writes, "and saw her growing smaller and smaller, her arms still waving. Then she was swallowed by the surrounding chaos."

He was still in India when the news reached him. His mother and his sixteen-year-old sister Belinda had been traveling by small plane from Kathmandu to Paphlu, in the Himalayan foothills, where Sir Edmund was working on a project. Shortly after takeoff, the young New Zealander pilot realized that the ailerons, devices on the wings to stabilize the aircraft's roll, were locked. The left wing tilted. The plane went into a vertical dive. It crashed nose-first into a paddy field. No one survived. By the time Peter Hillary got back to Kathmandu, his mother and sister had already been cremated. He went to the crash site. He saw the three-foot-deep crater the plane had made on impact. Wandering around the paddy field in distress, he found his mother's amber beads. The impact had broken them loose and they were scattered in the mud. He collected as many of them as he could find. All those years later, as he trudged across the ice to the South Pole, in his head he designed a display case for the beads, which he planned to set inside a coffee table.

His mother was the best friend he'd ever had. Her death had left a dark hole in his life, which had never been filled. So, although it was a little disquieting when she first appeared to him on the ice, he really wasn't surprised that she was there. She looked exactly as she did the last time he saw her. She was locked in time, forty-three years old, younger than he was now.

"It seemed natural as anything to walk along talking to her," he writes. "And I could feel her outlying quietness as I told her about my children, the grandchildren she never saw."

Hillary wondered if his team members ever caught sight of him apparently talking to himself, or smiling in quiet reverie. He never told them about the ghosts. He barely talked to them at all, for the entire trip. Relationships between them had deteriorated badly. When they were forced to communicate, about things necessary to keep the trip together, it was never without deep rancor.

Research into the psychology of polar travel, based mostly on records of polar trips taken in the nineteenth century, has found that life among a team comes to resemble the interactions of men confined to a prison cell. Frustration and boredom at being cooped up together in tents can lead to aggression and intimidation. On top of this are visual deprivation, hunger, and exhaustion. Hillary also factors in "huge egos, bitter resentments, nobody willing to blink, various states of emotional gangrene and incompetence."

Eric Philips and Jon Muir were younger than Hillary and generally moved faster across the ice. He often found himself far behind them, dreading a blizzard that would cover their tracks. Two weeks into the trip, fearing they might deliberately go so far ahead that he would lose sight of them—which could be deadly in such conditions and terrain—he always made sure he had enough on his sled to survive alone for a few days.

But the physical and social misery of the trip turned into an unexpected benefit for Hillary.

"To keep going, I had to do something with my mind," he says. "I couldn't just put it into neutral. I realized I had the opportunity to move back down through my memory banks, deep into the past. The loss of my mother, and my close climbing friends, they happened in such painful circumstances. That pain never leaves you, there's always a scar, but you have to get on with life, you don't want to summon the loss back in its full-blown reality, it's just too hard. So you keep it at arm's length and try to get by. Being out on the ice, with all that time for contemplation, was an incredible opportunity to bring it back full-force, to meet those people again. You can actually see them, like a projection."

On his many mountain expeditions, with teams that functioned better, he had never been able to summon up ghosts in the same way. It was the ice that made it possible. And the extreme physical and social isolation.

As their journey got ever more grueling, and Hillary became increasingly estranged from his two teammates, he came to depend upon the comforting companionship of the ghosts. But he firmly believes that these ghosts were simply projections of his own mind. The result of what he calls "psychological osmosis." That the harsh white world and endless effort of moving through it caused him to "dissociate" from reality.

"With nothing coming in," writes Hillary, "I believe everything is leached out of you like salt is leached from soil by fresh water. . . . The white world is a merciless therapist, one that derobes you and your secrets. My very essence, my history and my heart, were to be projected in front of me...."

Whatever the cause, the ghost encounters were thrilling, the most memorable part of the trip, bringing him a "rapture that overwhelmed the agonies, such that there was no confusion or ambivalence or doubt."

After suffering damage to their visual pathways, from glaucoma, cataracts, macular denigration, or diabetic retinopathy, some people develop Charles Bonnet syndrome—despite being partially or totally blind, they experience vivid visual hallucinations. According to a study reported in the British medical journal *Lancet,* of the five hundred visually handicapped elderly people interviewed for a research project, sixty admitted to having hallucinations, sometimes on a daily basis. The figures might be much higher, as often people prefer not to admit to such symptoms, for fear they will be regarded as crazy.

"Who would believe that a blind person was seeing clowns and circus animals cavorting in her bedroom?" writes V. S. Ramachandran, director of the Center for Brain and Cognition at the University of California, San Diego. "Given how common this syndrome is, I am tempted to wonder whether the occasional reports of 'true' sightings of ghosts, UFOs and angels by otherwise sane people may merely be examples of Charles Bonnet hallucinations. Is it any surprise that roughly one-third of Americans claim to have seen angels?"

According to Ramachandran's research, such visions could be projections of the body and mind. In one of his test studies, he sits with two volunteers, who are facing each other. One of them is blindfolded. While he taps and strokes the nose of the blindfolded person, he guides her index finger to tap and stroke the nose of the person opposite her. If the taps and strokes are random and in sync with each other, after about thirty seconds the blindfolded person may begin to feel that she is tapping her own nose at arm's length. Some of his volunteers say it's as if their noses have grown enormously. Others say their noses seem to leave their bodies and are floating in front of them. The experiment has a 50 percent success rate, and shows, says Ramachandran, that you can project your sensations outside of your brain, and that the mechanisms of perception "are mainly involved in extracting statistical correlations from the world to create a model that is temporarily useful."

It's a radical idea, especially when he extends the theory to inanimate objects. Ramachandran sits at a table with a volunteer who has one hand under the tabletop, completely hidden from view. Simultaneously, Ramachandran taps the top of the table and the volunteer's hidden hand. In many cases, the volunteer will gradually feel the tapping, not in his hand but in the table. Rationally, he knows that the table is beyond the boundaries of his body, but he experiences something totally different.

To find out if the volunteers really identified with the tabletop, Ramachandran hooked them to a galvanic skin-response device. He repeated the experiment, and when each volunteer started to experience the table as part of his or her own hand, Ramachandran produced a hammer and smashed it down onto the tabletop.

"Instantly there was a huge change in GSR," he reports, "as if I had smashed the student's own fingers. It was as though the table had now become coupled to the student's own limbic system and been assimilated into his body image, so much so that pain and threat to the dummy are felt as threats to his own body."

By implication, his theories reverse the idea that our "self" is attached to a single body, suggesting instead that our body image is an internal construct that can be manipulated.

If our body image is a phantom that can be profoundly altered, could it be feasible that the spirits that visited Joshua Slocum, Charles Lindbergh, Dick Rutan, and Peter Hillary were nothing more than bizarre extensions of themselves, brought on by the extremes of their situations? A phenomenon that some scientists have called a "phantom double"? Perhaps, but this doesn't explain the uncannily parallel experiences of Lou and Ingrid Whittaker.

In 1989, Lou Whittaker, a veteran North American mountaineer, was leading the first American expedition to climb Kanchenjunga. At Base Camp, he kept getting the feeling that someone was in his tent with him.

"I'd look around and think, *Who's here?* Then I would feel the presence of a Tibetan woman. There were no Tibetan women at Base Camp. But she was there every night. She was middle-aged, and dressed traditionally. It wasn't a strong image, more a sensation. There was nothing sexual about it. She was a friendly spirit, able to share my concerns. I felt she was communicating, without words, that everything was okay."

While he was on the mountain, his wife, Ingrid, was also in the area, leading a trek as far as his base camp. Eager to see him, she persuaded her group to skip the last resting stage of the trek and go straight from twelve thousand to sixteen thousand feet in one day. It was a mistake. By the time they reached the base camp, Ingrid was suffering from altitude sickness. For the next three days she had such an appalling headache that she never left Lou's tent. But she wasn't alone there. In the daytime, when Lou was climbing, she was kept company by a Tibetan woman.

"I always felt this local woman with me," she recalls. "She was wearing a headscarf and a long dress. She was shadowy and two-dimensional, like a silhouette. It was a good presence, very comforting. She would put her hand on my forehead and help me roll over. She was just kind of hovering around and helpful the whole time. She didn't speak but there was always a feeling of kindness, that this was a good person who was going to take care of me. It was like we were communicating mind to mind, without words. I thought, *Oh my God, I'm really sick, I'm hallucinating, I'm losing it, I'll probably die.* I didn't tell Lou about it; I was in such a lot of pain, we hardly spoke to each other the whole time I was there."

Once she managed to stagger down to a lower altitude, her symptoms abated. Two months later, when Lou returned to North America after the expedition, they talked about her visit to Base Camp. Hesitantly, Ingrid told Lou about the presence in the tent.

"That's weird," he replied. "I had the same feeling. This woman was there with me in the tent for the whole three months."

They are both convinced that it wasn't a hallucination. It was a real presence. Nothing like this has ever happened to them again and they have told few of their friends about it.

"Most of them would think we were making it up," says Lou.

Hearing this story, Dr. Pierre Mayer shrugs and says, "Hypnagogic dreams." Mayer, an expert in respiratory medicine and sleep disorders, has taken part in several mountaineering expeditions to the Alps, the Andes, and the Himalayas. As director of CHUM, the Sleep Disorders Investigation Center and Clinic of Montreal University Hospital, he is conducting research into dreams and hypoxia. At altitude, he explains, it is common for sleep cycles to be irregular and disturbed, something that in Ingrid's case was compounded by illness. Such disturbances made her and Lou more prone to having

hypnagogic dreams, which are often reported as hallucinations, varying from poorly formed shapes to vivid images of people and animals.
They happen mostly at the onset of sleep or during periods of relaxed
wakefulness. Similar dreams known as hypnopompic occur at sleep
offset. Both can be experienced in successive sleep cycles.

But this doesn't explain why the couple *both* sensed the same
Tibetan woman. Lou Whittaker has his own theory about the
visitation.

"There is such old history on Kanchenjunga. I think she was a
strong spirit that had enough influence to break through our reserves
and make us feel that she was there."

Like Lou and Ingrid Whittaker, many mountaineers have sensed
unexplainable presences in the high mountains. In 1983, the Australian mountaineer Greg Child was high on Broad Peak in Pakistan,
when his climbing partner Pete Thexton became seriously ill. For
hours, through darkness and a storm, Child struggled to get Thexton down the mountain. Throughout the ordeal he had the sense of
a presence behind him, gently guiding him in the right direction. "I
kept turning around, puzzled to find only darkness behind me," he
writes. "But there was definitely someone, or something, there."

Five years later, the British climber Stephen Venables became the
first person to ascend Everest by its Kangschung Face. He was forced
to spend a night just below the summit, where he was kept company
by an old man. As he began his descent, in an exhausted state, the
man encouraged him to keep going. Together they crawled down to
the South Summit, where they were joined by Eric Shipton, the long-
dead explorer, who helped to warm Venables's hands.

Steve Swenson, from Seattle, told friends about the "disembodied heads" he saw during a night he spent close to the summit of Everest in the late 1990s. The heads of a Japanese woman and a Punjabi man nagged him to stay awake until sunrise, then encouraged him to hurry as he broke camp. Finally, a third head gave him directions as he climbed down the mountain.

During an expedition on Kanchenjunga in 1978, Joe Tasker climbed alone to a snow cave on the mountain, where he sat waiting for the arrival of "an indistinct group of people I imagined were also on the climb with us." His climbing partners, Doug Scott and Peter Boardman, admitted to the same sensations. After reaching the summit, when they were heading back to the cave, Boardman was at the back of the group, convinced that there were others following him.

"It was not a thought that needed verification," writes Joe, "he was simply aware of the presence of someone behind him, just as firmly as he knew we three were in front of him."

On Everest, in 1975, Doug Scott sensed a presence that spoke to him and guided him while he was climbing difficult sections. Nick Estcourt, who would dream his death on K2 three years later, had a more dramatic experience. Early one morning, he was moving up the fixed ropes between Camps 4 and 5. When he was about two hundred feet above Camp 4, he got a feeling that he was being followed. Turning around, he saw another climber. He assumed it was one of the team, trying to catch up. He stopped and waited. The climber was moving extremely slowly. Estcourt shouted down to him, but got no reply. Eventually he decided to press on. Several times he turned around. The figure was still there.

"It was definitely a human figure with arms and legs," he recounted to Chris Bonington, the team leader. "At one stage I can remember seeing him behind a slight undulation in the slope, from the waist upward, as you would expect, with the lower part of his body hidden in the slight dip."

After a time, he turned around to find the slope below him empty. He could see all the way back to Camp 4—it was impossible that the person could have retreated without him knowing. And if he had fallen, he would have seen traces of that as well. When finally he returned to the rest of the team, he quizzed them as to who had been on the rope behind. No one had been there.

This phenomenon, of a phantom climbing partner, was reported by early Himalayan mountaineers.

"I have often felt the presence of a Companion on the mountain who is not in our earthly party of climbers," writes Howard Somervell, a member of the 1924 Everest expedition. He also reported a "curious sensation" while at the high camp of 26,800 feet. It was "as if we were getting near the edge of a field with a wall all around it—a high, insuperable wall. The field was human capacity, the wall human limitations. The field, I remember, was a bright and uniform green, and we were walking toward the edge—very near the edge now, where the whitish-gray wall said 'Thus far, and no further.'"

Frank Smythe, who took part in three attempts on Everest in the 1930s, writes, "There is something about the Himalayas not possessed by the Alps, something unseen and unknown, a charm that pervades every hour spent among them, a mystery intriguing and disturbing. Confronted by them, a man loses his grasp of ordinary things, perceiving himself as immortal, an entity capable of outdistancing all change, all decay, all life, all death."

On the 1933 Everest expedition, Smythe reached a height of 28,100 feet without oxygen—a record-breaking feat that was not to be repeated until 1982. At 23,000 feet, he sat down in the snow and shared his food with an imaginary companion. Later, when he was descending from his high point to Camp 6, at 27,400 feet, he looked up to see two dark objects floating in the sky.

"In shape they resembled kite balloons," he writes, "except that one appeared to possess short squat wings. As they hovered motionless, they seemed to pulsate in and out as though they were breathing. I gazed at them dumbfounded and intensely interested. It seemed to me that my brain was working normally, but to test myself I looked away. The objects did not follow my gaze but were still there when I looked back. So I looked away again, but this time identified by name various details of the landscape by way of a mental test. Yet, when I again looked back the objects were still visible. A minute or two later, a mist drifted across the northeast shoulder of Everest above which they were still poised. As this thickened the objects gradually disappeared behind it and were lost to sight. A few minutes later the mist blew away. I looked again, expecting to see them, but they had vanished as mysteriously as they had appeared. If it was an optical illusion, it was a strange one. But it is possible that fatigue magnified out of all proportion something capable of a perfectly ordinary and rational explanation. That is all I can say about the matter and it rests there."

When Walter Bonatti was two hundred feet from the top of the Matterhorn, during his famous solo ascent of its North Face in 1965, he saw a vision of a cross.

"In the sun which illuminated it, it seemed incandescent. The light which emanated from it dazzled me. It was a supernatural, mysterious thing, like the halo of the saints.... Then as if hypnotized, I stretched out my arms toward the cross until I could feel its metal substance right against my chest. And I fell to my knees and wept in silence."

At the Laboratory of Cognitive Neuroscience in Lausanne, Switzerland, scientists have been studying the link between mystical experiences and cognitive neuroscience. They point out that the fundamental revelations to the founders of the three monotheistic religions—Moses, Jesus, and Mohammed—occurred on mountains, and included such components as feeling a presence, seeing a figure, hearing voices, and seeing lights. These similarities of experience suggest to the scientists that exposure to altitude might affect functions relying on brain areas such as the temporoparietal junction and the prefrontal cortex. Prolonged stays at high altitude, especially when linked to social deprivation, can lead to prefrontal lobe dysfunctions, which are commonly found during ecstatic experiences. Also, the physical and emotional stresses of climbing at altitude release endorphins, which are known to lower the threshold for temporal lobe epilepsy, which in turn might evoke such experiences. All such phenomena, then, might relate to "abnormal body processing."

Tests conducted on climbers by British doctors Michael Ward and Jim Milledge, during Himalayan expeditions, indicate that above 18,000 feet, thought function and perception become increasingly impaired and above 28,000 feet hallucinations are common. Dr. Charles Houston, a legendary American mountaineer and the co-discoverer of high-altitude pulmonary edema, claims such hallucinations could be caused by miniature temporal lobe seizures, triggered by fatigue, low blood sugar, personal crisis, and anxiety. They could also be the result of hypoxia, in which there is a diminished supply of oxygen to the brain. By scanning the brains of hospitalized patients suffering from hypoxia due to other causes, scientists have shown neural irregularities, including fluid pockets and swelling of the brain, or edema. When the brain is hypoxic, control of the cortical function is weakened, which impairs the climber's judgment, but also creates a type of euphoria that makes difficult tasks seem easier. This euphoria is similar to the state of enhanced ability and senses brought about by biochemical changes during stress—the flood of endorphins—dopamine, serotonin, noradrenaline, and adrenaline.

Greg Child has a simpler theory. "Going to blow-your-mind high altitude creates a world inside of ourselves. When you're down here you're not so tuned into the same things as when you're up high or in some extreme circumstances, wondering if you're going to make it through the next few hours."

Adrian Burgess puts it even more succinctly. "The higher you go, the more weird things get."

Mountain ghosts have appeared at lower altitudes. One winter in the late 1960s, Dougal Haston, a Scottish climber, was staying with a friend in an alpine hut in Argentiere, near Chamonix, France. They were its only occupants. At around two a.m., Haston was woken by the sound of someone walking heavily across the floor of the room above them, then clumping down the wooden stairs. The latch to their room rattled. The footsteps went back up the stairs again. Then, silence. Haston believed in ghosts, but didn't want his companion to think he was crazy, so he said nothing. In the morning, however, his friend asked him if he had heard strange sounds in the night. They decided to search the place but found no trace of anyone having been there.

Bad weather forced them to spend another night in the hut. At two a.m., the footsteps returned. The door latch rattled. This time, they were ready. They sprang up and yanked open the door, but there was no sign of anyone in the hallway. Despite being brave mountaineers, neither could face going upstairs. They left the hut at first light. Just before heading out, Haston checked through the visitors' book, in which climbers recorded the routes they had completed on surrounding mountains. He was shocked to find a note about the hut guardian being killed in an avalanche. It was a fate that would befall Haston himself, a few years later.

Adrian Burgess stayed in the same hut in 1972. He didn't know about the ghost, and only learned about it later, when the hut was about to be demolished and there was a big discussion about whether its replacement should be built on the same site, because of the resident spirit.

He's skeptical about the idea of ghosts and spirits on mountains. "In some places I climb, if the ghosts of dead friends were coming to visit me there would be so many of them it would be pretty crowded. I mean, if it was true, the entire Alpine hut system would be crawling with howlers. Anyway, thankfully none of them have ever tapped on the tent door. I'd be scared shitless."

Like people suffering from Charles Bonnet syndrome, many climbers are reticent about admitting to paranormal experiences, for fear their peers will think them crazy. Not so the Mexican climber Carlos Carsolio, who in 1996, at the age of thirty-three, became the fourth and youngest person to climb all fourteen of the world's highest peaks. He never used supplementary oxygen and he's had many hallucinations, including the "third man" syndrome, which he says is a normal phenomenon up high. What he calls his "moments of extended reality" are quite another matter. They are, he says, "a step more" and it is to attain these that he climbed so hard and has taken so many risks.

One of his most profound experiences was in 1988, after his solo ascent of Makalu, the world's fifth-highest mountain. By the time he began his descent, night had fallen, and the wind was very strong. He was extremely weak, struggling with the beginning of pulmonary edema and beginning to freeze. His headlamp faded, the windblown snow had covered his tracks, and he was soon lost. He had been in desperate situations before; he knew what he must do to survive.

"I stopped fighting the cold. I became one with it. Then I became part of the mountain and I didn't get frozen. I used my energy in a positive way."

He started to talk to the mountain and the different entities it was revealing to him.

"Some of the seracs were female, some of the rocks were male. They were guiding me, telling me where to go. But some of the presences were evil and wanted me to die. The two sides were fighting over this. I was talking with them. With the friendly ones in a friendly way, with the bad ones in a fighting way."

These conversations went on for hours, as he struggled down through the storm, searching blindly for a narrow snow bridge that he knew was the only safe route through a section of dangerous crevasses. Suddenly he felt a strong presence. He recognized it as a climber he'd known who had died on Makalu—later, he would discover that the man perished in the exact area where he was picking up the sense of his spirit. Eventually, he came across the snow bridge, and from there reached his high camp. This would have been impossible, he believes, without the help of his climbing friend's spirit and the friendly entities.

"I cannot understand how else I found the bridge, in such a huge place with the wind and the dark night and no lamp and frozen glasses and my exhaustion. It was like finding a needle in a haystack."

He collapsed inside the tent, still wearing his crampons. Two hours later, when the sun woke him, he could barely breathe and was coughing up blood.

He had a tape recorder in the tent. He managed to record a brief message, saying good-bye to his family and friends. As he signed off, however, he decided he didn't want to die in a tent on the side of a mountain. He would prefer to die fighting. He started crawling and sliding down the mountain. After several hours a Polish team passed him on their way to the summit. He called to them, but they thought he was so close to death that they simply carried on, without offering help. By now, his team at Base Camp could see him through binoculars. They watched his tortuous progress—descending a few feet, then lying down for half an hour. Finally some Spanish climbers came by. They gave him oxygen, water, and food, and stayed with him until he felt strong enough to carry on alone to the safety of Base Camp.

He counts such harrowing experiences among the most memorable and treasured of his life.

"It's not about the adrenaline," he insists. "These extended moments are different. They take me to another dimension. They are why I wanted to climb alone and to do such hard routes, so that I could reach them."

Four years later he went to Kanchenjunga with a team that included Wanda Rutkiewicz, a legendary Polish mountaineer. They arrived at Base Camp in mid-March, but by early May they had made little progress on the mountain, and the team was ravaged by frostbite and illness. Only Carsolio and Rutkiewicz, twenty years his senior, were fit enough to continue. On their summit attempt, she set out two days ahead of him, but she was slowed by age and a nagging injury from a previous trip, and he soon caught up with her. They spent a night at Camp 4 and left at three the following morning. Determined to make the summit in a fast, light push and get back the same day, they took a minimum of food and water and no bivouac gear.

After a few hours of climbing, Rutkiewicz slowed down to a crawl.

She urged Carsolio to go ahead, insisting she would catch up with him after a rest. He climbed all day, regularly looking back at her figure growing ever smaller on the slopes below him. It was five p.m. before he reached the summit. The sun was setting, and already the cold of the night was seeping through to his bones. His food and water had run out. It was essential for him to descend as fast as possible. Carefully, he picked his way down the icy slopes, conscious that tiredness, hunger, dehydration, and hypoxia could easily add up to a fatal mistake. After three hours, when he was less than a thousand feet below the summit, he came across a familiar rope, and followed it to where Rutkiewicz was huddled in a tiny snow cave. Like him, she had nothing to eat or drink. Worse, she was inadequately dressed in a light down suit designed for lower altitudes. She asked Carsolio for his jacket, but he knew he must keep wearing it in order to get down without freezing. He encouraged her to descend with him to their high camp but she insisted she wanted to spend the night in that place. She would wait for the sun to come up and warm her, she said, and then she would go for the summit.

Carsolio was horrified. But he was too much in awe of her to argue. She was one of the world's best Himalayan climbers. She had years of experience behind her, and far more expeditions than he had undertaken. She was a legend, and he was her acolyte. He sat with her for fifteen minutes until he realized that he was becoming dangerously cold. He stood up. He bid her farewell.

See you later, Wanda.

It was a decision he'd always regret.

"I knew she was in a state of exhaustion and cold but I had not the guts to tell her to go down."

He waited for her all that night and for much of the next day at their high camp. Eventually he could wait no longer.

"As I was climbing down to Camp 2," he recalls, "suddenly I knew, right at that very moment, that Wanda was dying. She said good-bye to me. I was climbing down, the terrain was hard, I was much focused, but suddenly my mind was filled with her presence, her femininity. I felt it very strongly."

A storm forced him to stay at Camp 2 for much of the next day. When finally he set off, he left behind food and water for Wanda, even though he knew there was no hope. Wrung out by grief, physically spent after a week on the mountain, he started to descend a huge, steep wall of ice and rock. On the way up with Wanda, they had fixed this section with ropes, so it should have been straightforward. While he was moving from one rope to another, however, sorrow overwhelmed him; he lost his focus and forgot to tie a crucial figure-8 knot. Presuming he was secure, he stepped back into thousands of feet of air. The fall was short; his arm caught in a loop of the fixed rope. He was hanging, in shock, when he heard Wanda's voice.

Don't worry. I will take care of you.

"I have no doubt that it was real," he insists. "I was not hallucinating and I'm not crazy. I'm sure it was her. I received it as a message; it was not exactly in words, it was another dimension, a feeling, a presence. I started to cry because I felt guilty about not having told her to come down. I did not take care of her and now she was taking care of me."

He tried to gather himself, to start rappelling again, but huge sobs racked his body.

"I was crying and crying, and then I felt her presence again. It was very peaceful. It was like a mother hugging her child."

Finally, he reached the glacier, where the rest of his team was waiting.

"I was back in the real world, the normal world," he said. "But this experience—it was very deep."

Several weeks after Wanda Rutkiewicz disappeared on K2, her mother, Ewa Matuszewska, was woken in the middle of the night by the telephone. When she picked it up, she heard her daughter's voice, calling her by her pet name, Ewunia, which few others ever used. "I am very cold," the voice said. "But don't cry, everything will be fine. I cannot come back now." Then the line went dead.

Days after Alex MacIntyre was killed by a falling stone on Annapurna, his teammate John Porter was in Kathmandu, trying to contact MacIntyre's family so that he could break the news of the tragedy to them before it was reported in the press. This was long before the Internet and easy phone connections, and Porter had to book a call at the local post office. While waiting for the appointed time, he went back to his hotel room.

"I was lying on my bed, thinking about Alex, feeling really sad and dreading having to tell his mother what had happened," he recalls. "There was a half bottle of whiskey on the window shelf. We'd bought it on the flight from England, and it had been in the tent with us at Base Camp. It was a plastic bottle, unopened. I was lying there looking at it when it came flying across the room and dropped in the middle of the floor. The window wasn't open—there was no draft, no disturbance. There was nothing to propel it off the shelf."

Nothing, perhaps, except Alex MacIntyre's energy, winging down from the mountain.

Chapter 9

WANDERING SPIRITS

Regard as one this life, the next life, and the life between.

MILAREPA

They were in a steep-sided slot canyon, on the Illinois River. All of them were experienced Class V river kayakers. They knew that the water levels that day were twice the ideal rate. And rising. They spent a long while mulling over whether to put in. Finally they decided to go for it, and run everything as a tightly packed group. Each of them had a single kayak, except for Jeff Alexander and Dorie Brownell, who were in a little raft called the Shredder. The kayakers went ahead to scout each rapid, run it, then eddy out and wait for the raft to come through. Until they reached The Green Wall, a notorious rapid made impassable by the high water levels. The whole group portaged it, and got back onto the river. The worst was behind them.

Then Alexander and Brownell got stuck in a circulating eddy. At its edge, where two currents met, was a ramp of turbulent water that they couldn't punch through. The kayakers pulled ashore again, and scrambled over some boulders to check on their friends. Seeing them break free of the eddy, they headed back to their kayaks, unaware that Alexander and Brownell were arguing. She wanted to pull into another eddy on the right side of the river, to rest. He wanted to head left, for an eddy farther downstream. While discussing these options, they floated past Brownell's choice. A fatal mistake. They ran into a maelstrom of massive holes, whirlpools, and a twelve-foot standing wave. The boat flipped. Brownell grabbed it, climbed back on, and threw the safety line to Alexander. It fell short. She threw it again. She yelled, "Jeff, right behind you, the rope!" But he was facing the standing wave, as if mesmerized, being carried toward it.

That was the last she saw of him. The current had her in its grip and took her five and a half miles downriver, flipping her out of the boat seven more times. Five and a half miles and seven dunkings, in March, in cold, crazy water, hanging onto a boat that was bucking like a bronco. She saw a man standing on the shore and yelled to him. He shrugged—a gesture of helplessness—and she realized that he had flipped, too, and had no boat or paddles. As the river swept her along, she caught flashes of other figures clinging to the cliff walls. In the rising waters, a number of rafts and kayaks had capsized and several parties were stranded. That evening, the national news showed search-and-rescue helicopters plucking them to safety.

By the time the kayakers had climbed over the boulders, launched their boats, snapped on their spray skirts, and pushed off, Alexander and Brownell were lost from their sight. They raced down the river, trying to catch up with the raft. What they came across first was the top of Jeff Alexander's helmet, bright red, going round and round in a whirlpool. He was wearing a dry suit but the gasket at his neck had blown and the suit had filled with water. His life jacket kept him floating just under the surface. The water in his suit made him so heavy they couldn't get him ashore. Tying him to a tree, they pushed off to rescue Brownell. Because of the water levels, it was thirty-six hours before they could return to retrieve his body.

Sara Whitner was on a highway in South Michigan, on her way to Grand Rapids, when she got the call. She hadn't seen much of Jeff during the past two months. They lived in different states and it was hard for her to take a break from her job as a sales representative for an outdoor clothing company. Finally, in early March 1998, they made a plan for her to fly over and see him. As she was driving, she was thinking that in a week's time they would be together. Just outside of Ann Arbor, she was overtaking a truck, listening to messages on her cell phone. One of her coworkers, Tom, had called to tell her that Jeff Alexander was dead.

"I hit the redial button," Whitner recalls. "I was absolutely hysterical. Tom was saying, 'Sara, pull over. PULL OVER.' But there were guardrails, and no hard shoulder. I couldn't stop. He said, 'Where are you?' I was such a mess, I didn't know where I had just come from, or where I was going. It took me five minutes to even figure out I was somewhere in the state of Michigan. But I just kept driving to Grand Rapids. I took a wrong turn; I almost ended up in Chicago, four hours out of the way. At one point I pulled up at a gas station to ask directions and the attendant looked afraid of me."

She managed to make her way to the house of some friends, Larry and Melissa. It was here that she'd first met Jeff. She sat for hours in their kitchen, weeping uncontrollably, dwelling on all her regrets, all the things she'd been meaning to tell Jeff when they next met. Eventually they persuaded her to try to get some sleep. She took a shower first. When she stepped out of the bathroom, she found a note from Melissa.

Talk to Jeff. He's out there. He's listening.

The tears wouldn't stop. Eventually she cried herself into an exhausted sleep. At some point in the night she woke to find herself lying on her back with her hands folded together on her chest. She remembers thinking, *How strange.* She always slept on her side. Then she felt a pressure under her shoulder.

"It was like someone was floating just above me, with a hand hooked under my shoulder blade," she recalls. "Somehow I knew that if they let go they would float away like a helium balloon. I started to wake up more. I knew it had to be Jeff. I was thinking, *It's him, but oh my God, he's dead.* He floated there for a while and then he pulled in to hug me, but it was as if he came right through me, right inside, his whole body into mine. We stayed like that for the longest time until I got uncomfortable. I said, *I'm so sorry, Jeff, I need to roll over for a second.* I was scared I'd lose him but I rolled on my side and he was still there. We hung out together like that all night. It was so comforting."

The next night, she had a vivid dream of him sitting by a riverbank. Over the following weeks, several friends called to say they had been dreaming about him, too. The dreams were all startlingly similar.

"There would be a big crowd of us together—in most of the dreams, like in mine, it was on a river. In some of them it was at a party in someone's house. But Jeff was always sitting on his own to one side. That was really unusual for him; he liked to be in the thick of things. The dreamer would walk over to him and they'd have a quiet conversation. He'd say something like, *I just came to tell you I'm okay. It's really good where I am now.* He told one friend, Larry, that it was great, because now he could be in a hundred places at one time. That had always been his big issue, wanting to be everywhere and do everything all at once—and now it seemed he was finally able to do that."

.   .   .

There is no scientific proof that an individual consciousness can survive the destruction of the physical body. There's only a weight of anecdotal evidence, and an enduring need, it seems, for people to feel that such a phenomenon is possible. It is estimated that 68 percent of people in the USA believe in some form of life after death—meaning the survival of consciousness for a time, rather than immortality—while in Britain the figure is 43 percent.

Nine months after Jeff Alexander's death, Sara Whitner traveled to Ecuador. En route to an Andean village, she got talking to an old man, a respected elder in the community. She told him that her boyfriend had drowned, and recounted his apparent visitation while she was sleeping. The man looked at her and smiled.

"Did you have your hands on your heart?" he asked.

She nodded.

"Ah, I thought so," said the man. "When you lie in that way, that's how the spirits get in."

I'm sure Peter came back to me," said Dorothy Boardman, about her mountaineering son. It happened ten months after he disappeared on Everest in 1982, along with Joe Tasker. She was in bed at the time, so she presumes she was dreaming, although the experience was completely real and vivid.

"There was a knock at the back door. When I opened it, Peter was there. I said, *Oh Peter, I just knew you were all right.* He caught hold of my arms and looked down at me with compassion. He gave a smile of such regret, as if to say, *I'm sorry I can't stay.* He didn't say a word. Then I woke up. I thought, *Why did that happen now?* It was in March, not in May, which would be the anniversary of his death. I looked in my diary. It was a year to the day since I last spoke to him. The team had been on their way to Everest and he phoned from Hong Kong to say 'Cheerio.' So it was exactly the same day, a year later. It was quite extraordinary. And it was lovely."

Tibetan Buddhists believe that after the physical death of the body the consciousness goes through a series of stages called *bardo*s. During the initial "*bardo* of becoming," the direction of the spirit is determined by its body's life on earth. At first, the spirit returns home to meet family and loved ones, trying to talk to them and touch them. This *bardo* is said to last for forty-nine days, but in extreme cases, the spirit can linger for weeks or years.

"Think then of the moment of death as a strange border zone of the mind," writes Sogyal Rinpoche, author of *The Tibetan Book of Living and Dying*. "A no-man's land in which on the one hand, if we do not understand the illusory nature of our body we might suffer vast emotional trauma as we lose it; and on the other hand we are presented with the possibility of limitless freedom, a freedom that springs precisely from the absence of that very same body."

The British BASE jumper Shaun Ellison has no doubt that the dead inhabit a "no man's land" for a while. He calls it "a holding period," a time they spend around people before moving on to another realm.

"What that realm is," he says, "I don't know."

After Duane Thomas died in a BASE jumping accident in the Alps, Ellison felt his friend's presence at regular intervals, for months.

"It's a bodily experience. You get the sense of something coming all around you. An overwhelming warmth. It gives you pins and needles. Sometimes it's so intense your hair stands on end."

Gradually the sensations came less frequently and intensely, until they faded away. A year and a half after Thomas's demise, however, Ellison traveled to the Alpine valley where Thomas had plummeted to his death.

"I went to the same exit point and did a memorial jump for him," says Ellison. "And suddenly he was with me again. The feeling was really intense, especially when I was gearing up for the jump. It's a very methodical process. As you only operate one parachute system with BASE jumping, you don't have a second chance if things go wrong. So you prepare very carefully, always putting on your rig in a certain way, to avoid making any mistakes. While I was doing that I felt Duane around me very strongly. Like he was watching out for me, making sure I did everything right."

Ellison's closest friend was Andrew Stockford, an experienced white-water kayaker with numerous first ascents of rivers all over the world to his credit, and a skydiver with a log of 640 jumps from airplanes. He and Ellison shared many adventures together. The last had been a trek across the steppes of Mongolia, on foot and horseback. They had often stayed in *gurs*, the tent houses of local people. To their amusement, Stockford insisted on sleeping outside in his down bag, under the stars.

"He loved wild places," said Ellison. "He wanted to be close to nature all the time."

He was also on a spiritual quest. He had traveled through Thailand, staying in monasteries and studying with Buddhist monks. He went to see Sufi teachers, who told him they couldn't answer the hard questions he was asking. He and Ellison had many long conversations about the spirituality of nature, the importance of living in the moment, and what they were seeking through their risk-taking. Stockford had periods of depression, when he seemed defeated by his failure to find the answers he wanted. Ellison was used to his friend's patterns. He'd seen him through many troughs, and helped him climb back up to the peaks through their shared exploits in the outdoors.

In June 2006, they had planned to meet up one Sunday and go mountain biking. The day before, Stockford's mother rang Ellison to say that she couldn't get hold of her son by phone. She was worried. Could Ellison go around to check up on him? She knew he had keys to the house.

When Ellison got there, he found everything as usual. Stockford's car reversed and carefully parked in the driveway. His mobile phone on the hallway table, where he always left it when he came in. His shoes on the rack by the door. His jacket on a peg above it. Ellison called out his friend's name. Then he looked down the hallway, and saw Stockford's legs sprawling out from a small cupboard under the stairs.

"I thought he'd collapsed. I whipped the door open. He had hung himself. The sight of it will never leave me. I tried to pick him up, but he'd been there twenty hours. He was stone cold."

Ellison is convinced that Stockford's suicide wasn't an act of desperation. The cupboard was very low; he could have stopped the hanging process by simply standing up. His hands were clasped in front of him. He looked calm, relaxed. The decision to end his life, thinks Ellison, was the next stage on his path to a meeting with his true inner self—a self free of time and space, unhindered by hopes or desire.

"I believe he felt this was the only way he could find enlightenment. His choice had been made, he couldn't stop."

Ellison felt Stockford's "visitations" even more intensely, and more often, than those of Duane Thomas. He thinks that this was Stockford's way of trying to help him to deal with the trauma of finding his body.

"It was as if he was wrapping himself around me as much as he possibly could, saying, *It's all right, you're going to be fine.*"

A few days after Stockford's funeral, Ellison went mountain biking on his own. But he wasn't alone for long.

"I felt Andrew right next to me. The feeling that there was another entity with me was so strong I kept looking behind me for him."

After a month, the regularity and intensity of the contact began to decrease. One evening, Ellison was upstairs in the house he shared with his girlfriend, Kerry. She had also been close to Stockford, but since his death had not felt his presence. Ellison knew she was upset about this.

"When I felt him come to me, it was much less strong than on other occasions. I said, 'Andrew, I can tell you're starting to go away. Can you visit Kerry before you leave?'"

A few minutes later he went downstairs and found Kerry in tears.

"Andrew was here," she told him. "He was with me."

Ellison doesn't claim to know how or why he has sensed his friends' spirits. It's too big, too mysterious, to even begin trying to interpret.

"There is so much out there that we don't understand," he says. "Sometimes it takes situations like this to open your eyes to that fact."

Patricia Culver, whose husband Dan died on K2 in 1993, agrees wholeheartedly. Culver, a family counselor, believes she has had "connections across the veil" with Dan. And she's enormously grateful for these connections.

"They've been a really important part of my coming to grips with my own fears about death," she says. "That experience of letting go, surrendering to another experience, which is what I believe death is—we mirror that all through our lives. If we can get that one sorted—the fear of death—it's going to topple the dominoes all the way down. Our living can take on a different intensity. But we can't just get it intellectually, it has to be palpable. We have to feel it. That's one of the gifts that Dan's death gave me."

She met Dan Culver in 1991, at a personal growth workshop in Vancouver, British Columbia. They proposed to each other on Valentine's Day, 1992, and were married the following October. Dan had started climbing six years earlier, when he was thirty-three, and he had already climbed Everest. Nine months after their wedding, he set off with the American and Canadian Expedition to K2. Both he and Patricia were eager to have a child together, and he reassured her that this would be his last big endeavor in the mountains. She admits she was naïve about the risks he would be taking on K2. And she was sure that he would be protected. They both believed in guardian angels and she accepted without question his account of his grandfather's spirit being with him on Everest in 1991. "Grandpa George," his father's father, who had died many years earlier, had also been a climber. Dan Culver had talked to him as he was summiting Everest, and he was convinced he would be there for him on K2.

At SeaTac Airport, as she was saying good-bye to her husband, something broke through Patricia's equanimity.

"I erupted into tears. They were the sort of tears that once they start it's hard to stop. Driving back to Vancouver, I cried all the way. At some level, I think I knew that this really was good-bye."

As soon as she got home, she started writing letters to Dan, and she addressed her regular journal entries to him. She's convinced she was aware of some of the things that were happening on the mountain. It wasn't the kind of telepathy they had experienced before, when Dan was stuck overnight on a climb in the Coast Mountain Range near Vancouver. This time Dan wasn't sitting in his tent sending her messages. It was a deeper connection, a conduit through which information about him and what was happening on the mountain could pass.

"I had a sense of the team, what was going on with them psychologically and physically. The dynamics between them, when someone got a bronchial infection, decisions on who was going for the summit and when, all that stuff. When his letters came, and when I got to talk to the team afterward, a lot of what I had written was validated."

At about five thirty a.m. on July 7, she sat bolt upright in bed, shaking all over. She can't remember the details of the dream that woke her so abruptly, only that she was terribly upset. She got out of bed and started to write to Dan in her journal.

"I told him about waking up in a panic. As I was writing, I suddenly got a sense of his guardian angel growing to a huge size, all around him. And I knew Grandpa George was there with him, too."

One night, several days later, she was drifting off to sleep when the phone rang. It was Jim Haberl, Dan Culver's close friend and his climbing partner on K2. For a second, Patricia forgot that both men were away in Pakistan. She thought Haberl was calling from his home in Vancouver, as he often did, wanting to speak to Dan.

"I said, 'Hi Jim, how are you?' He said he was fine. But that he had bad news."

At three p.m. on July 7, the American Phil Powers reached the top of K2. As he was heading down, he met his teammates Jim Haberl and Dan Culver, heading up. He advised them that, due to the lateness of the hour and the fact that Dan was moving so slowly, they should think about turning around. Both men refused. An hour and a half later, they became the first Canadians to stand on the summit of the mountain. They lingered there until almost five p.m., taking photos and shooting video footage. Then they began their descent, unroped. Soon they were climbing down the Bottleneck, a narrow gully of forty-five-degree rock and snow, almost a thousand feet above Camp 4. Haberl reached the bottom of the gully first. As he was beginning the traverse to Camp 4, he heard a crashing noise from above and turned to see Culver tumbling down, "faster and faster, his blond hair in the tangle of the fall." Haberl watched in horror as his best friend cartwheeled past him, hit some rocks three hundred feet below, then bounced down the South Face of K2 and into oblivion. At that moment, in a different time zone, Patricia Culver sat up in bed, shaking with panic.

She's convinced that the spirit of Grandpa George and the angel she sensed growing around her husband were there to help the transition of his energy, as his spirit was released from his body.

"He loved life. He didn't want to be out of his body. Initially he was in shock and confusion and anger. He had a rocky transition at first."

She continued to feel Dan's presence, in different ways. When the K2 team flew back to Seattle, she went down to meet them with Dan's parents and his sister. They gathered in a friend's house to talk about the accident. Jim Haberl had a picture of the mountain, to show them their route.

"Just as Jim was pointing to the place where Dan fell, the door flew open and then banged shut. There was no wind, nothing to have made it happen. Everyone was startled."

On another occasion, she was meeting with Haberl at a coffee shop in downtown Vancouver. "We were sitting inside facing the large windows. There was no wind on that day either, but just as Jim started to talk about Dan, one of the chairs outside flipped over."

Dan Culver had loved great blue herons, and had named his company after them. Following his death, his family and friends had what Patricia Culver calls "heron visitations, in the strangest places at the strangest times." On the day of his memorial, his parents were woken early in the morning by a number of herons perched on the roof of their condo, making their primordial screeching sounds. Not long afterward, a close friend of Dan's was competing in an Ironman race. In the middle of a particular long, hard hill climb on a bike, a heron flew right across his path.

"And every time I was having a really hard day," says Patricia, "herons would suddenly appear in the most unlikely places."

The British biologist Rupert Sheldrake has done extensive surveys in the United Kingdom with the recently bereaved. He estimates that almost 50 percent of people he's surveyed claim to have seen, felt, or heard the presence of the person they've lost.

"Usually they appear to them as an apparition or they feel their presence or touch, or hear their voice. In about half the cases on my database, it only happens once. When it happens they know this person has come to say good-bye or they feel enormously comforted by it."

If spirits do wander back to their loved ones from faraway places, as ghosts, winds, or birds, how do they know how to find them? When I posed this seemingly childish question to Rupert Sheldrake, he answered it seriously. Memory, he says, lies outside the brain, and therefore survives death.

"The standard scientific view is that memories are stored in the brain, so that when you die, and your brain decays, all your memories are wiped out. That means no survival of bodily death is possible. The reason that scientists like this theory is that it's a one-step argument anyone can understand. Ask a fundamentalist Christian where memory is stored and they will say it's in the brain. As soon as they admit that, they are trapped, because the brain decays at death. All forms of survival theory depend on the survival of memory."

Sheldrake believes that all living organisms have morphic fields that impose patterns on otherwise random processes. They underlie the behavior and instincts of animals and contain a collective memory of the species, which is transferred through morphic resonance, the influence of like upon like across or through space and time. He argues that morphic resonance is the basis not just of collective memory but of individual memory.

"I don't think our memories are stored inside our brains. I think the brain is more like a receiver, a TV set picking up these things, than like a video recorder that's got memory stored inside. Scientists have been trying to find memories in brains for over a hundred years and they've always failed. If you have brain damage, then indeed you get loss of memory. Most people say it's because you've destroyed the memories. But in many cases people eventually get the memories back. And even if they have been destroyed, say with Alzheimer's disease, that doesn't prove the memories are stored in the brain, it merely proves that those parts of the brain that are necessary for tuning in have been destroyed. I could take away parts of your TV, and make it aphasic, so you couldn't get sounds, only pictures. But it wouldn't prove the sounds were in the bit I've damaged, it would only prove it plays an essential role in the reception of the sound."

Memory, says Sheldrake, is not stored anywhere. Morphic resonance leaps across time from the past to the present, so the whole of the past is potentially present everywhere. You can tune into it on the basis of similarity. So the question is, how can you access the memories when the physical brain decays?

"I can't say anything from science to give a clear answer," says Sheldrake. "But the morphic resonance theory of memory leaves that question open whereas the conventional theory of memory leaves that question closed."

On a May morning in 2000, Beth Malloy climbed onto her exercise bike for part of her daily workout. She was reading while she pedaled. After a while her attention wandered from the book. A thought went through her head. *I wonder if Seth isn't going to come back.*

Seth Shaw, her boyfriend of eleven years, was away climbing in Alaska with his friend Tim Wagner. Malloy wasn't unduly worried about him. She had confidence in his abilities and judgment—he worked as an avalanche forecaster, so she knew he paid close attention to snow and ice conditions.

Malloy was a climber herself and she had been on expeditions with Seth, in Alaska, Peru, and Canada, as well as the States, tackling routes that were difficult enough for her, but easy for him. She was not prepared to take the sort of risks he loved, so at least once every year he would take off with some friends to really push his limits.

Whenever Seth left on one of these trips, Beth would occasionally consider the possibility of his not returning, and what that would mean for her. Then she would tell herself not to dwell on such things, to think positively. That's how it had always been.

"But this was really different," she said. "The idea of him not coming back popped into my head again and with it I got the most serene feeling. I understood that whatever happened, it would be okay."

Seconds later, Seth Shaw materialized before her.

"I wasn't dreaming," she recalls. "I was wide awake and my eyes were open. I got a complete vision of him, standing right in front of me. He was so close I could see every detail of him, even his chest hairs. It was as if there was all this love around him, giving me a peaceful, calming feeling."

The vision only lasted a few seconds. When it faded, she shook her head. *Wow,* she thought, *that was bizarre.* But the peaceful feeling remained.

That afternoon, she came home from work to find the phone ringing. It was Tim Wagner's girlfriend, asking her if she had any news of the men. They were chatting when Malloy's father and stepmother walked into her house.

Her father said, "Beth, we need to talk to you. Hang up." She knew from the expression on his face that whatever he had to talk about wasn't good.

The previous night, at ten p.m., Shaw had been standing on Ruth Glacier when a serac broke off directly above him, burying him under thousands of tons of ice. Wagner survived the serac collapse, but broke his leg. He crawled to the base camp of another climbing party to ask them to radio the rangers. It was the next afternoon before they came to pick him up, flew by the site of the accident, and started to make the necessary calls. By then, Shaw had already appeared to Malloy. Hours before she knew he was dead.

"If it had happened after I knew he'd died," she says, "you could say that it was the stress causing me to imagine these things. But at the time I had no idea. It convinced me that something does happen after we die. That our souls do go on."

She never saw another vision of Shaw, but over the next few months she was often aware of him.

"I kept feeling he was in a really good place. That he was really happy and trying to give me a lot of loving energy. It made me stronger."

That summer, she went to Bolivia with some friends, on a rock-climbing trip. It was hard for her; she felt deeply lonely for Shaw.

"I had my own tent, and I was lying there one night thinking about Seth and wondering what his soul was doing. I was thinking, *Okay, Seth, where are you? Are you around?* Suddenly my tent lit up. I thought someone was on the way to the latrine and was shining their flashlight on my tent. Then I realized the light came from my own headlamp, lying next to me. It had turned on by itself, right at the moment when I was asking Seth questions in my head. I thought, *Oh my God.* I picked up the headlamp and started examining it to see if it had got jarred somehow. It had a little catch that you have to push over to turn it on. I have an engineering degree, so I was trying to work out exactly how much pressure would it take to turn this on. I tested it, turning it on and off lots of times. I realized that it would take a certain amount of force, that simply jarring it wouldn't work."

She lay down, pondering all this. Finally she drifted off to sleep, and into a vivid dream about Seth Shaw.

"Seth came to say good-bye. He said, *It's time for me to leave, Beth. I have to go on now.* I woke up just bawling. It was almost like a second death for me. When I first found out he was dead I felt his presence around. But when I had that dream, and I realized he was moving on, I felt so alone. It was really hard; it set me back for a while."

Since then she's sensed his presence only a few times—and always very faintly, like a distant shadow passing.

Shadows passing. When Alex MacIntyre died on Annapurna, his girlfriend Sarah Richard was tossing and turning in bed, thousands of miles away in England.

"I kept waking up throughout the night seeing a shadow walk across my vision," she recalls. "It happened maybe three or four times. I'd wake up and think, *Oh, what was that?* It was something walking."

In August 1971, Arlene Blum was on her way home from the university campus in Berkeley, where she was working on a Ph.D. in biophysical chemistry. She was also in the midst of planning the Endless Winter Expedition, a yearlong climbing trip to peaks around the world. One of the team was a man who had been her on-off boyfriend for the previous nine years. He was away climbing with friends in Alaska, and she didn't expect him back for a couple of weeks. But as she turned the corner onto her street she saw him on her porch. He had his back to her, and was just stepping through the front door. She ran up, thrilled that he was home early. Flinging open the door, she started calling his name. *John! John?* She ran from room to room, searching the whole house. He wasn't there. A week later she got news that he and three of his teammates had been buried in an avalanche on Mount Saint Elias. It had happened on the afternoon of August 11, a few hours before she saw him on the porch.

To try to explain such paranormal phenomena, parapsychologists have long cited Einstein's "spooky action at a distance"—the apparent ability of interacting, or entangled subatomic particles to affect each other no matter how far apart they are in the universe. The physicist and science-fiction writer John Cramer suggested a new twist on this: an electron or photon emits an "offer" wave that travels outward and forward in time at the speed of light until it encounters a particle that can absorb it. The absorbing particle then emits an "acceptance" wave that travels back along the route of the offer wave—both in space and time, arriving at the same time that the offer wave is emitted. The emitting particle "instantly knows" the quantum state of the absorbing particle, since the information waves travel backward and forward in time without taking any time to do so. A logical consequence of this is that all of the "information" about everything that has ever happened or ever will happen coexists simultaneously in temporal space. If people somehow become attuned to a frequency on which some of these information waves exist, they can receive information about future events, or events that are happening in real time. And if they latch onto the frequency of some dead person's experiences? Presumably they experience the presence of that person.

Contact with the dead is usually dismissed as wishful thinking, a projection, a fantasy, a hallucination. Something the brain conjures up to help the grieving deal with their loss. One psychiatrist I spoke to attributed Sara Whitner's experience of a floating ghost to extreme distress, exhaustion, and, in her half-dream state, harking back sub-consciously to childhood memories. Ghosts are often perceived as floating, and this could be a result of the mind recalling some of our earliest experiences, such as seeing people leaning over us as we lie in a crib.

I'm not so sure. I've had a few of my own ghost encounters. Whether they were the result of my own brain activity, another con-sciousness stretching out to touch mine, or some strange quantum effect, I can't say. What I do know is that they brought me comfort, then unease, and that eventually I was able to control them.

While Joe Tasker was away on his last expedition, to attempt Everest's then-unclimbed Northeast Ridge, I went on a rock-climbing course in the Lake District with some girlfriends. We were shar-ing a room in a hostel. One night I dreamed I was running down the village street, wailing and distraught. My friends remember me sitting bolt upright, crying out, *Joe's dead.* Three weeks later, news came that he had disappeared on Everest. When I traced it back, my dream had occurred only hours after he was last sighted on the mountain.

A few days after getting the news of Joe's disappearance, I asked my closest friend, Sarah Richard, to drive me from where I lived in Manchester to his house in Derbyshire. It was a dreadful journey, knowing I would not find him at home, not then or ever again. I sat in the car, distraught, feeling sucked toward a terrible finality. Sarah reached over from time to time to squeeze my hand.

I had driven that road countless times before, on my way to see Joe. Always, as I passed beneath a bridge on the edge of the city and caught a glimpse of the Derbyshire hills, my heart would lift with joy. That bridge felt like a marker between my old life and a new, happier one with Joe. This time, though, something different happened as I passed beneath it. Joe arrived. He was suddenly in the car, all around me. A warm, comforting, suffusing presence. My tears stopped; I hardly dared breathe, fearful that I would lose this sense of him. Gradually, I relaxed, basking in his reassurance. There was no vision, no sound, only a feeling of intense peace. The feeling I had always had when I woke up in his arms.

Sarah said nothing for the rest of the way. After half an hour or so we arrived at the little cottage she shared with Alex MacIntyre, and I slid over into the driver's seat. I wanted to go alone to Joe's house. I rolled down the window and she ducked her head in to kiss me. "Are you sure you're all right?"

I told her I was fine. I drove along a back lane. Sunlight filtered through an arch of tree branches, setting the leaves alight. Surrounded by Joe, I felt high, and happy. But when I got to the house and unlocked the door, the comfort of his presence was swept away for a while. I wanted so badly to be doing this with him, his warm, breathing body, not just his spirit. I wandered around distractedly, touching all the familiar things. Going into the bedroom was hardest of all. I lay down and wrapped myself in the duvet. As my nostrils filled with his smell, I felt him about me more powerfully than before. I talked aloud to him, cried, and finally fell into a deep sleep. When I woke, blinking at mid-afternoon sun streaming through the window, he was still there. He was in the car as I drove back toward Sarah's cottage. Only as I parked and walked up the narrow track did the feeling of him begin to fade.

Sarah was standing in the garden, watching my approach. The scene was like an impressionist painting. A tall, blond woman among overgrown grasses, one hand held up to shade her eyes against the bright light. Behind her, green fields and stone walls sweeping up toward the summery blue sky.

I began to tell her about Joe. She wasn't surprised. She'd felt him too, she said. In the car, when she was driving. A strong sense of his presence. It had started as we headed under the bridge.

"I wasn't going to say anything," she admitted, "in case it upset you."

I longed for Joe's presence to return, but I couldn't summon it at will. Occasionally, over the next few years, it would arrive without warning. While I was trekking across a high pass in Tibet. While I was writing a book about him. While I was kayaking on the ocean, close to my new home in Canada. And in dreams.

At first, the dreams were troubling. In them he was alive, he'd come back from Everest, but he was rejecting me. Sometimes we were at a party and he was with another woman. Once, I was calling him at his house and a woman answered the phone. She said she would go to fetch him. I was looking through the window of his house and I could see the phone, lying off the hook on a table in his living room. He never came to pick it up and speak to me.

After a few years, the dreams changed. He was alive and loving, and he wanted us to be together again. But by this time I was happily married, and I would wake up confused and conflicted. The space between these dreams increased, until they occurred only once or twice a year, but they were always intense, and disturbing. One morning, almost two decades after he died, I woke from such a dream feeling really angry. With my husband fast asleep beside me, I sat up and spoke aloud to Joe. I told him I loved him and always would. I forgave him and myself for the mistakes we had made in our relationship. It was time now, I insisted, for these dreams to stop.

"No more dreams, Joe," I said firmly. "It's over. Please get out of my head."

I went downstairs, made myself some tea, and sat looking out at the ocean, with one of our cats purring on my lap. Up in our loft bedroom, I heard my husband stir and yawn. *This* was my reality. And the dreams—were they my own creation, or had Joe's energy somehow been part of them? There's no way of knowing, but since that morning I've never had one again.

Part Four

And the point is to live everything. Live the questions now. Perhaps then, someday far into the future, you will gradually, without even noticing it, live your way into the answer.

RAINER MARIA RILKE, *Letters to a Young Poet*

Chapter 10

SPIRITUAL TOOLS

Climbing is the lazy man's way to enlightenment. It forces you to pay attention, because if you don't you won't succeed, which is minor—or you may get hurt, which is major. Instead of years of meditation, you have this activity that forces you to relax and monitor your breathing and tread that line between living and dying. When you climb, you are always confronted with that edge. Hey, if it was just like climbing a ladder we would all have quit a long time ago.

DUNCAN FERGUSON, "Life on the Edge"

Adrian Burgess was leading his twin brother, Alan, up a climb in the Dolomites. The pitch was a right-facing corner, his ropes were swinging on either side of it and one of them got caught in a protruding piece of rock. As Adrian pulled the rope free, a big chunk of the rock sheared off. It hit the face twenty feet above the ledge where Alan was on belay, and shattered into several pieces.

"I saw this rock coming at me," Alan Burgess recalls. "I dived in, trying to flatten myself against the face. I thought, *I'm going to take it on my helmet or my back.* All this must have lasted about a second, even though it seemed a lot longer at the time."

The next thing he knew, the rock that had been coming straight for him was sitting on top of his daypack, next to him on the ledge. He stared at it in disbelief. It was twelve inches across, eight inches wide, and eight inches deep. Too big to be sitting cushioned on that pack. But that's where it was. Later, his brother told him that the rock seemed to be heading right at him when, at the last second, it stopped and floated off to the right.

"If the rock had gone over my head and down the face, I would have said, *Holy shit, that was close,*" says Alan. "But it didn't. It floated off to one side and landed on my pack. I leaned over and tipped it off. I was shaking after that. We still had to climb a thousand feet and the face was really loose. It was scary as hell. When we got to the top, Adrian said, 'Good job you've been doing your yoga, youth.' Typical Adrian. Not saying what he was really thinking."

After the climb, when Alan Burgess told people about what he calls "the floating rock," they would usually say he had a guardian angel, or that God was watching out for him.

"As if I had nothing to do with it," he snorts. "What that rock did is supposedly impossible. But maybe there are other realities. Maybe just occasionally, in times of duress, we can observe them. What I think now is that I ripped a little corner of our usual reality. Just for a millisecond, I moved into a different reality where gravity isn't fixed. And that what happened was to do with my own energy."

Burgess believes in the power of chi, a universal life energy that, according to Chinese philosophy, animates all things. Highly trained martial artists claim to be able to put up walls of chi energy around them, something Burgess feels he might have done unwittingly, as the rock fell toward him. He's convinced that the change in its trajectory wasn't a freak occurrence.

"Maybe it was the gathering of all my hopes, fears, and whatever else was going around—I'll accept a guardian angel if that's what it was—so that for a millisecond something else played out."

Something that he can't explain, but believes in nonetheless.

For the last decade, Alan Burgess has practiced and taught Ashtanga yoga, in which breath is synchronized with movement. He's convinced that high-altitude climbers are practicing yoga without realizing it.

"It might be a crude form of yoga, but it's happening. They're doing it, twenty-four hours a day on the mountain. They're living it. Imagine the breath control at high altitude. You've got to slow it down so much, for long periods of time, hour after hour."

When he guides his yoga students through meditation, he tells them to create the waters of a lake, and to quiet the surface so they can observe the bubbles coming up from the bottom—bubbles that represent their true selves. It's a process that he remembers happening naturally in the mountains.

"Being high up, surrounded by immense natural forces, the chatter automatically dies away. Then there are the deep levels of relaxation you reach when you're lying in your bivouac or at base camp, recovering. Without even realizing it you're practicing *shavasana*—the corpse pose."

He recalls a time in the Alps when he was climbing a hard ice route with his brother and two other alpinists. By nightfall they had finished the route, but as they still had at least another half-day of climbing to get to the top of the mountain, they set up a bivouac. There was no big ledge for them all to lie on, so each just had to find a suitable place to spend the night.

"I found a perfect site in the shelter of a huge block," says Alan. "I didn't need to be tied on. I could stretch out fully, on my back. I remember totally relaxing, and not letting my head get into the fear of tomorrow because there was nothing we could do about it. There were so many other times like that, when we were really cold, sat on small ledges in the Alps or the Himalayas, without much food or fluid. Just enduring things. All we had was our breath. I used to focus on breathing and relaxing to generate heat. I wasn't having mystical experiences, I was just surviving. But I do think I was tapping into methods that are ancient spiritual tools. Anyone at high altitude, breathing concentratedly without oxygen, taps into a spiritual world."

So, are climbers, and other types of adventurers, on a spiritual search? "They have to be," says Burgess. "But you know how climbers are. They will give you flippant answers to questions like this, so you can't discover their deeper motives."

Tomaz Humar, a Slovenian mountaineer, is far from shy about his spiritual motives. Humar started climbing in his late teens, in the mountains near his family home. Slovenia has a long tradition of mountaineering, and in a country of two million people there are approximately forty climbing clubs, filled with people who have put up new routes throughout the Alps and the Himalayas. To make his mark, Humar knew he would have to do something extra-special. He set off to find spiritual tools that would enable him to climb in the severest of conditions. He began to see everything in nature, and especially mountains, as alive. He taught himself how to feel the energy of a mountain, to communicate with the mountain and respect what it told him.

"I understand the mountains not just with my muscles but with my third eye," he says. "This is my secret weapon. With my third eye I can measure people, what sort of energy they have, I can read their chakras. And I use it to talk to the mountains. I never solo-climb unless the mountain face calls me. If the mountain doesn't accept you, and if you don't meet her wishes, she will destroy you."

His Himalayan career began in 1994, when he climbed Ganesh V in Nepal. Over the next five years he made a number of ascents that stunned the mountaineering world. He summitted Annapurna alone, via the French Route, in a blizzard, ignoring the commands of his expedition leader that he turn back. He put a new route up the Northwest Face of Ama Dablam and traversed its southwest ridge in conditions that had defeated four other expeditions on the mountain at the same time. He soloed Bobaye, a virgin peak in Western Nepal. In one year he climbed Lobuche East, Pomori, and the West Face of Nuptse, where his climbing partner was blown off the summit by hurricane-force winds. He ascended Reticence Wall, the hardest ascent in Yosemite Valley.

In November 1999, he spent ten nights and eleven days alone on the South Face of Dhaulagiri—a face mined by enormous overhanging seracs and loose rock. Humar climbed it solo, on a new route, mostly without any form of protection. On the second day of the climb, a series of seracs broke off above him, and for four hours he was battered by avalanches of ice and snow, leaving him bruised and bloodied. On the sixth day he developed a bad toothache, and performed some emergency dental work on himself, using a Swiss Army knife to dig a hole through a filling and release the pus underneath. For the last two nights he was forced to bivouac at 26,600 feet on exposed ledges, without food, water, or oxygen. He credits his survival on that expedition, and the others that preceded it, to the mystical powers that he had been developing for years. He slowed down his heartbeat, drew most of his blood into the core of his body, separated from the physical world so that he could withstand the cold, thirst, hunger, and pain. He opened his "third eye." Such powers, Humar believes, point to where the future of mountaineering lies.

"With our third eyes open," he writes, "we will be able to understand and accept the danger which has so far been unforeseeable. We will have to cross the threshold of earthly life and concentrate on other dimensions, which are still beyond western comprehensions."

Back in Slovenia, he was doing some building work on his house when he fell into the cellar and broke both legs. But that only slowed him down for a while. Between 2002 and 2004 he climbed several Himalayan peaks and made two attempts on Nanga Parbat.

As usual, before starting each climb he meditated at the base of the mountain, waiting to receive its call. When the call came, it was so strong, he likened it to "a telephone, buzzing." It's because of this connection, he believes, that he has survived, while so many of his friends have died climbing. On his second attempt to climb Nanga Parbat, however, his spiritual connection with the mountain failed him. Or he failed it.

His aim was to put a new route up the Central Pillar of the fearsome Rupal Face, the biggest mountain wall in the world. Among Humar's base camp team was Natasa Pergar, a bio-therapist who had been working with him for four years, guiding his spiritual development. Pergar claims to be able to read the auras of both people and mountains. She is reported to have told Humar that she saw a green aura emanating from the Rupal Face, which she interpreted as the mountain expressing anger. Despite this, and despite the marginal weather conditions, Humar pushed ahead with his solo climb, possibly because two other mountaineers had just arrived at base camp, intent on climbing the same route.

When Humar was halfway up the Rupal Face, fog closed around the mountain, and a series of avalanches and rockfalls began rain-ing down, forcing him to lie huddled in a bivouac, slowly freezing, starving, and becoming seriously dehydrated. He had always boasted that he only climbed routes where rescue wasn't possible, so that in difficult situations he would have to rely on himself, his special powers, and God. But after nine days stuck on the Rupal Face, realizing that even if conditions improved he would be too weak to climb down, he radioed his Base Camp, calling for a helicopter rescue. Two pilots from the Pakistan Air Force executed an extraordinarily difficult maneuver, unprecedented at that altitude. Hovering in their machines perilously close to the face, they managed to pluck Humar off the ledge. But in the stress of the moment, he forgot to unclip from his anchor. As he was hauled up, his lifeline to the mountain turned into a potential death line, threatening to tug the helicopter from the sky. At the last second it snapped, saving all their lives.

In the mountaineering world, his epic was fiercely criticized as a fiasco, the result of him bending to the pressures of sponsors and his own ambition, and making bad judgment calls. For a while he lay low. Until, in 2007, he quietly headed off to Annapurna, and, without any pre-publicity spent four days climbing solo to the summit. His spiritual connection, it seems, was back in place.

Humar is not alone in his description of a third eye opening at the threshold of life and death. During his solo monoplane flight from New York to Paris in 1927, Charles Lindbergh experienced limitless vision. "My skull is one great eye, seeing everywhere at once," he writes. "…I'm on the border line of…a greater real beyond, as though caught in the field of gravitation between two planets, acted on by forces I can't control, forces too weak to be measured by any means at my command, yet representing powers incomparably stronger than I have ever known."

For the Canadian freediver Mandy Rae Cruickshank, something akin to a third eye screens out any distraction during the lead up to a competition. Before a 213-foot constant ballast dive in Kona, Hawaii, in 2002, she spent about seven minutes "breathing up" to get as much air as possible into her system.

"There was a boat full of people hanging beside me watching, there were cameras all over, there were people right beside me yelling in my ear, but I got so internally focused, everyone literally disappeared," she says. "And during the dive, I don't remember seeing the safety divers or video cameras or the still camera flashes. I have no idea how I did the dive. This only happens when I have to perform. It's amazing how far you can get pulled in when the time is ready."

For Reinhold Messner, it happens during or just after a particularly challenging climb.

"Everything goes black in front of my eyes," he writes, about approaching high camp after completing his solo climb of Everest. "Slowly, very slowly, I let myself dissolve. With each further step downward, with the marker poles in front of me, the first moraines in sight, the whole world stands revealed within me. I see my whole being from without. 'Here' is now somewhere else. I am transparent, made of glass, borne up by the world."

The commitment and discipline of such extreme adventurers, and the concomitant rewards, echo those of Eastern mystics. Han Shan, a hermit and poet of the eighth-century T'ang Dynasty, wrote most of his poems while living in caves in China's T'ien-t'ai Mountains, where he was said to have experienced profound mystical awareness and altered states of consciousness. In the 1990s, author George

Crane visited some of Han Shan's haunts. "Incidentally, these sages were fine climbers," he writes. "During the Cultural Revolution the Red Guards swarmed up into the T'ien-t'ai to destroy the inscriptions these lone holy men had left on the cliffs; they had to use elaborate rappel systems. . . . to reach them."

Milarepa, a Tibetan saint, wandered the Himalayas for years, surviving on nettle tea that was said to have turned his skin green. He dwelt in caves for whole winters, practicing *tumo,* the raising of mystical heat, to keep warm.

"To spend the winter in a cave at an altitude that varies between 11,000 and 18,000 feet, clad in a thin garment or even naked, and escape freezing, is a somewhat difficult achievement," writes Alexandra David-Neel, a French explorer. "Yet numbers of Tibetan hermits go safely each year through this ordeal. Their endurance is ascribed . . . to *tumo.*"

Between 1914 and 1918, David-Neel lived in a cave—albeit one with carpets—at thirteen thousand feet in northern Sikkim. During this period she made her first visit to Tibet, secretly crossing the border. In the 1920s she was the first foreign woman to visit Lhasa, and over the next several decades she traveled extensively in Tibet, studying and writing exhaustively about its spiritual practices.

In *Magic and Mystery in Tibet* she outlines the complicated stages of activating *tumo*—demanding yoga *asanas,* deep concentration, visualizations of fire in the spine, and prolonged retention of the breath. She also describes the tests that *tumo* neophytes are subjected to by their gurus: "[They] sit on the ground cross-legged and naked. Sheets are dipped in the icy water, each man wraps himself in one of them and must dry it on his body. As soon as the sheet has become dry, it is again dipped in the icy water and placed on the novice's body to be dried as before. The operation goes on in that way until daybreak.

Then he who has dried the largest number of sheets is acknowledged the winner of the competition."

The American climber Stephen Koch automatically practiced a form of *tumo* during a night he spent alone and badly injured on the slopes of Mount Owen in the Teton Range of Wyoming, in the spring of 1998. He was solo-climbing on the north side of the mountain, hoping to do the first snowboard descent from its summit. It was a warm, sunny day, and, as he planned to be down the mountain and on his way home by mid-afternoon, he was lightly dressed and carrying little extra gear. But as he was nearing the top of Koven Col, the sun loosened the slopes above him, triggering a big avalanche that carried him a thousand feet down the mountain, and over a big cliff.

"I knew while it was happening that my body was getting broken apart," Koch recalls. "I remember thinking, *Oh, there goes my right knee, there goes my left knee, next it's going to be my head. I'll hit my head on a rock and it will be all over.* Suddenly everything got super-quiet, and I thought, *It's over, it's done, I'm dead.* Then I realized I was in the air, going over the cliff. I landed hard, which is probably when I broke my back, and I kept going down the slope. I was thinking, *I'm still alive, I should try and stop.* I was on my stomach, so I clawed at the snow with my fingers, trying to self-arrest. It must have worked but as I slowed down the wet snow kept going. It filled my mouth and throat and it tore up my esophagus."

He found himself lying on the surface of the slope, in bright sunlight. His right knee was dislocated and the anterior cruciate ligament of his left knee was ripped. His back was broken in two places. He had smashed some ribs, and he was covered with cuts, scrapes, and bruises. The slopes above him were still laden with snow and he knew another avalanche was imminent. To survive, somehow he had to move.

"I managed to drag myself to the side. It wasn't easy with two legs that didn't work. And my right knee was a flopping mess, barely held on with skin. I sat in the sun for a while, drifting in and out of consciousness. The next avalanches started coming down, there were big bowling balls of snow going every which way. I remember thinking, *Oh please, don't hit my leg.*"

For several hours he lay in the sunshine. But gradually the shadows lengthened, until he was in the shade, and temperatures were quickly dropping. He started crawling and sliding down the mountain, trying to reach the place where he had left a stuff sack earlier in the day. By nightfall he had made it. Inside the sack were two candy bars, a head band, and a couple of "shake and warm" hand heaters. The avalanche had ripped away his backpack, so he had no extra clothes to put on, and nothing to drink. He lay down and prepared to endure the long night ahead. He was too badly injured to do calisthenics to keep warm. All he had was his breath.

He spent the entire night focusing on breathing deep and fast to fend off the beginning stages of hypothermia. From time to time he also tried to send out mental messages to people, that he needed help. A close friend of his got worried when Koch didn't come back from the day trip, and rang the park rangers. Early the next morning, a search was mounted.

"They followed my tracks, saw the avalanche debris, and found me," says Koch. "As soon as they were there I went into hypothermia; I started convulsing with cold. I knew I was in their hands and safe, so I could finally relax."

Alexandra David-Neel also described the Tantric discipline of *lung gom,* which translates to "wind concentration" and is a psychic state enabling its adepts to walk great distances, at speed, for long periods, without rest. After witnessing such an adept, David-Neel wrote, "The man did not run. He seemed to lift himself from the ground proceeding by leaps. It looked as if he had been endowed with the elasticity of a ball and rebounded each time his feet touched the ground."

These runners, known as *lung-gom-pa,* were said to be able to travel nonstop for forty-eight hours or more, covering at least two hundred miles a day—a feat that would impress the best of today's ultramarathon runners. In *The Way of the White Clouds,* Lama Anagarika Govinda, a German-born explorer of Tibet and its mysticism, explains the practice and meaning of *lung-gom. Lung* signifies air, as well as psychic force. *Gom* means the concentration of one's entire being on a single thing. A *lung-gom-pa,* then, is someone who can control and channel his energy through the ancient practice of *pranayama*—yogic breathing. To qualify as a *lung-gom-pa,* the trainee had to master deep-breathing techniques and visualizations in which they imagined their own body to be as light as a feather. "The *lung-gom-pa* method does not aim at training the disciple by strengthening his muscles," writes Lama Anagarika Govinda, "but by developing his psychic states that make these extraordinary marches possible."

After years of preparation, the *lung-gom-pa* were allowed to demonstrate these skills. Some, like the man David-Neel witnessed, at times became so light they seemed to float through the air. To prevent this actually going out of control, they would wear heavy chains around their necks.

Ancient stories of people floating or flying might be ascribed, in part, to practices similar to *lung-gom.* Milarepa was said to have flown to the top of Mount Kalias. Saint Joseph of Cupertino apparently was often seen levitating, sometimes for up to two hours at a time. Saint Teresa of Avila experienced levitating during states of rapture, and was reported by Sister Ann of the Incarnation to have floated a foot off the ground for thirty minutes. Saint Teresa wrote of these occurrences, "It seemed to me, when I tried to make some resistance, as if a great force beneath me lifted me up." She stayed conscious throughout the levitations, and described looking down on her body and seeing it being lifted up—a classic example of what is now known as an OBE—an out-of-body experience.

The British alpinist Andy Parkin once found himself looking down on his own body. It happened in the 1990s, during a winter climb in the Alps.

"I was soloing Les Droites, a thousand-meter [three-thousand-foot] face, one of the hardest in the Alps," says Parkin. "I was aware of the vast expanse of this face, it was very harsh, very cold, but I was moving like the wind, totally at ease, totally confident. Then, when I was about halfway up, suddenly I was looking at myself. It was like I was floating out in space, watching myself climb. There was a part of me still on the face thinking, *Come back here, this is not a good moment to drift off.* I had to force myself to pull back into my own body. It didn't happen because I was gripped—you can't allow yourself that emotion when you're soloing. But I was in a state of hyper-awareness. It's happened occasionally when I've been in that state. Maybe it's a chemical thing."

In 1993, Marshall Ulrich was running the Badwater course, trying to break his own record. He set out at six p.m., watched the sun go down, and carried on running into the night. At some point, around the forty-mile mark, he felt himself leave his body. Suddenly the effort of running was gone—from above, he watched his lone figure pounding along the road, he could hear his footfall and see his support team waiting at certain stages with food and water. He saw himself eating and drinking as he ran.

"It was like watching myself on a movie screen," he says. "I lost all sense of time. It could have been only ten minutes that had passed, but then I realized that dawn was coming, the sun was about to rise. I knew it was time to go back into my body."

He was reluctant to tell anyone about this, particularly other runners. "I was sure they'd think I was nutty." Then he met Yiannis Kouros, the legendary, world-record-breaking Greek ultramarathoner, who now lives in Australia. Kouros is unabashed about the spiritual component to his running.

"It is not easy," he writes, "to grasp what is taking place in the mind and the soul, in the senses and beyond the senses of a runner due to the refusal of the body. Only if the runner achieves his transcendence, and especially in the metaphysical level, he is then able to continue."

When he heard Ulrich's story, he fully understood. And he told him how to get back to that place.

"He said I have to break myself down until there's nothing left— until I transcend the limits of my physical body and enter a new realm of existence."

And how does it feel to leave that new realm of existence and go back into a body that has just run right through the night?

"Painful," he says. "I wanted to get up and out of myself again."

According to polls done in the United Kingdom, approximately 10 percent of people claim to have had OBEs, yet scientists know very little about the phenomena. They are often a symptom of another strange occurrence—the NDE, or near-death experience, in which people, while apparently dead, go through a series of vivid sensations and emotions before eventually returning to life.

In Tibetan Buddhism, people who appear to die and then come back to life are referred to as *delok*s. During the period between life and death they find themselves traveling in the *bardo* state, where they report visits to heavenly and hellish states, and encounters with protective deities. Alexandra David-Neel described an encounter with a *delok* in the 1920s.

"She said she had been agreeably astonished by the lightness and agility of her new body," writes David-Neel. "She could cross rivers, walk upon waters, or pass through walls. There was only one thing she found impossible—to cut an almost impalpable cord...which lengthened out indefinitely."

The term "near-death experience" was introduced by Raymond Moody, an American physician, in the 1970s. In his book *Life After Life*, he outlines nine elements that generally occur during NDEs, almost all of them pleasant, including a buzzing or ringing noise, a sense of peace, the feeling of moving down a tunnel toward bright light, a review of one's past life, and a reluctance to return to that life. Some people, like *delok*s, reported negative and often terrifying experiences. But even in these cases there was a conviction that if a final boundary was crossed, there was no going back.

Hilary Rhodes went through many of those stages when she was avalanched while heli-skiing in the Alps in 1982. There were eleven people in her group, and when the helicopter dropped them off she was the third to set off down the mountain. She had almost reached the end of the run, and was skiing down the final moraine, when the remaining skiers all pushed off from the top, one right after the other. Their combined weight set off a slab avalanche, about nine hundred feet long and wide, which caught up with Rhodes in seconds. At first she managed to ski on its surface, but as she grasped the scale of the monster, she was consumed with anger that it was probably about to kill her. Her husband, Peter Boardman, was climbing Everest at the time; he had promised it was to be his last big expedition and on his return they were planning to start a family.

"I was fighting to stay on my skis," she recalls. "And I was scream-ing out loud, 'It's not fair! Not now, it can't be now!'"

She reached the bottom of the slope and had come to a stop when the tail end of the avalanche engulfed her. She was buried under three feet of snow.

"I can remember a terrifying feeling of concrete setting around me," says Rhodes, "and not being able to move or breathe. Then it was just like going into oblivion until suddenly I found myself in this amazing tunnel. I was going round and round and round, like water going down a sink. It was amazingly peaceful, but exciting as well, in a strange way."

The skiers above her had managed to pinpoint where she had been buried, and within fifteen minutes they were digging her out. They soon knew they had the exact spot, because they heard her screaming under the snow.

"Once they started to get the weight of snow off my chest and I could breathe again, the pain was horrendous," she says. "But I hadn't been physically injured. I think it was the pain of my spirit having to come back into my body."

Many scientists would say that her experiences were hallucina-tions brought on by lack of oxygen and intense fear. That her peace-fulness and euphoria, for example, were the result of a massive release of endorphins, which may also have caused seizures in the temporal lobe—long suspected as the trigger for a range of religious and mys-tical experiences. Susan Blackmore, a British psychologist and the author of *Dying to Live,* further explains Rhodes's NDE through her "dying brain hypothesis": as the outer senses begin to fail, the brain struggles to construct a model of reality by drawing on inner data, using memory and imagination. These inner processes are perceived as outer events—a result of changes in the visual cortex brought

about by anoxia and the effects of massive releases of endorphins to
the frontal lobe. To explain the tunnel effect, Blackmore has developed some computer mapping of the effects of increased electrical
noise in the visual cortex—the part of the brain that processes visual
information. Brain activity is kept stable by some cells inhibiting
others. When disinhibition occurs—for example, due to anoxia—an
excess of brain activity, or neural noise, occurs. Blackmore's mapping
produces a series of images that look like a dark tunnel with a glow-
ing light at the end.

"According to this theory, the tunnel would come to an end when
all the cells cease to fire," she says. "Alternatively, if the oxygen supply
is returned before this stage is reached, the inhibition would resume,
the light would dim, and the movement reverse. In this case one would
presumably have the sensation of going back down the tunnel."

What the person having an NDE sees and hears, as described by
Moody and a host of other reports, are, says Blackmore, "a fiction
they are creating, to make sense of this extreme situation they find
themselves in."

Sam Parnia was sixteen years old, studying in England and dreaming of becoming a doctor, when he came across Raymond Moody's
book on NDEs. He was struck by the similarities of people's experiences, and the stories stayed with him as he worked hard to qualify
for medical school. Toward the end of his training, he took a place-
ment at the Mount Sinai Medical Center in New York. One morning
he spent a pleasant hour on a ward, chatting with a patient. Not long
afterward, he got a cardiac-arrest call. He ran to help the team of doctors. The man they were frantically trying to resuscitate was, Parnia
realized, the very patient he had been conversing with earlier that day.
When the doctors failed to bring him back, Parnia began wondering what had happened to the person he had laughed and joked with

shortly before. Had he been floating out of his body, watching the attempts to resuscitate him? Did his consciousness survive in some form, or was it lost with the death of his body?

"I really wanted to know," says Parnia, "but the answers were not available. After I qualified as a doctor I decided the best way to find out was to do the work myself."

He teamed up with Dr. Peter Fenwick, a London-based neuro-psychiatrist, who had just published a book on NDE, in which he critically examines three hundred such reports. In 1997, the two physicians began a pilot study in the coronary care, emergency, and medical units of Southampton Hospital, interviewing patients who had suffered heart attacks and who, until responding to resuscitation, had for a short time been clinically dead, with no pulse or respiration and with fixed, dilated pupils. Of sixty-three patients interviewed, only six had memories of sounds, visions, or emotions while they were "flatlined." But as news of the study spread, Parnia was contacted by more than five hundred other people who had survived a close brush with death. Their stories were remarkably similar to the patients in Parnia's study, and the cases that had been reported by Moody. In 2005, Dr. Parnia published his findings, and now, with Dr. Fenwick, he is leading more wide-ranging studies in a number of hospitals, in the United Kingdom and the United States.

Needless to say, their work comes under criticism from the scientific community. Christopher French, a professor of psychology at Goldsmiths College, University of London, claims that "virtually all the aspects of the NDE have been reported in other contexts," including out-of-body experiences reported by patients when the right angular gyrus of their brain was stimulated. However, even Professor French is not totally dismissive of the experience itself.

"I think it will be a long time before we fully understand the

NDE," he said, in a BBC-broadcast debate on the subject. "It's an incredibly fascinating and profound experience for the people that have it and it would certainly be a mistake for science to close its eyes to those kinds of experiences. Potentially they can tell us an awful lot, not only about the way the brain might operate at those kinds of extremes but also about everyday consciousness."

A few weeks after Hilary Rhodes was avalanched, her husband, Peter Boardman, along with Joe Tasker, disappeared on the Northeast Ridge of Everest. It was ten years before Boardman's body was found on the mountain. During those years, Rhodes took what she had learned as a mountaineer and a competitive skier—discipline, focus and fear management—and channeled them into a spiritual path. She joined an ashram, and during long hours of meditation had experiences that were "far more wild" than many she'd had as an athlete. But she recognized the value of all the time she had spent in the mountains—including the avalanche.

"I think the avalanche was given to me as a gift," says Rhodes. "It taught me that it doesn't actually hurt to die, that once one is in the death process, it is just incredibly comforting. There was no physical pain, it was just a whizzing along into a new experience. So I've always thought that the peaceful and exciting feeling I had is what happened to Pete at the end. I'd been allowed to experience it, so that I would know what it was like for him."

Chapter 11

BEYOND EXTREMES

We must live in the free fall of infinity. Standing at the edge, the heart opens.

THOMAS MOORE

It is often the hardest, most challenging experiences of our lives that crack us open, For some people, these experiences are chosen, or accepted as a consequence of risk-taking. For others—for most of us—they come without warning. Unlikely gifts that rip away our layers of insulation, allowing us glimpses of the mysterious, the ineffable—the infinite realms of human consciousness.

During one of my long university summers, I traveled through Morocco with three girlfriends. We went to all the usual places—Marrakech, Fez, Casablanca, Rabat—then took a local bus down the Atlantic coast as far as a small village called Mirleft. Back then, Mirleft was one dirt street and a long row of joined houses, their doorways shaded by stone colonnades. As we wandered along the street, carrying our backpacks, small whorls of red dust rose up around our sandals. Outside the butcher's shop, a goat's head lay in a pool of bright blood. Next door, in a tiny restaurant, the remainder of the goat was being turned into a slow-cooked *tajine,* the only item on that night's menu. The owner called to us as we passed: "Come for dinner!" Men sitting at a table watched us curiously, these young women from another world, without husbands, children, or apparent cares.

An old man called Mohammed offered to rent us a room in his house. Bare except for straw mats on the floor, it had two shuttered windows opening onto a courtyard. We took it. Next morning, Mohammed brought us sweet mint tea and cookies. We asked him where we could go swimming and he told us about a beach, almost a mile away. "Take care," he said. "The sea is dangerous."

The beach was at the bottom of a sandy bluff that curved to form a half-moon bay. As we headed down the steep path, I gazed over the Atlantic, its cobalt surface flecked with whitecaps. Below us, a few wooden boats lay upturned, with tangles of nets and ropes around them. No fishermen were out, and no one was in the water save for a group of tourists bodysurfing in the breaking waves. Leaving our bags and towels on the sand, we waded into the shallows. Feeling the undertow suck at our legs, we remembered Mohammed's words; none of us were strong swimmers and we decided that this was far enough.

Then a shout went up. Several men sprinted down the beach and splashed past us, yelling that their friend had swum out beyond the wave break, and was in trouble. They linked hands, forming a human chain, calling for others to help. My friends wisely backed away, but, caught by the excitement, I offered my hands. In an instant I was committed, part of the chain and moving out. A wave surged around my chest, lifting me off my feet. The one that reared up behind it was much bigger than all the rest. I gazed at its smooth, glassy green belly and its curling head, dazzlingly white against the blue sky. Then a shock of noise, the crashing impact that swept me out of the chain and tumbled me round and round like a rag in a washing machine. My head popped up, the beach was close, and I flailed with my feet, expecting to touch bottom. But this time the sea sucked me out, pulling me into its maw, away from my friends, who were standing in a silent tableau on the shore, their faces full of confusion.

Later, I learned of the treacherous riptides in that bay; that it was a place feared by the men who fished there; that no one who had fallen afoul of its strong currents had survived. I didn't know these things as I was carried out. All I knew was the malevolence of the sea as it overwhelmed me, hammering me in the face, forcing water down my throat. Panicked and out of control, I clawed for life against this monster. At first I wasn't alone; others were caught in the rip. Someone moved toward me; I saw dark hair plastered against a narrow, bearded face. "Calm down," the man shouted. "I'll help you." I threw my arms around him, clinging so hard I pulled us both beneath the surface. He wriggled free of my grip, and when I lunged at him again, he pushed me away, punching me in the chest. "I'm sorry," he said, then turned and swam for shore.

Body and mind separated. I have only fragmented memories of the physical side of drowning: the flailing limbs, the awful inhalations of water, the gagging and choking. But I clearly recollect the mental processes, which were lucid and unhurried. I accepted that I was about to die, and wondered what would come next. I thought about my parents receiving the news of my death, and felt huge regret for their suffering. I remembered the cross words exchanged with one of my friends that morning, and wished we had resolved our spat. I realized I would never turn twenty-one, never have the big party I'd planned, never meet the love of my life and get married. I've no idea how long this strange disparity between fight and reflection went on. But when a wave lifted me so that I could see the beach, and how tiny the figures on it had become, I decided that the struggle was too hard, that it was better to get it over with. Calmly, I let myself sink beneath the water.

Opening my eyes, I stared down at my body, curled into the fetal position, floating like a child in the womb. Light shafting from the surface disappeared into darkness. Horror flooded through me; I didn't want to drift into those bottomless depths. I didn't want to die! With one kick I broke the surface and gasped for precious air, just as a wave reared up and crashed against my open mouth.

After that, all I remember is a rushing sound and the sense of moving fast through clouds, cradled by unseen hands. The rest is blank. Blackness. Until I was gazing at a forearm, strangely familiar, with grains of sand caught between the fine hairs of its skin. It was mine. I was lying, stomach-down, on the beach. With great puzzlement, I thought, *I'm alive.*

The young German tourist almost didn't go to the beach that morning. He'd hung around the village and smoked a chillum with some locals. But it was hot, a swim would be good. He ambled along, taking his time. On reaching the top of the bluff, he saw the waves, and the people running about like ants. Too busy, he thought, and then remembered another path, down at the far end of the bay where the waves were usually smaller and it would be easier to swim. It was a less trodden route, through prickly bushes that grabbed at his pants, slowing his progress. He was almost at the bottom when he noticed the body washing to and fro in the surf, long hair streaming. Rushing in fully clothed, he grabbed me by my hair. My lips were blue and swollen, and I was no longer breathing. Seemingly, I was beyond hope. But, as people ran along the beach to help him, he began mouth-to-mouth resuscitation.

When I regained consciousness, they carried me up the bluff and into a jeep. The drive back to the village was agony. At every bump in the road pain seared through me, and with every breath I took, a knife was plunged into my lungs. In our room, my friends piled up all our sleeping bags to make a soft bed for me. But in my delirious state, I was convinced that if I went to sleep I would stop breathing and die. Throughout that first night I hallucinated wildly—snakes crawled up the walls, shadows jeered at me, the faces of people leaning over me split apart. Around dawn, finally I closed my eyes. When I awoke, strong sunlight was seeping through cracks in the shutters. Our landlord knelt at my side, mumbling prayers and touching his head to the floor, giving thanks for the miracle of my survival.

A week passed. As I gradually recovered, I retreated from my friends. They were giddy with relief, and their conversations seemed flippant and silly. I wanted to be away from them, alone. One afternoon, when I felt strong enough to walk, I made my way out of the village, and up a small hill. I sat there for hours, watching scrawny sheep graze on the thorn bushes, listening to the clunking of the bells around their necks. I thought about my time in the ocean. About the man who decided at the last moment to come down to the beach by a different path. About the fine line between being alive on this barren hillside and rolling around, dead, on the ocean floor. The sun was slipping away, bathing the desert in a palette of golds and reds. Suddenly I was overwhelmed with a sense of profound gratitude—for the beauty of the sky, for the softening colors of the land, for the air that now moved easily in and out of my lungs. At that moment I knew without question that whatever had brought me back from the edge of death was linked to all of these things; that I was deeply connected to the earth and its forces; that my survival had been no coincidence. Tears poured down my face as I whispered my thanks, until the wavering edge of the sun slipped from sight, like a drowning swimmer.

For everyone
The swimmer's moment at the whirlpool comes,
But many at that moment will not say
"This is the whirlpool then."
By their refusal they are saved
From the black pit, and also from contesting
The deadly rapids, and emerging in
The mysterious, and more ample, further waters.
And so their bland-blank faces turn and turn
Pale and forever on the rim of suction
They will not recognize.
Of those who dare the knowledge
Many are whirled into the ominous centre
That, gaping vertical, seals up
For them an eternal boon of privacy,
So that we turn away from their defeat
With a despair, not for their deaths, but for
Ourselves, who cannot penetrate their secret
Nor even guess at the anonymous breadth
Where one or two have won:
(The silver reaches of the estuary.)

The Swimmer's Moment
Margaret Avison

ACKNOWLEDGMENTS

First, I thank my literary agent, Susan Golomb, for asking, "Have any of the mountaineers told you about ghosts?" and setting me on the journey that led to *Explorers of the Infinite*. I am also grateful to Mitch Horowitz of Tarcher Penguin for his support and patience. And I acknowledge and thank the Canada Council for the Arts and the BC Arts Council for their financial assistance.

At various stages of the book's development, I had the good fortune to work with a number of gifted editors. During the first Mountain Writing program at the Banff Center, Marni Jackson and Tony Whittome helped steer me toward a new start on the manuscript. Gabrielle Moss, at Tarcher Penguin, buoyed me with her great enthusiasm for the book, offered invaluable advice during its final drafts, and has been unfailingly helpful and good-natured. During the early stages of the project and during its final incarnations, Isabelle Gutmanis came on board with me once more, bringing her fearless, incisive, and much appreciated editorial skills. My thanks to you all, and to Peter Gutmanis for checking a number of the scientific references. Any mistakes are entirely my own.

I thank Olga Gardner Galvin for her thorough copyediting and Nicole LaRoche and David Walker for their design work on the book.

A multitude of thanks to Bernadette Macdonald, Shannon O'Donaghue, Brian Hall, John Porter, Julie Tait, Rick Silverman, and Arlene Burns for welcoming me to their mountain festivals and helping me to make contacts that have proved crucial for the book; Margo Talbot for her careful reading of the manuscript, her suggestions, and her encouragement; my sister-in-law, Gail Coffey, for her enthusiasm at a time when it was very much needed; and my old friend Claire David for sharing her vivid memories of our time in Morocco.

In exploring the links between adventure and spiritual, mystical, and paranormal experience, I stand on the shoulders of other writers who have tackled elements of this topic. Two books, in particular, were important early signposts and references: *Bone Games* by Rob Schultheis and *In the Zone* by Michael Murphy and Rhea A. White. Many of the other books that informed and inspired all elements of my research are listed in the reference section. A number were recommended or given to me by thoughtful friends. For this I thank Joanie Bick, Kaz Connelly, Christin Geall, Mike Hawkes, Marni Jackson, Tom Lucas, Carol Matthews, Joan Skogan, and Clint Willis. I'm also grateful to Colleen Campbell, Ania Korzun, Geoff Powter, Royal Robbins, Shandell Susin, Alison Watt, and Colin Wells for other helpful materials.

Without the following people, there would be no book. For the stories and the expertise they shared, I thank Leanne Allison, Arlene Blum, Dorothy Boardman, Cherie Bremer-Kamp, Jim Buckley, Wesley Bunch, Adrian Burgess, Alan Burgess, Greg Child, Carlos Carsolio, Mandy Rae-Cruickshank, Patricia Culver, Sam Drevo, Dr. Jimmy Duff, David Eagleman, Reverend Neil Ellis, Shaun Ellison, Mark Fawcett, Will Gadd, Justin Harvey, Karsten Heuer, Peter Hillary, Charlie Houston, Tomaz Humar, Clay Hunting, Stephen Koch, Anna Levesque, Ed Lucero, Warren MacDonald, Beth Malloy, Dr. Pierre Mayer,

Dr. Tim Noakes, Timmy O'Neill, Andy Parkin, Gavin Perryman, John Porter, Dean Potter, Hilary Rhodes, Royal Robbins, David Roberts, Dick Rutan, Rupert Sheldrake, Rabbi Shifren, Marlene Smith, Cheryl Sterns, Tanya Streeter, Shandell Susin, Margo Talbot, Kristen Ulmer, Marshall Ulrich, Ed Webster, Sara Whitner, and Lou and Ingrid Whittaker.

While researching and writing *Explorers of the Infinite*, I was touched by the interest it sparked in so many people, leading to countless conversations that all contributed in some way to the end result. I regret that I can't list everyone I spoke to, but please—each of you—know how much your input meant to me.

Finally, more thanks than I could ever adequately convey are due to Dag Goering, my husband, best friend, and soul mate. Two years before I met him, at a time when my life was very dark, a friend persuaded me to have a tarot reading. During that reading, Dag was described to me in detail; future happiness was promised. Was it pure coincidence that I stumbled into him, as predicted, when we were both far away from our homes? I'll never know. But I do know that he's brought me the greatest joys of my life. And that without his encouragement, love, support—and at times some necessary goading!—this book would never have been completed.

Selected References

Part One

Einstein, Albert. "The World As I See It." *Living Philosophies.* New York: Simon & Schuster, 1931.

Chapter 1. Spiritual Addiction

Duane, Daniel. *Caught Inside.* New York: North Point Press, 1996.
———. "Anatomy of a Big One." *Outside* (May 1998).
Elliot, Neil. "The Spirituality of Snowboarding." Working paper 8, University of Central England, Birmingham, 2003.
Misra, Neelesh. "Reading Winds, Waves May Have Saved Ancient Tribes on Remote Indian Islands." Associated Press, January 5, 2005, 2007.
Schultheis, Rob. *Bone Games.* New York: Breakaway Books, 1984.
Sheldrake, Rupert. "Listen to the Animals." *The Ecologist* (March 2005).
Shifren, Nachum. *Surfing Rabbi.* Los Angeles: Heaven Ink Publishing, 2001.

Part Two

Muir, John. *The Yosemite.* New York: The Century Company, 1912.

Chapter 2. Fear

Cloninger, C. R., D. M. Svrakic, and T. R. Przybeck. "A Psychobiological

Model of Temperament and Character." *Archives of General Psychiatry* 50, no. 12 (December 1993).

Dillard, Annie. *Pilgrim at Tinker Creek.* New York: Harper's Magazine Press, 1974.

Ebstein, Richard, Olga Novick, Roberto Umansky, et al. "Dopamine D4 Receptor (D4DR) Exon III Polymorphism Associated with the Human Personality Trait of Novelty Seeking." *Nature Genetics* 12 (January 1996).

Finnegan, William. "Playing Doc's Games." *The New Yorker* (August 1992).

George, Leonard. *The Ultimate Athlete.* New York: Viking, 1975.

Graham, Stephen. *The Gentle Art of Tramping.* London: E. Benn Ltd., 1931.

Hariri, Ahmad, and Daniel Weinberger. "Imaging Genomics." *British Medical Bulletin* 65 (March 2003): 259–270.

MacFarlane, Robert. *Mountains of the Mind.* London: Granta, 2004.

Mitchell, Edgar D., with Dwight Williams. *The Way of the Explorer.* New York, G. P. Putnam's Sons, 1996.

Newberg, Andrew, and Eugene d'Aquili. *Why God Won't Go Away.* New York: Ballantine Books, 2001.

O'Neill, Maureen. "Queen of All She Surveys." *Leading Out: Mountaineering Stories of Adventuring Women.* Seattle: Seal Press, 1992.

Otto, Rudolph. *The Idea of the Holy.* New York: Oxford University Press, 1958.

Petit, Philippe. *To Reach the Clouds.* New York: North Point Press, 2002.

Pluming, R., M. J. Owen, and P. McGuffin. "The Genetic Basis of Complex Human Behaviors." *Science* 264 (1994): 1733–1739.

Phelps, Elizabeth, Mauricio Delgado, Katherine Nearing, et al. "Extinction Learning in Humans." *Neuron* 43, no. 6 (September 16, 2004): 897–905.

Roberts, Andy. "Panic on the Streets of Staffin." *The Angry Corrie*, no. 38 (August–September 1998).

Roper, Robert. *Fatal Mountaineer.* New York: St. Martin's Press, 2002.

Rosenthal, Sol. "Hardwired for Thrills." Interview, *As it Happens*, CBC Radio, February 25, 1998.

Rosner, Dalya. "Is Mountaineering Addictive?" www.thenakedscientists.com, July 2004.

Ulmer, Kristen. "I Hate Couloirs." *Skiing.* www.kristenulmer.com, 2004.

Unsoeld, Willi. *Wilderness and Spirit.* Graduation address to the 1974 Park Ranger class, Horace M. Albright Training Center, Grand Canyon, Arizona.

Willis, Clint. *Why Meditate?* New York: Marlowe and Company, 2001.

Chapter 3. Focus

Ackerman, Diane. *On Extended Wings.* New York: Atheneum, 1985.

Bevan, William. "Mountain Mavericks: Patrick Vallencant." *Snow News* (January 2003).

Burdick, Alan. "The Mind in Overdrive." *Discover* (April 2006).

Eagleman, David. *Ten Unsolved Problems of Neuroscience.* Cambridge, MA: MIT Press, 2004.

Greenfield, Susan. *The Private Life of the Brain.* London: Penguin, 2001.

Goldberg, Ilan, and Rafael Malach. "When the Brain Loses Its Self: Prefrontal Inactivity During Sensorimotor Processing." *Neuron* 50 (April 20, 2006): 329–339.

Griffiths, Jay. *Sideways Look at Time.* New York: Tarcher, 1999.

Ingram, Jay. *The Theatre of the Mind.* Toronto: HarperCollins, 2005.

LaChapelle, Dolores. *Sacred Land, Sacred Sex, Rapture of the Deep.* Durango, CO: Kivaki Press, 1988.

———. *Deep Powder.* Durango: Kivaki Press, 1993.

Lindemann, Hans. *Alone at Sea.* Translated by Peter Bandtock. Oberschleissheim, Germany: Poller Verlag, 1993.

Matthiessen, Peter. *The Snow Leopard.* New York: Bantam Books, 1980.

———. *Ends of the Earth: Voyages to Antartica.* Washington, DC: National Geographic, 2007.

Murphy, Michael, and Rhea White. *In the Zone.* New York: Penguin, 1995.

Rao, Stephen, Andrew Mayer, and Deborah Harrington. "The Evolution of Brain Activation During Temporal Processing." *Nature Neuroscience* 4 (March 2001): 317–323.

Tolle, Eckhart. *The Power of Now.* Vancouver: Namaste Publishing, 1997.

Chapter 4. Suffering

Armstrong, Lance. *It's Not About the Bike.* New York: Berkley, 2001.

Askwith, Richard. *Feet in the Clouds.* London: Arum Press, 2004.

Becerra, Lino, Hans Breiter, Roy Wise, et al. "Reward Circuitry Activation by Noxious Thermal Stimuli." *Neuron* 32, no. 5 (December 6, 2001).

Coyle, Daniel. "That Which Does Not Kill Me Makes Me Stranger." *The New York Times,* February 5, 2006.

——. "The New American in Paris." *Outside* (July 2006).

Harnden, Philip. *Journeys of Simplicity.* Woodstock: Skylight Paths Publishing, 2003.

Jackson, Marni. *Pain: The Science and Culture of Why We Hurt.* Toronto: Vintage Canada, 2002.

Johnson, Kirk. *To the Edge.* New York, Warner, 2001.

MacKenzie, Vicki. *Cave in the Snow.* London: Bloomsbury, 1999.

Matthews, Todd. "Going the Distance." *Outside* (July 2006).

Messner, Rheinhold. *The Crystal Horizon.* Seattle: The Mountaineers, 1989.

Noakes, Timothy D. "The Limits of Human Endurance." Academic paper, Department of Human Biology, Sports Science Institute of South Africa, Cape Town, South Africa, June 1, 2006.

Nietzsche, Friedrich. *Joyful Wisdom,* Book 4. New York: Unger, 1973.

O'Donoghue, John. *Anam Cara: A Book of Celtic Wisdom.* New York: HarperCollins, 1998.

Petit, Philippe. *On the High Wire.* New York: Random House, 1985.

Rasmussen, Knud. *Across Arctic America.* New York: G. P. Putnam's Sons, 1927.

Tasker, Joe. *Savage Arena.* London: Methuen, 1982.

Tilman H. W. "Voyage to the Îles Crozet and Îles Kerguelen." *Geographical Journal* 127, no. 3 (1961): 310–316.

Twight, Mark. *Extreme Alpinism.* Seattle: Mountaineers Books, 1999.

Chapter 5. Only Connect

Abram, David. *Spell of the Sensuous.* New York: Vintage, 1997.

Bernbaum, Edwin. *Sacred Mountains of the World*. Berkeley: University of California Press, 1998.

Berman, Morris. *The Re-enchantment of the World*. New York: Cornell University Press, 1981.

Biggest Wednesday: Condition Black. IMAX documentary. Ventura Distribution, 2000.

Boyer, Pascal. *Religion Explained*. London: Heinemann, 2001.

Heuer, Karsten. *Being Caribou*. Seattle: Mountaineers Books, 2005.

Lewis, David. *We, the Navigators*. Honolulu: University of Hawaii Press, 1994.

London, Scott. "The Ecology of Magic: An Interview with David Abram." *Insight & Outlook*, National Public Radio, 2006.

Norgay, Jamling Tenzing. *Touching My Father's Soul*. San Francisco: Harper-Collins, 2001.

Popham, Peter. "Social Climbers: Pioneers of the Peaks." *The Independent* (London), December 22, 2006.

Rumi, Jelaluddin. "A Great Wagon." *The Essential Rumi*. Translated by Coleman Barks. Edison, NJ: Castle Books, 1998.

Schama, Simon. *Landscape and Memory*. New York: Vintage, 1996.

Sheldrake, Rupert. *The Rebirth of Nature*. Rochester, VT: Park Street Press, 1991.

———. A New Science of Life. Rochester, VT: Park Street Press, 1995.

Sheldrake, Rupert, and Matthew Fox. *Natural Grace*. New York: Image, 1997.

Vyse, Stuart A. *Believing in Magic*. New York: Oxford University Press, 1997.

Chapter 6. Remembering the Future

Bremer-Kamp, Cherie. *Living on the Edge*. London: David and Charles, 1987.

Carroll, Lewis. *Through the Looking-Glass*. London: Macmillan, 1872.

Domhoff, G. William. *The Scientific Study of Dreams*. Washington, DC: American Psychological Association, 2003.

Folger, Tim. "Newsflash: Time May Not Exist." *Discover* (June 12, 2007).

Foulkes, David. *Dreaming: A Cognitive-Psychological Analysis.* Hillsdale, NJ: Lawrence Erlbaum Associates, 1985.

Greene, Brian. *The Fabric of the Cosmos.* London: Penguin, 2004.

Hall, James. *Patterns of Dreaming.* Boston: Shambhala Publications, 1991.

Kaster, Joseph. *The Wisdom of Ancient Egypt.* New York: Barnes and Noble, 1993.

MacKenzie, Norman. *Dreams and Dreaming.* New York: The Vanguard Press, 1965.

Rumi, Jelaluddin. "Unmarked Boxes." *The Essential Rumi.* Translated by Coleman Barks. Edison, NJ: Castle Books, 1998.

Schneider, Daniel E. "Dream Flying and Dream Weightlessness." *Journal of the Hillside Hospital* 4 (1960).

Ullman, Montague. *Dream Telepathy.* Charlottesville, VA: Hampton Roads Publishing, 2003.

Webster, Ed. *Snow in the Kingdom.* Colorado: Mountain Imagery, 2000.

Wheeler, John. *Geons, Black Holes and Quantum Foam.* New York: Norton, 1998.

Chapter 7. Strange Intuitions

Bergson, Henri. *The Creative Mind.* New York: Andison, 1946.

Bullimore, Tony. *Saved.* London: Time Warner, 1998.

Crawley, Susan, Christopher French, and Stephen Yesson. "Evidence for Transliminality from a Subliminal Card-Guessing Game." *Perception* 31 (2002).

Evernden, J. F., ed. "Abnormal Animal Behavior Prior to Earthquakes." U.S. Dept. of Interior Geological Survey, Conference I. Menlo Park, California, September 23–24, 1976.

Gladwell, Malcolm. *Blink.* New York: Little Brown, 2005.

Herzog, Maurice. *Annapurna.* New York: Dutton, 1952.

Sheldrake, Rupert. *The Sense of Being Stared At.* London: Hutchinson, 2003.

Suyehiro, Y. "Unusual Behavior of Fishes Prior to Earthquakes." Scientific report, Keikyu Aburatsubo Marine Park Aquarium, 1 (1968): 4–11.

Tributsch, Helmut. *When the Snakes Awake.* Cambridge: MIT Press, 1982.

Utts, Jessica. "An Assessment of the Evidence for Psychic Functioning." Academic paper, Division of Statistics, University of California, Davis, 1995.

Zhang Jun and Douglas Williams. "China's Zoos Are on Earthquake Watch." *Shanghai Daily,* February 26, 2007.

Chapter 8. Spirit Friends

Arzy, S., M. Idel, T. Landis, and O. Blanke. "Why Revelations Have Occurred on Mountains." Academic paper, Laboratory of Cognitive Neuroscience, Brain-Mind Institute, Ecole Polytechnique Federale de Lausanne, Switzerland, 2005.

Brugger, Peter. "Phantomology." Paper given at Phantom Limb Conference, Goldsmiths College, University of London, 2003.

Child, Greg. *Thin Air.* Seattle: The Mountaineers, 1998.

Connor, Jeff. *Dougal Haston: The Philosophy of Risk.* Edinburgh: Canongate, 2002.

Hillary, Peter, and John E. Elder. *In the Ghost Country.* Edinburgh: Mainstream, 2004.

Jordan, Jennifer. *Savage Summit.* New York: William Morrow, 2005.

Levin, Abraham S. "Psychometric Considerations in Selecting Personnel for Unusual Environments." *Personnel Psychology* 13 (September 1960).

Lindbergh, Charles. *The Spirit of St. Louis.* New York: Scribner, 2003.

Ramachandran, V. S. *Phantoms in the Brain.* London: Fourth Estate, 1999.

Rebuffat, Gaston. *Men and the Matterhorn.* London: Oxford University Press, 1967.

Rilke, Rainer Maria. *Letters to a Young Poet.* Translated by Stephen Mitchell. London: Vintage, 1989.

Slocum, Joshua. Sailing Alone Around the World. New York: Dover Publications, 1956.

Smythe, Frank. *The Mountain Vision.* London: Hodder and Stoughton, 1949.

"Spatial Disorientation." *Flight International,* RAF Institute of Aviation Medicine, March 1980.

Tuenisse, J. P. "Visual Hallucinations in Psychologically Normal People: Charles Bonnett Syndrome." *The Lancet* 347 (1996).

Wilson, Stephen. *The Bloomsbury Book of the Mind.* London: Bloomsbury, 2004.

Chapter 9. Wandering Spirits

Blum, Arlene. *Breaking Trail.* New York: Simon & Schuster, 2006.

Broks, Paul. *Into the Silent Land.* London: Atlantic Books, 2003.

Chang, Garma, trans. *The Hundred Thousand Songs of Milarepa.* Boston: Shambala, 1999.

Gauld, Alan. *Mediumship and Survival.* London: Heinemann, 1982.

Gribben, John. *In Search of Schrondinger's Cat.* London: Corgi, 1985.

Rinpoche, Sogyal. *The Tibetan Book of Living and Dying.* New York: Harper-Collins, 1994.

Sabom, Michael. *Recollections of Death.* New York: HarperCollins, 1981.

Chapter 10. Spiritual Tools

Blackmore, Susan. *Dying to Live.* London: Prometheus, 1993.

Chotzinoff, Robin. "Quoting Duncan Ferguson, Life on the Edge." *Denver Westworld News,* October 1995.

Crane, George. *Bones of the Master.* New York: Bantam, 2001.

David-Neel, Alexandra. *Magic and Mystery in Tibet.* New York: Dover, 1971.

Fenwick, Peter. *The Truth in the Light.* New York: Berkley, 1997.

Fox, Mark. *Religion, Spirituality and the Near-Death Experience.* London: Routledge, 2003.

French, Christopher. "After Death, What?" BBC Radio 4 debate, January 26, 2004.

Govinda, Lama Anagarika. *The Way of the White Clouds*. Woodstock, NY: Overlook Press, 2006.

Humar, Tomaz. *No Impossible Ways*. Ljubljana, Slovenia: Mobitel, 2001.

Moody, Raymond. *Life after Life*. New York: Bantam, 1982.

Parnia, Sam. *What Happens When We Die?* Carlsbad, CA: Hay House, 2007.

Talbot, Michael. *Mysticism and the New Physics*. London: Arkana, 1993.

Yogananda, Paramahansa. *Autobiography of a Yogi*. Los Angeles: Self-Realization Fellowship, 1998.

INDEX

ABOUT THE AUTHOR

Maria Coffey is the author of twelve internationally published books, including four titles for children and *Visions of the Wild: A Voyage by Kayak around Vancouver Island*, which she coauthored with her husband, Dag Goering. Her previous book, *Where the Mountain Casts Its Shadow: The Dark Side of Extreme Adventure*, was serialized in *Outside* magazine and won the prestigious Jon Whyte Award for Mountain Literature at the Banff Mountain Book Festival. A native of England, Maria now lives on Vancouver Island, Canada, where she and Dag run Hidden Places, an adventure travel company. Maria's Web site is Hiddenplaces.net.